James Long

Scripture truth in Oriental dress

Emblems explanatory of Biblical doctrines and morals

James Long

Scripture truth in Oriental dress
Emblems explanatory of Biblical doctrines and morals

ISBN/EAN: 9783337279752

Hergestellt in Europa, USA, Kanada, Australien, Japan

Cover: Foto ©Lupo / pixelio.de

Weitere Bücher finden Sie auf **www.hansebooks.com**

SCRIPTURE TRUTH IN ORIENTAL DRESS,

OR

EMBLEMS EXPLANATORY

OF

BIBLICAL DOCTRINES AND MORALS,

WITH

PARALLEL OR ILLUSTRATIVE REFERENCES

TO

PROVERBS AND PROVERBIAL SAYINGS

IN THE

Arabic, Bengali, Canarese, Persian, Russian, Sanskrit, Tamul, Telegu and Urdu Languages.

THE REV. J. LONG.

"Without a parable spake He not to the people."

Mark iv. 34.

PREFACE.

This little manual is designed merely to *introduce* the important subject of Biblical truth illustrated from Emblems, Oriental Proverbs and Proverbial sayings, and the Author hopes that some one of more leisure and learning will carry out the plan in a more elaborate manner. His simple object is to furnish *some* raw materials to those wishing to convey the Doctrines of Christianity to the millions of India through popular preaching or schools for the masses—to point out to natives of India non-Christian how thoroughly Oriental the Bible is both in its subject and style—and to open out to European readers a new mine for illustrating Christian truth by Oriental Proverbs and Proverbial sayings which enshrine the wit and wisdom of the multitude.

Emblems, parables, pictures, proverbs are even in Europe regarded as of great value in instructing the masses, how much more ought they to be used in Eastern lands, where it is so important when announcing new dogma to fix them in the mind by illustrations which excite interest and arrest attention. Chrysostom in Constantinople and Latimer in London well knew the value of these in their popular addresses.

The field of illustration drawn from the book of nature and man's social condition is very wide, but the limits assigned to this manual have excluded a variety of other illustrative matter and especially anecdotes, Fables, Historical references; various doctrines which did not admit of illustration by Scripture emblems have been necessarily omitted.

J. LONG.

Calcutta, 15th June 1871.

CONTENTS.

Introduction	i—ii
Index	iii—viii
Emblems 252 of Bible truths with commentary, illustrations from Bible history, Oriental sayings...	1—216
Badaga Proverbs illustrating Bible	217—218
Malayalan ditto	218—219
Tamul ditto	219—221
Chinese ditto	221—222
Panjabi ditto	222
Persian ditto	222—226
Urdu ditto	226—228
Telegu ditto	228—230
Veman's Telegu ditto	230—239
Russian ditto	239—241
Turkish ditto	241—242
Abu Talib's Arabic ditto	242—245
Bengali ditto	245—250
Sanskrit ditto	251—258
Arabic ditto	258—262
Canarese ditto	262—263
Scripture Similes illustrating texts	264—266
Oriental Customs ditto	266—268
Specimens of Questions on Emblems	265—689

CHRISTIYA TATVA PURBADESH RESHE,

OR,

CHRISTIAN TRUTH IN ORIENTAL DRESS.

———o———

ALL Orientals are fond of apologue, fables, and figurative language, and love to clothe ethical and religious truth in the graceful and pleasing drapery of metaphor, thus engaging the attention, impressing the memory, and strewing the path to abstract dogmas with flowers; even dictionaries have been composed by them in verse.

The Bible as an oriental book is imbued with this spirit, as is exemplified in the lyrical odes of the Psalms, the proverbial writings of Solomon, the dramas of Job, and Solomon's song; while of our Lord it is said,—without a parable or simile spake He not to the people; He represented moral and spiritual truths by imagery drawn from nature, the relations of society, and the common occupations of men.

While parts of the Bible from the Historical and Geographical references, as well as from frequent allusions to the Jewish system, must be obscure to the masses of India; on the other hand, there is an ample storehouse in the figurative language of Scripture, as well as in its emblems and similies, drawn from God's glorious and open picture Book, the familiar scenes of Nature, which none observes with more interest than the Indian peasant, calculated to interest an Oriental race, as well as to make its great doctrines more intelligible to them.

Among the Fathers Chrysostom, in France Saurin and Massillon, and even in England itself Jeremy Taylor, South, Latimer, Fuller, Hall, Flavel, and a host of writers of former days, availed themselves of this storehouse in their writings and pulpit discourse; even proverbs were not thought beneath the dignity of pulpit oratory, and in modern times, some of the greatest pulpit orators have followed in the same track.

Numerous works have issued from the Press in England and Germany on the Emblems, Similies, Parables, and Proverbs of the Holy Scriptures, which have been found of great use in popular preaching, in school teaching, and in the family circle.

In India, where a Christian Vernacular Literature is rising to great consequence, where Native Pastors are rapidly on the increase, where Christian Vernacular Education is becoming one of the great needs of the day, and where the mode and manner of Missionary Preaching to Orientals is of great consequence, there is a wide field opened for works of this description.

This Manual is designed as a contribution towards supplying this want, and is constructed on the following principles :—

(1.) A selection of *texts* illustrating Christian truths in their Doctrinal and Ethical variety by emblems, metaphors, and proverbs to be committed to memory in schools, and form the subjects of short addresses to village congregations.

(2.) Brief notes and comments on these texts, pointing out the applicability of the emblems as illustrative of Biblical truths, accompanied by illustrations drawn from natural objects, Scripture History, from Oriental Proverbs, Sayings, and Similies.

The author has found these of great use to teachers in school, as well as to Catechists preaching to the heathen or to Native Christians; and some of them might form useful popular tracts for distribution.

Ample use has been made of such works, as those of Boyle, Wemyss, Jones, Gotthold, Harris, Greenhill, Burder, and Kitto. on Scripture Similies; while in Sanskrit and Arabic, reference has been made to the Trabodh Chandrody, Chanyakea Sloke, Niti Shatak, Drishtanta Shatak, Ramayan, Bhagavat Gita, Freytag's Arabic Proverb, the Gulestan, Bostan, Mason Good, Trower's Scripture Similitudes, Nicolson on Solomon's Proverbs, explained and illustrated from other parts of Holy Scripture, Keach's Scripture Metaphors, &c., &c.

INDEX.

Adder wicked as a deaf, 36.
Abu Talibs Arabic Sayings. 242.
AFFLICTION, A Chastising, 103. A Cup, 156. A Furnace, 142. A refining 37. A Rod, 145. As Sparks, 112.
Almsgiving a watering, 65.
Altar Christ, an 192.
Anchor of Hope, 22.
ANGELS, Encamp, 131.
ANGER in Fool's Bosom, 149. Of God as Smoke, 165. From strife 137.
Ant Teaches Sluggard, 20.
Apples of Eye. Providence Keeps as, 152. Of Good Words, 181.
ARABIC PROVERBS. 258.
Arms Everlasting of God, 77.
Arrows of Vengeance, Gods 163.
Ass wild, Man as, 39. Man contrasted with, 95.
ATONEMENT, an Altar, 191. A Blotting Out, 73. A Bitter Cup, 144. A Making White, 85. A Propitiation, 180.
Axe, Of Punishment for Sin. 127.

BADAGA PROVERBS, 217.
Bags of Holiness, Not worn out 101.
Bear Robbed of Whelps, a Fool as, a 106.
BEAUTIFUL and Ignorant as Jewel in swine's Snout 15. Fade as a Leaf, 12. as a Moth, 17.
Belly of Glutton His God. 128.
BENGALI PROVERBS. 245-250
BIBLE as Milk, 12. A Seed, 16. A Sword, 193.
Blind Sinner, are, 172.
Body Crushed like the Moth, 17. an Earthen Vessel, 157. As Grass, 202. A House of Clay, 2, 17. A House, 161. Of Faith, 35. a Tabernacle, 192. A Living Sacrifice, 191. A Tent, 1.
Bones Rottenness of Envy i , 5.
Born again by Conversion, 177.
Bread cast On waters, 51. Christ, 163. Unleavened of Sincerity, 215.
Book of Life at Judgment, 132.
Bosom of Fool's Anger in, 149.

Bottle for Righteous Tears. 127.
Brand Plucked from Fire Converted are, 203.
Brass Sounding Lip Love as, 117. Brow of Obstinate Such 174.
Brook Deceitful Brethren as, 32.
BROTHERLY Love, a Threefold Cord, 25 : 109.
Brethren Who Christs are, 134.
Brow of Brass Obstinate 174.
Builder God a, 187.
Buried with Christ, who 156.
Burthen of Sin, 127.
Butter Words of Hypocrite as, 114. As butter from milk so strife from wrath 137.

Camel in Needle's Eye.—rich as 28.
CANARESE PROVERBS. 262.
Captives wicked are 144.
Clay man as God the Potter. 10.
Chains of darkness devils in 196.
City heaven as a 182.
Chaff wicked as 127.
CHASTISING of Sin 103. As a rod 145.
CHILDREN Christians as 49. Mocking their Eyes Eaten 189.
CHINESE PROVERBS. 221.
CHRIST, Altar 192. A friend 186. A head. 160 A lily 205. A root 197. A physician 115. A lamb 120. A rainbow 92. A rock 79. A rose 78, 146. Coming as a thief 183. Bread 163. Epistles of Christ 212. First fruits of Sleepers, 212. Foundation 206. His legacy 146. Looking to 211. Sun 34. Star, of morning 67. Sun of righteousness 195. Well 202. Way 118. Woman's Seed 9. Second coming of as lightning 158.
CHRISTIANS, Children 49. Inheritance of 211. as Jewels 29. as Merchants 133. Silver 37. as Soldiers 63. Stranger 152. Watchmen 72.
Coals of fire of love melt an enemy 111, 198.
Cord of love threefold 25, 109.
Clay man as 10. Body a house of 17.

INDEX.

Cloud the fickle as 64. Without water wicked are, 130.
Corn death of righteous as a shock of 90.
COURAGE, of righteous as a lion 88.
Crows eat eyes of bad sons. 189.
CRUEL troubles his own flesh 175.
CHURCH, A garden 122 Christ the head believers members, 160. a Family 166. A kingdom. 184 Moon, 96.
COMPANY, bad as darkness. 129.
Conversion a new birth 177 brands from burning 203.
CONSCIENCE, Seared, 154. Worm of 173.
COVETOUSNESS, root of all Evil 112.
Crown of glory for old age, 182.
Crucifying flesh by believer 198.
Customs Oriental, 266.
CUP, bitter of Christ, 144. of salvation, 156.

Darkness bad company as, 129, chains of outer darkness 187, for Satan 196.
Day of Eternity, 60. a shadow. 132.
DEATH, Congregation of 110. A sleep 146. A Valley, 104. Wages of sin 181.
DEAD, bury dead, 23; 55. Keys of 14. Righteous and corn 90. Tree 89. as water spilled 9. Warfare of 37.
Debt of sin, 73.
DECEIT, bread of as gravel 110.
DECEITFUL as a brook, 32.
Dew fickle as 64. Providence as 58.
Disease of sin, 42.
Dogs, holy things thrown to 81. living dog and dead lion 101. Taking by ears intermeddlers. 109.
Door of heart Christ knocks at 102.
Dove Christian as, 141.
Dross wicked as 89.

Eagles' wings of Christians, 26. Riches as 55. time as 20.
Earnest of the Holy Spirit, 158.
Ears wicked have but hear not, 176.
Earthen vessel the body an, 157.
EMBLEMS 1-211.
Encampment of angels, 131.
ENVY, rottenness of the bones, 5.

Epistles Christians are 212.
ETERNITY, as a day, 60.
Ethiopians skin sin as. 25.
Eye mote in 15. Mocking parents eaten by crows 189. Single of purity, 107. Rivers from 102.

FAITH, a body 35. as Gold 87. A Shield 216. A stronghold 141.
Family Church a great 166.
Father God a 82. His House in heaven 190. Of lies Satan 169.
Feet keep in God's house 120.
Fickle as morning cloud and dew 64.
First fruits of sleepers Christ 212.
Fire tongue a 90.
Flesh of cruel troubled 175. Fool eats his own 102. Sowing to 84.
Flies dead little sins as 140.
Flood human life as a 28.
Flower life as a 108.
Foxes wicked are as 21.
Fool as a bear 106. Brayed in a Mortar 74. Eats his own flesh 102. In the congregation of the dead 110.
Forehead Gods name on the righteous 114.
Foundation Christ the sure 206.
Fountain God a 150.
Fowler Satan a 209.
Friend Christ a 186.
Fruits righteous have 94.
Furnace of affliction 142.

Garden enclosed Church as a 122.
Garment waxes old so Earth 147.
Gate the narrow one of holiness 189.
Girdle of truth 75.
Glass dark world a 40. Looking glass like hearers not doers 119.
GLUTTON, his belly his God 128.
GOSPEL a net 201.
Goads words of wise are . 174
Goats wicked as 30. Wild righteous protected as 210.
GOD a builder 187. House of 120. a Fountain 150. A father 82. A Judge 137. a Potter 10. Right hand of 213.
Gold faith more precious than 87.
GRACE a river 178.

INDEX.

Grass Man's flesh as 202.
GRATITUDE as ox. 95.
GRAVE, a rest in the 138.
Gravel and deceit 110.
Groaning with burthen of body 192
Guide safe God a 196.
Craving on palm of hand by Providence 200.

Hand right of God 213.
Hart Christian thirsty as 124.
Head of wife husband 150. Hoary a crown of glory 182.
HEARERS, not doers a looking glass 119. As House on Sand 175.
HEAVEN, a city 182. Father's house 190. A treasure house 170.
HEART of sinner stony 6.
HELL, fire of outer darkness 188. A prison 71.
Hen Providence shelters as a 40.
Helm tongue a 160.
Hidden man of the heart woman's ornament is the 118.
HOLINESS, a brotherhood 134. God's name on forehead 114. A Gate 189. A race 125. A service 179. a Walking with God 216. White raiment 140.
HOLY SPIRIT, an earnest 158. An oil 197. As Rain 97. Seals 133. Water 50. Wind 121. Quench not 216.
HOLY THINGS, cast not to dogs 81.
HOPE, an anchor 22. Of hypocrite a rush 156. Vain a spiders web 11.
House, body of clay 17. God's house 120. Drops through 122. In old age 135. On sands of profession 175. Heaven a 190.
HUMBLE, as a reed 55.
Husbandry righteous God's 41.
HUSBAND, head of the wife 150.
HYPOCRITE as spiders web 10. Whited sepulchres 19. Words butter 114.

IDLENESS, makes house drop through 122.
Ignorant and beautiful as jewel in Swines snout 15. as Swallow 204
Incense of prayer, 110.
INGRATITUDE, man has more than ass, or ox 95.

Inheritance of Christian, 211.
Inner Man of the soul, 177.
INTERMEDDLERS, like taking dog by ears, 109.

Jewel's God's people are his 29. In swines Snout 15.
JOY worldly crackling thorns 4.
JUDGMENT DAY, book of life opened on 132. God a judge, 137.

Keys of death with Christ, 14.
KINGDOM, of Christ, immoveable 184.
Kings believers are as, 194.

Lamb Christ, a 120.
Lamp of wicked put out, 75.
Leaf mans life, as 12.
Legacy Christs to believers, 146.
Leprosy sin as 117.
LIBERALITY, as bread on waters, 51. Watering watered, 65.
Lily Christ a 205.
LIFE, Christians on Eagles wings, 26. As a Flood 28. A flower 108. A night. 60. A post 26 a—shadow 122. As Vapor 38. A Warfare, 167.
Lion Christian as 88. Dead and dog 101. Oppressor as a crouching, 116.
Lightning, Christ's coming as, 158.
Looking to Jesus, 211.
Looking-glass hearers not doers. like a, 119.
Locusts wicked as 209.
LOVE, to Christ as a lily 205. A rose 78 146, to enemies as coals of fire, 111.

MALAYALIM PROVERBS 218.
MAN, clay 10. inner man of Heart woman's ornament 118. As a leaf, 12, as a worm 65.
MEEKNESS as dove's 141.
Melting power of love to enemies, 111.
Members of Christ believers as 160.
Merchant Christain a, 133.
Milk God's word as, 12.
MISERY, remembrance of as water passed away 113.
Mocking God by oppressing poor 161

Mortar a fool brayed in as, 74. Untempered a false peace 102.
Moon and Church 96.
Mote in brother's eye, 15.
Morning Star Christ the 67.
Moth body as, 17.

Nails words of wise as, 174.
Naked wicked are, 214.
Neck hardened of the obstinate, 173.
Net of the Gospel 204.
Night of life 60.

Obstinacy, neck hardened 173. as a Brazen brow, 174.
Oil Holy spirit like 197.
Ointment of Christ's name, 197.
Old Age, an old house 135. Of righteous a crown 182. Or a shock of corn 90. Or an unsetting sun 193.
Oppression, as a crouching lion 116. A Mocking God 161.
Oriental Customs, in the Bible 266.
Ox more grateful than sinner 95.

Palm, righteous flourish as a 31.
Peace, false as untempered mortar 106.
Persian Proverbs. 222.
Physician Christ a 115.
Pilgrims Christian's on earth 99.
Pit of destruction 220.
Plough of Gospel 204.
Poison of sin 96.
Post time as a 26.
Potter God as a 10.
Prayer, as hart thirst 125. Eagles wings 26. Incense 110.
Providence, Arms 77. Graves his people 210, a refuge 201. Dew 58. Hen 40. Guards as apple of eye 152. Wall of fire 3. Everlasting Shepherd 171. Safe guide 196. Stay 199.
Prison of hell, 70.
Punjab Proverbs. 222.
Proverbs, Abu Talibs Arabic, Arabic, Bagada, Bengali, Canarese, Chinese, Malayalim, Persian, Punjabi, Russian, Sanskrit, Tamul, Telegu, Turkish, Urdu, Veman's Telegu. 217-263.
Punishment, as an arrow 163, as an axe 127, as a storm 76, death wages of 181.
Purity as a single eye 107. Seeing God 199.

Quench not the Spirit 216.
Questions on Emblems 268.

Race, Christians of holiness 125.
Raiment white of holiness 140.
Rainbow Christ a 92.
Rain God's influence as 97.
Redeeming the time 186.
Reed humble as 56.
Refuge Providence a 201.
Rending of repentance 191.
Repentance, a rending of the heart 191. Tears of 127.
Rest of the grave 138.
Resurrection, a sowing 113.
Rich, needle's eye 28. Money of as eagles wings 57. Love of money root of all evil 112. Lion 88. Palm 31. Salt 7. Stewarts 159.
Righteous, God's husbandry 44, as palm tree 31, protected as a mountain goat 210, as Salt 7 Sheep 85. Stars 130. Trees planted by water side 209.
Rivers of water for sin 102, of God's grace 178.
Rock Christ the 79.
Rod of chastisement God's 145.
Root Christ a 197. Covetousness root of all evil 112.
Rose, Christ a 146.
Rottenness of bones envy 5.
Rush in the mire worldly hope 156
Russian Proverbs. 239.

Sacrifice of body 194.
Salt of the earth righteous as 7.
Sanskrit Sayings Atmabodh, Banarastak, Bhagavadgita, Chanakyea, Maha Mudgar, Malati Madhava,

INDEX.

Mrichhakati, Naba Ratna, Niti Shatak, Pancha Ratna, Prabodh Chandrody, Raghuvansa, Santi Shatak, Uttar Ram Charita, Vikram Urvasi. 251—258.
SATAN, father of lies 169. In chains 196 a fowler 209. 196.
Scarlet sins red as 85.
SCRIPTURE SIMILES. 264.
Seared conscience 154.
Sealing of Holy Spirit 133.
Sea troubled wicked as 52.
Seed Woman's bruises Serpents head 9 of God's word 46.
See God by purity 199.
Sepulchres whited hypocrites as 19.
Serpents head 9, poison sin as 96.
Servants Christians are 179.
Shadow our days as 132.
Sheep righteous as 85, 171.
Shepherd Providence a 171.
Sleep death as a 146.
Shield of faith 216.
Shipwreck of soul 173.
Silver refined believers as 37.
Sincerity unleavened bread of 215.
Smoke Gods anger as 176.
Spiders web hypocrite 10.
Ship time as a swift 26.
SIN, burthen 127. a debt 74, disease 42. Ethiopians Skin 25. Leprosy 117. little as dead flies. in ointment 140. Poison of Serpents 96 wages of 181.
SINNERS, blind 172.
Sleep death of righteous a 146.
SLUGGARD, taught by ant 20.
Soldier Christian a 63.
Soul Ship-wrecked 173.
Sowing to flesh 84.
Sparks affliction as 112.
Sting of sin death 198.
Stone Sinners heart as 6.
Star Christ the 67 righteous as 130.
Stay Providence a 199.
Stewarts rich are only 159.
Sting of death sin 198.
Stranger Christian a 152.
Stork knows time not sinner 33.

Storms of God's wrath 78.
STRIFE, beginning of letting out water 129.
Stronghold God the 141.
Sun Christ the 34. Christ rising as a 195 unsetting sun of christian's old age 193.
Sword bible word of God as 193.
Swallow ignorant worse than 204.
Swine jewel in snout of 15.

TALKING, not doing Sounding brass. 117.
TAMUL PROVERBS. 219
TELEGU PROVERBS. 223
Tent body as a 1.
Thief Christ as a 183.
THORNS, Crackling of so worldly Joy 4, wicked are 78.
TIME, as an eagle a post 26, redeeming 186, a shadow 132, a ship 26.
SUITABLE time, Stork knows 33.
TONGUE, a fire 90, a helm 160, wheel of nature fired by 184.
Tree man revives not as 39, righteous as 209, 94.
Treasures in earthen vessels 157 in heaven 170.
TRUTH, a girdle 75.
TURKISH PROVERBS. 211.

URDU PROVERBS. 226.

Valley of shadow of death 104.
Vapor life as a 38.
VEMANS TELEGU PROVERBS 230.
Vessels earthen heavenly treasures in 157.

Wages of sin death is 181.
Wall of Providence 3.
Walking with God 216.
War of death 37. Of life 167.
Water letting out of as strife 129. Spilled dead as 9. Holy Spirit as 50. Liberal as 65. Passed away remembrance as 143. Waterer watered 65.
Watchmen Christians are 72.

INDEX.

Way Christ the 148.
Web of Spider vain hopes as 11.
Well Christ a 202.
Wheel of nature fired by tongue 184.
Whirlwind, wicked pass as 16.
Wind Holy Spirit as 121.
WICKED as adder 36. wild Ass 39. Captive 144. Chaff 128. Clouds without water 130. Dross 89. Ears hear not 176. Foxes 21. Goats 30. Lamp put out 75. Sea 52. Thorns 78. Whirlwind 16. Wolves 208.
Wilderness world a 69.
Wings of riches 57. Of sun 195.
WITNESS false one as a sword 188.

Wolves wicked are 208.
World a dark glass 40. A night 62. An old garment 147. A wilderness 69.
Worm of conscience 173. Man a 65.
WORDS Apples of gold 181. Good 174.
WORKS bags not old 101. Fruit 94.
WRATH as butter from milk 137. Storm of God's 76.
WOMANS ornament hidden man of the heart 118. Seed bruises 9.
Writing belivers Gods 212.

Yoke of Christ Easy 200

CHRISTIAN TRUTH

IN

ORIENTAL GARB.

(1) THE BODY A TENT.

2 Cor. v., 1, 4.

ALL men are but passengers and pilgrims through this world; not real possessors of anything, but only tenants and occupiers in this transitory life. Some dwell in stately palaces; and many more in poor cottages; but all are born to the same mortality. If the poor man's hut drops into decay, he dies never the sooner; and if the house of the rich is founded upon a rock, he lives never the longer.

The holy patriarchs, *Abraham*, *Isaac*, and *Jacob*, inhabited no lofty cities, built no strong holds, but lived in tents or tabernacles, with which they removed from place to place, as God was pleased to order them. This was very remarkable in their case, because they did it in a land which God had promised to them for an inheritance: thereby signifying, that they did not accept of the earthly land, but looked for a *better country, that is, an heavenly*. When the *children of Israel* were journeying to Canaan, they lived by encampments in a wilderness, removing their tents from place to place for forty years, and ending their days in that unsettled way of life. Even when the people were fixed in Canaan, good men still devoted themselves to live as sojourners and pilgrims; thus the *Rechabites*, who renounced the pleasures and possessions of the world and dwelt in tents as their holy fathers had done before, Jer. xxxv., 6. Even God himself was pleased to partake of the condition of his people; making himself even under the law, that stranger upon earth which he was to be afterwards under the Gospel as the place of his worship in the wilderness, and long afterwards, was not fixed as a house, but moveable as a tent and a *tabernacle ;* and when Christ the Word was made flesh he is said to have *tabernacled* amongst us; living as one who renounced this world and all its possessions; more unprovided with house and land, than the foxes of the earth or the birds of the air. The passage from this world to the other is much more easy to those who live in this manner. The man of the world, who fixes his abode here, is violently torn away at his death, like the Banyan tree pulled up by the roots, and has no prospect after it: but he who lives in a tent is easily removed.

The soul dwells in a *house of clay,* the foundation of which is in the dust, and which is crushed before the moth, Job. iv., 19. This comparison reminds us of our frailty, and so ought to check in us "the pride of life" and all high or vain imagination, showing that we are "strangers and pilgrims upon earth."

It was an act of faith in *Abraham* to dwell in tabernacles in the land of promise as in a strange country. His practice in this respect was a perpetual confession that he regarded himself only as a stranger and traveller on the earth, and that "he looked for a city which hath foundations, whose builder and maker is God." The *feast of tabernacles* was appointed to remind the children of Israel of the wanderings of their forefathers in the wilderness (when they dwelt in tents), and thus to suggest to them continually the same thought, that this life is only a pilgrimage, and that our true home is elsewhere, that we have here no continuing city, but seek one to come. The Jews even now live in tents or booths made of trees when this feast comes round.

By faith, a Christian continually regards his body as a tent or tabernacle, a frail and uncertain habitation, suited to the condition of one who is only a traveller to his true home, offering no effectual protection against the many dangers to which he is exposed—a dwelling-place which may be struck or taken down in a moment, open to heat or cold, rain or lightning.

The Probodh Chandroday says *you should consider the society of friends as a momentary flash of lightning.* The Shanti Shatak writes: *Our place is like a terrible wilderness; our body like a building with much fleshy lattice-work in it; our earthly friends are like travellers whom we meet by chance and are soon separated from.*

The Moguls lived often in tents, miles in circumference, and which cost many lacs of rupees, being decorated with silk and gold; still they were but tents, and exposed to being blown down by storm, or consumed by fire.

(2) God a Wall of Fire to protect the Good.

Zech. ii., 5.

Babylon had walls 300 feet high and 70 feet thick, so that six carriages could drive abreast, yet the city was taken owing to the gates having been left open when the people were drunk. The walls of Gaur in Bengal were 100 feet high. The walls of Jericho were high, but they fell down at the command of God, Jos. vi, 20, so he destroys walls by earthquakes.

It was a practice of the eastern shepherds and travellers, in order to protect themselves and their flocks from the attacks of wild beasts at night, to make fires all around them, over which the most furious animals dare not pass; this custom is still adopted by travellers, in various parts of the world, where there are many wild beasts. Even the tiger, being afraid of fire, mounts not this wall.

The Christian is travelling as a pilgrim through this world a howling wilderness, the devil is a dragon, and the wicked as lions are ready to devour him, but he sleeps secure, surrounded with God a Wall of Fire; so the Jews walked through the Red Sea, the waters standing up on both sides as a wall, Ex. xiv., 22.

(3) WORDLY JOY AS THE CRACKLING OF THORNS.
Eccl. viii, 6.

Thorns at first blaze under a pot as if they would give out a mighty heat, but the water in it is cold—such is worldly enjoyment: all noise and smoke—no heat; cold as moonbeams, such is drunkenness—a sweet poison.

All earthly things are like the *earth* founded on nothing; they are like *Absalom's Mule*, they will most fail us when we have most need of them, 2 Sam. xviii., 9; a velvet slipper cannot cure the gout. The wicked are compared to thorns, because they are very troublesome and useless, and often cause great pain; their crackling is quickly over and with little effect, as thorns when alight though they make such a noise and fire yet give out little heat to the water: Similar is the Bengali Proverb *a fire of rags*.

Cowdung dried was the fuel commonly used for firing, but this was remarkably slow in burning. On this account the Arabs would frequently threaten to burn a person with cowdung as a lingering death. When this was used it was generally under their pots. This fuel is a very striking contrast to thorns and furze, and plants of that kind would doubtless be speedily consumed with crackling noise.

Wordly joys are short. Herod the king was gorgeously arrayed, so that the people worshipped him, but he was soon after devoured by worms, Acts. xii., 23. Queen Jezebel, a handsome woman, enjoyed her grandeur but a short time, and was eaten up by dogs, 2 Kng. x., 36. Belshabzar in his grand banquet at

Babylon, a city larger and mightier than Delhi, had his empire taken away at once, as foreshewn by a handwriting on the wall, Dan. v., 5, 6.

(4) ENVY THE ROTTENNESS OF THE BONES.
Pr. xiv., 30.

If the bones, the mainstay of the system, be rotten, the whole body becomes sick; a slow and torturing death takes place—so is it with envy.

Envy converts the happiness of which it is the witness into worm-wood and gall for its own cup, and transvenoms the honey of another man's comfort into the poison of asps for its own bosom: it is an instrument of selftorment—a burning ulceration of the soul—a crime, which, partaking of the guilt, partakes as largely of the misery of hell. We see it in *Cain*, the first murderer, who slew his brother at the instigation of this vice, Gen. iv., 4, in the dark, and gloomy, and revengeful spirit of *Saul*, who, under the influence of envy, plotted for years the slaughter of David, 1 Sam. xviii, 25. In *Ahab*, the king of Israel, when he pined for the vineyard of Naboth, and shed his blood to gain it, 1 Kng. xxi., it was envy that perpetrated that most atrocious crime on which the sun refused to look, and at which nature gave signs of abhorrence by the rending of the rocks—the crucifixion of Christ: for envy the Jews delivered our Lord, Acts viii., 14, 15. The envious man is a man of the worst diet, for he consumes himself, and delights in pining: a thorn-hedge covered with nettles; a peevish interpreter of good things; and no other than a lean and pale carcass, quickened with a fiend.

Envy is painful to ourselves, therefore called "the rottenness of the bones," it arises from pride, and is carried out in covetousness and evil desire, ending in discontent. Envy is discontentedness at another man's good and prosperous estate, holiness, esteem, renown, and ability. In carnal things it is sordid, in higher things it is devilish; in the one we partake with the beasts, who ravenously seek to take the prey from one another; in the other with the devils and evil angels, who being fallen from happiness, now malign and envy those that enjoy it, St. James—iii., 14—calls it "bitter envying," to distinguish it from that holy emulation which makes us strive who shall excel each other in the ways of godliness; as also from true zeal for God's glory. It proceeds from the overflow of gall and choler, that root of bitterness that is in the heart; it is bitter to ourselves and others, it makes us unpleasant to those with whom we converse; and though it be sweet for the present, yet, when conscience is opened, and we taste the fruits of it, it proves bitterness in the issue. Envy is but a cockatrice egg, that soon brings forth strife. The world had an early experience of it in *Abraham* and *Lot's* herdmen, Gen. xiii., 7, then in *Joseph* and his brethern; "When his brethren saw that their father loved him more than all his brethern, they hated him, and could not speak peaceably unto him," Gen. xxxvii., 4. They envied him, and they conspired to slay him. So in *Saul* and David; "And Saul eyed David from that day and forward," 1 Sam. xviii., 9.

The Bengali Proverb is "*in seeing another's wealth, it is not good to have the eyes smart.*" Sàdy in the *Gulistan* writes: "I can avoid injuring the mind of any one, but what shall I do to the envious man who carrieth the injury in his own breast, die thou envious wretch since thou canst not be cured of the disease under which thou laborest, but by death."

(5) THE SINNER'S HEART STONY.
Is. xxxvi., 26.

The heart of the wicked is compared to a stone, as—
Hard yields not to a blow, hence Job—xli, 24—refers to the heart of the crocodile hard as the nether millstone, arrows and spears are as stubble to him, they

will not enter—such were *Stephen's* murderers' hearts, Acts vii., 57. There are stones in India on which the rains and winds have been beating for many thousand years, yet they are not worn, while the instruments used to break these stones are often broken themselves, Lk. iv., 28.

2. *Senseless* no feeling, Eph. iv., 19, the wicked go as an ox to the slaughter, feeling no danger of their lives; they have no shame, but a brow of brass, Is. xlviii., 4; the seed that falls on stony soil springs not up, as there is no moisture in a stone.

3. *Heavy and the Motion downwards.*—The thoughts of the wicked are not up to heavenly things, but down to earthly, their God is their belly, they are of the earth earthy.

3. *No motion*, therefore no life.

4. *Cold* as being without life.

But God's Holy Spirit has a hammer, his word, Jer. xxiii., 29, which breaks the rock in pieces like the great steam hammers and gives a heart of flesh, such as *Paul*, who from a persecutor became a preacher of Christianity, so the hardened *jailor* when he became softened, he began to cry out, Act. xvi., 29, this hammer fastens conviction as a nail in a sure place, Is. xxii., 23, it softens and smashes the hardest rock.

---

(6) THE RIGHTEOUS THE SALT OF THE EARTH.
Mt. v., 13.

SALT is remarkable for its own peculiar savour, by which its presence in any substance with which it can unite itself is at once detected; spreading itself through any thing with which it is thus mixed, it imparts its own quality of saltness to the previous taste or savour. It has also the quality of preserving from corruption, even for a number of years, many substances that would otherwise perish; hence it is an emblem of what is enduring or perpetual.

God appointed that salt should be used in all the sacrifices offered to him: salt was the opposite to *leaven*, for it preserved from putrefaction and corruption, and signified the *purity* and *persevering fidelity* that are necessary in the worship of God. Every thing was seasoned with it, to signify the purity and perfection that should be extended through every part of the divine service, and through the hearts and lives of God's worshippers. It was called 'the salt of the covenant of God,' because, as salt is incorruptible, so were the covenant and promise of Jehovah. Among the heathens *salt* was a common ingredient in all their sacrificial offerings; and as it was considered essential to the comfort and preservation of life, and an emblem of the most perfect corporeal and mental endowments, so it was supposed to be one of the most acceptable presents they could make unto their gods, from whose sacrifices it was never absent. The delights of life, repose, and the highest mental serenity, are expressed by no other term than *sales*, among the Romans. It has also been applied to designate the honourable rewards given to soldiers, which are called "salarii," *salaries, i.e.*, salt money.

Salt is the symbol of *wisdom*, Col. iv., 6, of *perpetuity* and *incorruption*, Numb. xviii., 19, 2 Chron. xiii., 5, 4, of *hospitality*; and of that *fidelity* which is due from servants, friends, guests, and domestics, to those that entertain them, and receive them at their tables: it is used in this sense, Ezra, iv., 14, where *maintenance from the king's table* means *salted with the salt of the palace*. In Russia at the present day when the Emperor visits any of his subjects, bread and salt are presented to him as an emblem of hospitality.

A little salt seasons much meat, and prevents its perishing; so *Lot* was the salt of Sodom, and had there been ten righteous persons in it, the city would have been preserved, Gen. xviii., 32. Salt preserves the human body from worms, so the righteous save society from corruption.

(7) THE DEAD AS WATER SPILLED UPON THE GROUND.
2 *Sam.* xiv., 14.

The dead return no more to this world ; they are as water spilled on the ground which cannot be gathered up again, like Pharoah and his host which went to the bottom of the Red Sea, or David when he lost his child, and stopped weeping saying—I shall go to him but he shall not return to me, 2 Sam. xii., 23.

Solomon uses a similar emblem of the *tree* fallen rising no more, Eccl. xi., 3. The sound of the woodman's axe gives note that some giant of the forest is about to fall: soon the crashing boughs tell plainly that the work is done and the pride of the summer foliage is brought down to the ground. A gap is made in the screen of wood, and the eye can now wander over the soft meadows, and the distant village, that were hid before ! The fallen tree lies in the direction in which it fell. While it still flourished in its pride and glory, the direction as well as the period of its fall was uncertain. It was possible that it might fall toward the north, or toward the south: nor was there any reason why it should not enjoy the sunshine, and the rain, through many a verdant summer. But the word was given that the axe should be laid unto its root ; and now the direction in which it should fall is no more a question. It is a fixed and unalterable fact. The period during which one or the other direction could have been given to its fall is past and gone for ever. So the stroke of death fixes the direction and the character of our future state of being.

The Bengali Proverb is *the milk once drawn never enters the cow's dug again.*

(8) THE WOMAN'S SEED BRUISES THE SERPENT'S HEAD.
Gen. iii., 15.

In the Iceland Mythology the Deity is said to have bruised the Serpent's head, so among the Hindus Krishna tramples on the Serpent's head, who bites his heel.

Jesus Christ was the seed of the woman born of the Virgin Mary; he destroyed the Serpent's, *i.e.*, Satan's head, or power; The head of the Serpent is the seat of life. Satan is like a Serpent, the old Serpent, Rev. xii., 9.

Satan is like a *Serpent*.

1. *Subtle,* lies in wait in holes to catch his prey, so the Egyptians behaved to the Babylonians.

2. *Poisonous,* Deu. xxxii., 24, yet Paul by Divine aid shook off a viper, Acts xxviii., 8.

3. *Watches opportunity* to sting; so Ahab could not sleep on account of Naboth's vineyard.

4. Feeds on dust; Satan's food, sin.

5. Fair in appearance; so are hypocrites.

(9) Man as Clay; God as the Potter.
Is. lxv., 9.

All things made of earth are frail, and easily broken: and, though they are finely figured, painted, and gilded like porcelain, they are but earth still, and a fall destroys them.

Man comes from the hands of the Maker, as clay from the hand of the potter; and is called a *vessel,* because he has capacity to hold either good or evil, a vessel of wrath or a vessel of destruction. Paul is called a chosen vessel, and the wife the weaker vessel.

We are as clay in God's hands, and formed of the dust; He had the most absolute right to form us as vessels to honour or to dishonour, and to endue us with powers of mind and body of such extent, capacity, and efficiency, as might seem good unto Him. He had a right to determine the duration and conditions of our being, to appoint the bounds of our habitations, and all the circumstances on which our happiness and welfare in any degree depend. He was pleased to create man in his own image as a vessel unto honour;

a little lower indeed than the angels, but still endued with noble faculties, and crowned with dominion over the beasts of the field, when man "marred" this Divine image and beauty by his own sinful folly. God had the most absolute right either at once to "dash him in pieces as a potter's vessel," or to continue his existence, and appoint him a new probation, on such conditions as he might see fit to enjoin with! whatever advantages or disadvantages He might be pleased to assign.

---

(10) HYPOCRITES' TRUST LIKE THE SPIDER'S WEB.

Job viii., 14.

The Italians to express the community of goods between true friends, say they tie their purses with a spider's web, *i.e.*, easily broken.

The spider weaves its web out of its own bowels, and with wonderful skill prepares a net-work which far surpasses the most curious product of human workmanship, even the Kashmir shawl in the regularity and fineness of its texture. It is said of her, that "she taketh hold with her hands, and is in kings' palaces." She succeeds in fixing herself even in the mansions of the great, and clings tenaciously to the haunt or home which she has chosen. Her web is admirably woven for the purpose which she has in view; and such insects, as are incautiously entangled in it, become an easy prey to their artful enemy. Yet is it also so frail and slight that a breath might rend it; and at last it is brushed away in a moment by the meanest servant of the house, the sweeper. So the hypocrite's hope is spun out of his own fancies, as the spider's web out of her own bowels; and it consists either in a groundless conceit of his own merits, or in an equally erroneous notion of God's character. By art and subtlety, however, he often succeeds in gaining his end; which is to obtain the praise of men, and a large share of earthly prosperity.

The spider when he suspects his web—here called his house—to be frail or unsure, leans upon it in different parts, propping himself on his hinder legs, and pulling with his fore-claws, to see if all be safe. If he find any part of it injured, he immediately adds new cordage to that part, and attaches it strongly to the wall. When he finds all safe and strong, he retires into his hole at one corner, and supposes himself to be in a state of complete security; the web looks very beautiful in sunshine, in a moment, however, any accident, to say nothing of a dirty brush or the metre's broom, sweeps away himself, and his house.

(11) God's Word like Milk.
1 Pt. ii., 42.

Newly converted Christians are compared to babes as God is their father, Jerusalem above the mother of all, Gal. iv., 26; 2, of the same nature with the parents that which is born of the flesh is flesh. 3, harmless; 4, helpless; Christ carries the lambs in his bosom, Is xl., 10; 5, ignorant, when I was a child I thought as a child. Peter showed himself as a babe when he did not believe in the humiliation of Christ, Mt. xvi., 22, and when he refused to eat food ceremonially unclean.

Milk means the plain truths of Christianity, salvation by faith in Christ, regeneration by the Holy Spirit. Milk nourishes, so does God's Word, Mt. iv., 4; 2, desired by babes; 3, restoration in disease; in Russia many people are cured of consumption by drinking mare's milk. One of the blessings of Canaan was that it was a land flowing with milk and honey.

The Mysterious Doctrines of Christianity, such as the Trinity, God's foreknowledge, are described as strong meat which babes cannot digest, Heb. v., 14.

(12) Man fades as a Leaf.
Is. lxiv., 6.

In Europe owing to the climate the greater part of the trees lose their leaves every year; it is not so in India.

The leaf becomes pale from a green hue when about to fall. How gradually does the change come on! We scarcely perceive a difference from day to day; but after the interval of a week it is distinctly seen; and then the breeze of autumn snaps the link by which the shred was joined to its branch, and wafts it to its resting-place under the parent tree, or it serves as fuel and manure.

And such is the strength of man. "We all do fade as a leaf light and unsubstantial." The freshness of youth soon passes into the maturity of manhood; and thus, by gradual but rapid steps, the feebleness of age comes on. Thus is "our strength, but labor and sorrow, so soon passeth it away, and we are gone."

Let it not be said of us, "Gray hairs are on him yet he knoweth it not." In youth and health let us think on our common frailty, and put away from us "the pride of life;" remembering that we must soon return to the dust from whence we came.

The leaves with which the earth is strewn, and which serve to manure, it will know no second spring, but our great Redeemer has won for us a resurrection from the grave.

How does a leaf fade? Two main features characterize the manner of its fall—certainty and uncertainty. In one aspect nothing is more fixed, and in another nothing more fluctuating. All those myriads that now glitter in the sunshine or flutter in the breeze will be strewn on the ground ere the year die out; but when this one shall fall, and how long that one shall hang, no tongue can tell. One falls smitten by a mildew soon after it has burst from the bud in spring; a second is withered by a worm at its root in early summer; a third is shaken off by a boisterous wind; and a fourth is nipped by frost in autumn. In what part of the year any leaf will drop is wholly uncertain; that all will be down ere the year be over is absolutely a sure. We may see in this fragile mirror the reflection of our own frailty. The generation now living, though composed of 1,000,000,000 of people, will, in a few years, be all beneath the dust; but the departure of each is as uncertain as the dropping of the leaves. Some drop in childhood's spring, some in the bloom of youth, some in the maturity of manhood, and some hang on till the winter of age arrive. These two things are clear—the time is short to all, and the short time is uncertain to each.

The conquerors in the great Grecian games of running, wrestling, &c., were crowned with leaves that looked very handsome for a time, but they soon faded away, not so the righteous man—though his outer man decay as the leaves, yet his inner man shall be like an ever green leaf.

(13) CHRIST HAS THE KEYS OF DEATH AND HELL.
Rev. i., 18.

Silence was represented by the Greeks as a golden key on the tongue.

Christ said to Peter *I will give unto thee the Keys of the Kingdom of Heaven*, Mt. xvi., 19, as stewards of a great family, especially of the royal household, bore a key, probably a golden one, in token of their office; the phrase of giving a person the key naturally grew into an expression of raising him to great power, Is. xxii., 22, Rev. iii., 7. This was with peculiar propriety applicable to ministers, the stewards of the mysteries of God, 1 Cor. iv., 1. Peter's opening the kingdom of heaven, as being the first that preached it both to the Jews and to the Gentiles, may be considered as an illustration of this promise; as also the power given of binding and loosing; authority to explain the law and the prophets was given among the Jews by the delivery of a key; in the case of one rabbi after his death they put his key and his tablets into his coffin, because he did not deserve to have a son to whom he might leave the ensigns of his office.

When a person is put into office, he is often intrusted with keys; thus a jailer has the keys of a prison. Ancient keys were often made of wood; and, to be strong, they were very large, so that they were carried on the shoulder; and, in the east, the carrying of a key on any great occasion was a mark of a person's holding some office of rank and power. Thus it is said of Jesus, "And the government shall be upon his shoulder;" that is, he shall have power as one that carries the key to mark his authority.

Jesus Christ says he who believes on him shall never see death, *i.e.*, Spiritual death.

---

(14) IGNORANT BUT BEAUTIFUL AS A JEWEL IN A SWINE'S SNOUT.
Pro. xi., 22.

Chanakyea says: a *handsome youth of high family, but without learning, is like the palasi tree, fair to see but without scent.*

A body may be beautiful but the soul loathsome—such were Absalom and Jezebel.

A Hindu Dramatist writes: *men are foolish in cherishing the gay blossoms of the palasa, whilst they neglect the fruit bearing amon, because its flowers are insignificant.*

The Bengali Proverb is *outside smooth and painted, inside only straw*—like Hindu idols stuffed with straw.

The *Drishtanta Shatak* states a bad person, though decorated, remains the same as cowdung which, though it be fertile, does not become pleasing.

A Russian Proverb is *a head without a mind, is a mere statue.* A Hindustani, *the fruit of the colocinth is good to look at, not to taste.*

---

(15) LOOKING AT THE MOTE IN A BROTHER'S EYE, WITH A BEAM IN YOUR OWN.
Mt. vii., 3.

The Russians have a proverb—*a pig came up to a horse and said your feet are crooked, and your hair* is worth nothing. The Bengalis say, "*the sieve says to the needle you have a hole in your tail.*"

Christian humility teaches us to regard others as better than ourselves. St. Paul, though the chief apostle, called himself the chief of sinners.

---

(16) THE WICKED PASS AWAY AS A WHIRLWIND.

Pro. x., 25.

In eastern countries so rapid and impetuous sometimes is the whirlwind, that it is in vain to think of flying; the swiftest horse though running a mile in two minutes, or the fastest sailing ship could be of no use to carry the traveller out of danger. Torrents of burning sand roll before it, the firmament is enveloped in a thick veil, and the sun appears of the colour of blood. In the frightful deserts of Senaar is pointed out a spot among some sandy hillocks, where the ground seemed to be more elevated than the rest, where one of the largest caravans which ever came out of Egypt, to the number of several thousand camels, was covered with sand, and every one perished.

The destruction of Sennacherib's army (2 Kng. xix., 35) was probably effected under the direction of an angel by the blast of the hot pestilential south wind blowing from the deserts of Lybia, called the Simoon. Sennacherib and his immense army had come like a whirlwind, threatening to bear down all before them, but they quickly vanished; one hundred and eighty-five thousand Assyrians being destroyed in one night, 2 Kng. xix., 35.

The world of the ungodly perished by the flood, Gen. vii., 21.

In one day three and twenty thousand Israelites, who had joined Baal-peor, were killed, Numb. xxv., 4, &c., 1 Cor. x., 8.

Solomon writes the hope of the ungodly is like dust (thistle-down), that is blown away with the wind; like a thin froth that is driven away with the storm; like as the smoke which is dispersed here and there with a tempest, and passeth away as the remembrance of a guest that tarrieth but a day.

The life of the wicked like a whirlwind rises *suddenly*, Acts ii., 2. Jonah's ship was caught in a whirlwind, Jon. i., 4; it is very *swift*, hence said, to have wings, 2 Sam. xxii., 14; *very destructive*, 1 Kng. xix., 11.

Yet God who holds the wind in his fists, Pro. xxx., 4, made a whirlwind to serve as Elizah's chariot to heaven, 2 Kng. ii., 11.

—

(17) MAN'S BODY A HOUSE OF CLAY, CRUSHED LIKE THE MOTH.
Job iv., 19.

These words were spoken by a spirit from the other world who addressed Job at midnight.

The grave is called the house appointed for all living, Job xxx., 23. The body is compared to a house of clay which is easily swept away by torrents, the walls of which, owing to rents, are the abodes of snakes. Swallows make their houses of clay.

In Arabia, the houses in general are built of white clay, and covered with reeds. Their foundations are laid in the dust or sand, the country affording no firmer basis on which to build; they are exposed to all the accidents of that climate, such as violent winds, and large moving pillars of sand, called sand-floods, by which they are liable to be blown down, or overwhelmed and crushed to the ground, together with their inhabitants, unless they can effect a timely escape.

Oftentimes they are crushed before the moth-worm, which lodges either in some part of their dress, or in the furniture of the dwelling; and not unfrequently survives man, secure for a time from the general ruin by reason of its slender form, and of the soft and yielding nature of the material which it occupies.

These desolating calamities more generally begin about sunrise, and usually continue till towards evening; and thus men perish from the morning to evening, without any one regarding it.

Robbers easily dig through the walls of houses of clay as is the case very often in Bengal *Sindkata*, Job xxiv., 16.

Manu calls the body "a mansion with bones for its rafters and beams; such a mansion let the soul cheerfully quit, as a tree leaves the bank of the river, or as a bird leaves the branch of a tree; thus he has his body delivered soon from the ravening shark the world."

The moth is a small insect which noiselessly, and gradually eats through garments, though very feeble, Job xxvii., 18. The rich are no more spared than the poor, but it especially attacks things not kept clean, and does its works secretly, spoils by degrees; so God gives cleanness of teeth, the palmer worm, the pestilence, Am iv., 8; the moth eats the inside when the outside is good, so *Sampson* said when his locks were gone, I will rise up; so the Jews, 2 Kng. xv.

Small things, as *lice*, *flies*, are a great plague. In Arabia and parts of India people drink bad water from which comes an egg that produces a worm in the body, from which often come palsy, gangrene, death.

The clothes-moth is of a white, shining, silver, or pearl colour. It is clothed with shells, fourteen in number, and these are scaly. This insect eats woollen stuffs; it is produced from a gray speckled moth, that flies by night, creeps among woollens, and there lays her eggs, which, after a little time, are hatched as worms, and in this state they feed on their habitation, till they change into a chrysalis, and thence emerge into moths. The young moth, or moth-worm, upon leaving the egg which a *papilio* had lodged upon a piece of stuff, commodious for her purpose, finds a proper place of residence, grows and feeds upon the nap, and likewise builds with it an apartment, which is fixed to the groundwork of the stuff with several cords and a little glue. From an aperture in this habitation, the moth-worm devours and demolishes all about him; and, when he has cleared the place, he draws out all the fastenings of his tent; after which he carries it to some little distance, and then fixes it with the slender cords in a new situation.

This perishing condition of *a moth-eaten garment,* as also of *the insect itself,* is referred to in Is. li., 6: "*The earth shall wax old as doth a garment,* and they that dwell therein *shall die in like manner.*"

He who buildeth his fortunes by methods of injustice, is by Job, xxvii., 18, compared to the *moth,* which, by eating into the garment, wherein it makes its habitation, destroys its own dwelling. The structure referred to is that provided by the insect, in its larva or caterpillar state, as a temporary residence during its wonderful change from a chrysalis to a winged insect.

---

(18) HYPOCRITES ARE WHITED SEPULCHRES.

Mat. xxiii., 27.

Sepulchres were beautiful without, loathsome within; hence they were away from cities, as those who touched the dead were accounted polluted.

Chanakyeu says, v. 16, a friend who injures your business in your absence, but speaks smoothly when you are present, should be shamed as *bishkumbhang payamukhang,* a bowl of poison with milk on its surface. The Bengali proverb says, *the heron is (in appearance) a saint as long as the fish is not in sight. The female devotee pretends not to eat fish, but there are three on her leaf; she does not talk with men, but three are hidden in her house.*

Hypocrites likened, Lk. xi., 44, to graves that appear not because covered with grass and weeds.

Paul called Ananias a whited wall, Acts xxiii., 3.

These hypocrites worshipped God with their lips, while their hearts were far from him, Mat. xv., 8, and by their extortions they devoured widow's houses, Mat. xxiii., 14.

Cain was a hypocrite in worshipping God without sacrifice and pretending not to know where his brother was when he had killed him, Gen. iv., 49; so Judas when he kissed Christ after he had betrayed him for 30 rupees, Mat. xxvi., 49.

(19) THE SLUGGARD TAUGHT BY THE ANT.
Pro. vi., 6, 8.

Animals teach us in scripture—thus the ass knowing his owner while man knows not God, Is i., 3; the crow has no barns, yet God provides for it; the swallow knows his time to emigrate, but man forgets his time for departure from the world, Jer viii., 7, so the ant here teaches. *Chanakyea* gives the lessons which the dog teaches us, of contentment with little—vigilant watching, gratitude and fortitude, the power of patience, indifference to cold and heat. The crow teaches Providence for the future and agility—the cock—early rising, sharing food and protecting women.

The bee, like the ant, is a pattern of diligence. As often as the sun shines, she goes out to work, and never loses any opportunity of gathering and laying up her honey. There is an idle sort of bees in the hive, which are called drones; these are killed and cast out by the busy bees; and it is a rule amongst them, as it ought to be amongst Christians, that "if any will not work, neither should he eat;" as being one who is unworthy to live. If any man eat without working, somebody else must work the more for it. If one of the legs should be benumbed, and will not walk, the other leg must do the work of both.

The bee, to look upon, is a poor little brown fly, with no beauty to make us admire it; yet it is the wisest of all insects. So is the nightingale, or *kokil*, with all its musical notes, which fill the woods, and charm the ear in the spring time in England, a little brown bird, not so handsome as a sparrow. The excellence of these creatures is in their art and wisdom, not in their outward form and beauty. The painted butterfly is very much admired, but it never makes any honey. The peacock has feathers embroidered with gold, and shining like the rainbow, but its voice is little better than the braying of the ass.

With respect to Ants their uniform care and promptitude in improving every moment as it passes, the admirable order in which they proceed to the scene of action, the perfect harmony which reigns in their bands, the eagerness which they discover in running to the assistance of the weak and the fatigued, the readiness with which those that have no burden yield the way to their fellows that bend under their load, or when the grain happens to be too heavy, cut it in two, and take the half upon their own shoulders, furnish a striking example of industry, benevolence, and concord, to the human family the skill and vigour which they display in digging under ground, in building their houses, and in constructing their cells, and their prudence and foresight in making use of the proper seasons to collect a supply of provision sufficient for their purpose are admirable, and should not be passed over in silence.

(20) THE WICKED LIKE FOXES OR JACKALS.
Lk. xiii., 23.

The jackal is a beast between the wolf and the dog, partaking of the nature of both, to the fierceness and shyness of the one joining the impudence and familiarity of the other.

Herod the king was called a fox, because he tried to catch Christ by cunning, Lk. xiii., 32, Mat. ii., 8, false teachers are also so called, Ez. xiii., 4, they used rough garments to deceive, Zech xiii., 14, in imitation of the true teachers, who wore sackcloth and hairy garments.

The wicked are like foxes in—

1. *Craftiness;* the fox when pursued and caught pretends to be dead: he uses his tail to catch crabs, he has many entrances to his den; so he moves crookedly and steals up lightly, Neh. iv., 3.

2. Cruel and destructive, he destroys more than he kills, Kng. xxii., 34; he makes havoc among grapes.

3. Attacking at night.

4. Greedy, eats all kind of filthy putrid things, lives on filth, digs up dead bodies.

5. Move in packs to destroy; so Samuel used three hundred of them with lighted brands to their tails to fire the corn, Jd. xv., 4, the wicked combine to do evil.

Christ said even the foxes had holes, but he had not where to lay his head, Lk. ix., 48.

---

(21) HOPE IN CHRIST THE ANCHOR OF THE SOUL.
Heb. vi., 19.

Every man has some kind of hope. Sangkar Acharyea, in the *Maha Mudgar,* writes: "Day and night, evening and morning, winter and spring come and go, time sports with our passing age, still the wind of hope ceases not. The body dissolves, the head gets gray, the mouth becomes toothless, the handsome stick trembles in the hand, yet hope ceases not to jest with us."

This world, full of uneasy cares and unlimited desires, is likened to the sea, which is ever restless; treacherous in its smiles; swept by frequent tempests; full of hidden rocks and quicksands, the ruin of many a gallant ship. The Apostle speaks of some on this sea "who make shipwreck concerning faith;" the Church of God has, however, to cross its wild and stormy waves before it can reach "the haven where it would be." The ark of Noah, borne up in safety above the waters of the flood, was in this respect a type of the Church of Christ.

As then the Christian has to cross a sea, which is so full of hidden rocks, and so much exposed to tempestuous winds, he is provided with an anchor which may help to save him from making shipwreck, and from being the sport of many a storm that would otherwise drive him up and down, without any sure knowledge of the course which he ought to take. This anchor is the hope which is set before sinners in Jesus Christ.

Hope is also compared to a helmet, 1 Thes. v., 8 protecting the head against spiritual enemies. The Arabs call a water-melon hope, because of its tendrils which cling to a prop. The merchant trades and the ploughman ploughs in hope. Hope deferred makes the heart sick, Pro. xiii., and the hope of the wicked is as the giving up the ghost, Job iv, 20, *i.e.*, like the last puff of breath when the person is dying. Hope is compared to a rush, a flag, a house built on the sand, Job xv., 2.

The Christian's hope in Christ is like an anchor.

(1) The anchor secures the vessel against tides or storms, Heb. x., 34.

(2) The anchor is out of sight, so hope dwells on things invisible, as Abraham, Rom. iv., 18, hoped against hope in reference to the birth of Isaac waiting 25 years. So Paul in the case of shipwreck, Acts xxiv., 15.

(3) This anchor rests not on the mud of this world, but on Christ the rock of ages, and they who have this hope or desire of future good will make efforts to realise the object.

---

(22) LET THE DEAD BURY THEIR DEAD.
Lk. ix., 60.

Christ said these words to one of his disciples whose employment was preaching, but who wished to go and bury his father. How can one dead man bury another? This can never be, unless the word *dead* be taken in two different senses; for, then, a man who is dead, in one sense, may be buried by another, who in a different sense is as dead as he; that is, *dead in trespasses and sins*. To be carnally minded is *death*, saith the Apostle: and the poor prodigal son in the parable, having lived in that state of mind till his conversion, the father says of him, " This thy brother *was dead, and is alive again.*"

Man has a soul and a body, each of which dies in its own way; and so either of them may be alive while the other is dead. There is a sense in which Adam died on the day when he sinned; and there is another sense in which Adam lived nine hundred and thirty years. Adam delivered down a natural life to all us that are born of him: but the only inheritance he could leave to our spirits was that death to which he was fallen. It is this death of the spirit which makes it necessary for every man to be born again.

We may preach all day long, to those not living to God, and do no more good by it than if we were to preach to a man in his coffin. If we were to cry into their ears, or blow a trumpet, to give them warning of the fire of judgment, and of eternal damnation, they would hear nothing.

If we offer to them the bread of life, they want it not: for a dead man has no appetite. Were the souls of men as visible as their bodies, we should see as much difference betwixt devout christians and the children of this world as betwixt a living healthy body and a dead corpse.

Wordly people are twice dead as St. Jude says: dead once by nature, and dead again unto grace. The pleasures of this world will extinguish the life of a Christian. " She that liveth in pleasure is dead while she liveth." When an affection to this world enters into the mind, and takes possession of it, all heavenly affections will die out.

A good man is described as while dead yet speaking, *i.e.,* by his works.

(23) Man's Corruption like the Ethiopians Skin.
Jer. xiii., 23.

The Russians have as illustrative proverbs: "The wolf changes his hair, but yet remains the wolf.—However you bind a tree, it will always grow upward; though you put oil on a dog's tail it will never become straight." The Hindustanis say: "If you put a crow in a cage will it talk like a parrot." The Sanskrit proverb is: "The Nim Tree will not be sweetned though you water it with milk." "The *Niti Sar* states "Though the crow's beak be gold, and his feet diamonds, yet the crow cannot become a swan."

Though the corruption from Adam cannot be changed by nature, yet God's Spirit can do it by supernatural power: thus Paul from being a persecutor of the Christians in three days so changed afterwards as to become a preacher of Christanity.

---

(24) Brotherly Unity a Threefold Cord.
Eccl. iv., 12.

There is more pleasure in what is shared with another —if one man, as Joseph is in a pit, he requires some one to take him out. God said of Adam in Paradise, "It was not good for man to be alone."

The Ramsanchis, a sect of western India, say regarding society: "A solitary lamp, however brilliant, casteth a shadow beneath it; place another lamp in the apartment, and the darkness of both is dissipated."

Soldiers union is their strength. A Father, on *his death bed*, represented unity by a bundle of sticks.

Love like *fire* streams forth by natural results and unavoidable emanations; like the *vine*, it withers and dies, if it has nothing to embrace.

The Apostles were sent forth two by two, Lk. x., 13, in the body all instruments of action are by pairs, hands, feet, eyes, ears, legs. The live *coal* left alone soon loses its vital heat. Iron sharpens iron, Pro. xxvii., 9, 17, Ex. xviii., 7, 9.

(25) Time compared to a Dak-post, Swift Ships, Eagles.

Job ix., 25, 26

In Job's days human life was gradually shortening.

A Bengali proverb states: " There is no hand to catch time."

The Persian messengers could, by royal authority, press horses, men, or ships, so as to expedite them, Esth. iii., 15.

The Dromedary post, though not as quick as a horse in a given space, yet maintains an uniform continued progress. By this Agency Mordicaia issued letters.

The Italians say: " Time is an *inaudible file*." The Greeks: " Man is a bubble."

Time is like a post.

(1) The postman rides on *swift horses*, 150 miles a day, while the caravan move at 2 miles an hour.

(2) *Changes* in order to increase speed.

(3) *Delays* little for rest or mere salutation.

(4) *Allows no obstruction on the road*.

The post may be stayed, but the sun never stops.

Time, in its rapid devastating course, is compared to a flood, Ps. xc., to a tale that is told, Ps. xc.

Swift ships, *i.e.*, made of papyrus of the Nile, which cut through the water with easy speed.

---

(26) The Believer's Life amounting on Eagle's Wings.

Is. xl., 30, 31.

1. The Eagle is the *king* of birds as the Lion is of beasts, so the Saint's are the excellent in the Earth, Ps. xvi., 2, 3, more excellent than their neighbours, Ps. xii., 26, 1 Cor. iv., 9, of whom the world was not worthy, Heb. xi., 38. Believers are sons of God of royal blood, Rev. i., 5, while the wicked feed on the wind, or husks, Heb. xii., 1, the righteous have manna, and Angels as attendants.

2. *Quick sighted*, Job. xxxix., 29, hence a man, 2, Sam. xiv., 20, is called eagle-eyed. The eagle can look at the sun, or see from above fish in the water, so believers behold the glory of God with open face, 2 Cor. iii., 18. The secrets of the Lord are with them that fear him, Ps. xxv., 14; they see the end of the wicked.

3. *Swift*, they have long wings; hence *Solomon* says: "Riches makes themselves wings and fly away like an eagle." *David*, lamenting the death of Saul and Jonathan, says: "They, as friends, were stronger than lions and swifter than eagles, 2 Sam. i., 23." *Nebuchadnezzer* came as an eagle against the temple, Heb. viii., 1, Jer. xliv., 22. Job compares life to an eagle, ix., 28, viii., 1 Ps. cxix., 59, 60, Rev. xiv, 6; hence, Nebuchadnezzar is represented as a great eagle with great wings, long feathers, having various nations in his empire, and took the highest branch of a cedar.

4. *Mount high*, out of sight lost in the clouds above the tempest and lightening; worldlings are moles, or worms which grovel in the earth, but believers have their conversation in heaven, Ph. iii., 20, mounting up on the wings of faith and prayer, Cor. iii., 3. *Nebuchadnezzer* built his nest on high, but for purposes of pride, Dan. iv., 30.

5. *Not tired.* Believers do not faint, Gal. vi., though the flight to heaven be long yet the wings of faith and love bear them up, Ps. xxvii., 13.

6. *Aim at high things*, not at flies or worms. An English proverb says: "Eagles catch no flies;" not like the crow who goes out early for this purpose, Job. xxxix., 27.

7. *Nestles on high*, Is. xxxiii., 16, amid lofty rocks above the clouds, where no enemy can come.

8. *Lively in old age*, by moulting his youth renewed Ps. ciii., 5. Believers put on the new man, the old is cast-off; angels have immortal youth. The eagle is so strong as to be able to carry away a lamb or a child.

9. *The young are borne on the mother's wings*, Deut. xxxii., 11, 12, so the Jews, Ex. xix., 4, Jer. iv., 13,

Lev. iv., 19. The *Aitareya Veda* says: "*Though* 100 *bodies like iron chains hold me down, yet like a falcon I quickly rise.*"

27. Life Quick as a Flood.
Ps. xci., 4, 6.

This Psalm was composed by Moses towards the close of his wandering in the desert when human life had been shortened, and when out of 3,000,000 Jews that came into the desert only two adults were allowed.

There are more than one thousand millions of people in the world, composed like the Ganges and Brahmaputra, streams of streams of many nations; they make a great noise, like a flood rise as suddenly and as suddenly go down to the Ocean of Eternity. Some of these floods fertilize the soil, while others sweep away cattle and villages, so some men lead the lives of lions, others of goats.

28. Trusting in Riches as a Camel through a Needle's Eye.
Mat. xix., 24.

When Christ says it is easier for a camel to go through a needle's eye than for a rich man to enter the kingdom of heaven, he explains: He meant those who trusted in riches rather than God; for *Abraham* was a rich man, yet good, Gen. xiii., 2, so *Isaac*, Gen. xxvi., 13, so *Joseph*, Gen. xlv., 8, *Joseph of Arimathea*, Mat. xxvii., 57. It is those who use riches for pride, oppression, sensuality, Jas. ii, 6; as Haman, Est. v., 11., *Esau*, Gen. xxxvi., 7.

An Oriental Proverb represents impossible things, thus

Unmitigated evil is as rare
As wings upon a cat, or flowers of air,
As rabbits horns, or ropes of tortoise hair.

The Bengali proverb is, "putting an elephant into a narrow dish; a horses eggs, or a flower in the air."

The Persians express the idea, thus saying of a needle's eye: "A needle's eye is wide enough for a friend, the whole world is too narrow for foes."

(29) GOD'S PEOPLE HIS JEWELS.
Mat. iii., 16, 17.

Jewels are much valued in every country; hence the New Jerusalem's gates are represented as made of pearls, Rev. xxi., 18, 21, Is. liv., 12. The jewels on the High Priest's breastplate symbolise the twelve tribes as dear to him. An esteemed wife is called by the Hindus a jewel of a woman.

The righteous are like jewels.

1. *Jewels are dug out of the earth*, except the pearl found in the oyster; the diamond is only crystalised carbon or coal hardened in the earth; so believers at first of the earth earthy (1 Cor. xv.) dead in trespasses. They are called little ones, like Zaccheus, who though a little man was privileged to receive Christ into his house.

2. *Jewels receive a fine polish.* A wheel is used for this purpose, so adversity polishes Christians to put on the new man as it did to *Job, David, Polycarp*; the polishing comtinues till all the flaws are removed, thus the Church hereafter will be without spot or blemish.

3. *Jewels are rare.* Many stones and metals are not equal in value to a small one, so Christians a little flock, Luke xii., 32, not many wise called. Silver and gold were as stones in Solomon's times, 1 Kng. x., 27, so again in the New Jerusalem.

4. *Jewels are very beautiful*—yellow, green, purple; so the Christian graces are beautiful—as love with *John*, humility as in *Mary*, patience as in *Job*, a putting on Christ—whatever things are lovely, Phl. iv, 8. Believers like Jewels shine in the dark, so believers are the light of the world, so Peter John's boldness was admired, though they were ignorant men, Acts iv., 5. Stephen's face shone when dying, Acts.

5. *Jewels are durable;* such was the Kohi Nur of Ranjit Sing. This is one cause of their value, so the hidden man of the heart, 1 Peter iii. 4, when earthly jewels shall be destroyed at the last day the righteous shall shine forth, Mat. xiii., 43; many seeming jewels are only glass as in Ceylon, so with hypocrites.

6. *Jewels are very valuable;* so Christians are the pearls of creation, of great price, Mat. xiii., 45, believers redeemed not with curruptible things, 1 Peter i., 17, the precious sons of Zion were esteemed by the Chaldeans as earthen vessels, Lam. iv, 2, yet regarded as the apple of God's eye, Zech. ii, 8. Ten jewels, *i.e.*, good men would have saved Sodom could they have been procured.

7. *Jewels are ornamental, set in a crown, ring, or seal;* so the Christian's crown will be an ornament to Christ's crown. Used by brides and kings, to angels is manifested the love of God to man. Christians a purchased people; Christ glorified in his saints who are his jewels, and bears them on his breastplate, Ex. xxviii., 49.

8. *Jewels collected from the sea and mines amidst rubbish;* many jewels are buried and lost.

9. *Jewels are kept carefully;* so Christians are kept by the power of God; angel have charge over them, Mat. iv., 6. The Lord is their shade.

10. *Jewels take long in making and polishing;* so religion in the soul a work of time, Phil. i., 6, liable to being marred in the making.

---

(30) THE WICKED COMPARED TO GOATS.
Mat. xxv., 31, 33.

The Devil is worshipped in some countries under the form of a goat. The Goat like the wicked—

1. *Feeds among sheep;* so hypocrites in a church, so tares and wheat—but the Shepherd will separate them at the judgment day. *Chanakyea* compares an uneducated man in society to a *bak* (crane) among swans.

2. *Mischievous;* destroys trees, plants, hence bad princes so called, Zech. x., 3.

3. *Unclean,* stinks; so the wicked, Rom. i., 26, 27.

4. *Greedy;* 100 goats will eat as much as 1,000 sheep, so *Ahab* coveted *Naboth's* vineyard though he was so rich himself. The Bengalis have a proverb " what will not a goat eat or a fool say."

---

(31) THE RIGHTEOUS FLOURISH AS THE PALM TREE.
Ps. xcii., 11.

Linnus called palms the princes of the vegetable kingdom, but the Palm of Scripture was far finer than the palm of Bengal: Palmyra was so called from its palms, 2 Kng. viii., 4.

The righteous are like the palm.

1. *The palm tree grows in the desert.* Earth is a desert to the Christan; true believers are even refreshed in it as a palm is in the Arabian desert, so *Lot* amid Sodom's wickedness, and *Enoch* who walked with God amongst the antediluvians.

2. *The palm tree grows from the sand, but the sand is not its food;* water below feeds its tap roots, though the heavens above be brass. Some Christians, not as the lily, Hos. xiv., 5 by green pastures, or willow by water-courses, Is. xliv., 4, but as the palm of the desert, so *Joseph* among the Cat-worshippers of Egypt, *Daniel* in voluptuous Babylon, faiths penetrating root reaches the fountains of living waters.

3. *The palm tree is beautiful,* with its tall and verdant canopy, and the silvery flashes of its waving plumes; so the Christian virtues are not like the creeper or bramble tending downwards, their palm branches shoot upwards, and seek the things above where Christ dwells, Col. iii., 1; some trees are crooked and snarled, but the Christian is a tall palm as a son of the light, Mat. iii., 12, Phil. ii., 15. The Jews were called a crooked generation, Deut. xxxii., 5, and Satan a crooked serpent, Is. xxvii., bu

the Christian is upright like the palm. Its beautiful, unfading leaves made it an emblem of victory, it was twisted into verdant booths at the feast of Tabernacles and the multitude, when escorting Christ to his coronation in Jerusalem, spread leaves on the way, Mat. xxi., 8, so victors in heaven are represented as having palms in their hands, Rev. vii., 9. No dust adheres to the leaf as it does with the *balirce;* the Christian is in the world not of it, the dust of Earth's desert adheres not to his palm leaf. The leaf of the palm is the same—it does not fall in winter and even in the summer it has no holiday-clothing, it is an ever-green; the palm trees rustling is the desert orison.

4. *The palm tree is very useful.* The Hindus reckon it has 360 uses. Its shadow shelters, its fruit refreshes the weary traveller, it points out to water, such was *Barnabas,* a son of consolation, Acts iv., 36, such Lydia, Dorcas, others, who on the king's highway showed the way to heaven, as Phillip did to the Ethiopian eunuch, Acts ix., 34. Jericho was called the City of Palms, Deut. xxxiv., 3.

5. *The palm tree produces even to old age.* The best dates are produced when the tree is from thirty to one hundred years old: 300lbs. of dates are annually yielded; so the Christian grows happier and more useful as he becomes older, knowing his own faults more, he is more mellow to others, he is like the sun setting, beautiful, mild, and large, looking like Elim where the wearied Jews found twelve wells and seventy palm trees.

---

(32) DECEITFUL BRETHREN AS A BROOK.
Job vi., 7, 15.

Job lived in the barren dry desert of Arabia, where no river is, and water is scarce, there are torrents in winter swelling from the melting of the snow on the hills as the Ganges does, *very noisy,* but in summer dried up or absorbed in the sand. The Arabs call a false friend a mirage, or a torrent, swelling, noisy in prosperity, but soon absorbed in the sand, Jer. xxxv., 7. Valleys in Arabia, that have a quarter of mile breadth, mile wide of water in winter, are yet quite dry in summer.

Tyre trusted in its walls and port and is now become only a place for fishermen to dry their nets on. The rich fool trusted in his wealth, Lk. xii., 19, and it left him. Solomon states: "Confidence in an unfaithful man in time of trouble is like a broken tooth and a foot out of joint." That affection which is knit in God alone is indissoluble. The Jews trusted the Egyptians who proved like a broken reed (Is. xxxvi., 6), which not only fails the hand that leans upon it, but pierces and wounds it.

The Bengali proverbs state: "A loose tooth and feeble friend are equally bad. A dam of sand and the love of the vicious have the same fate." Chanakya says: "A wicked person, though sweet speaking, is not to be trusted; honey is on his tongue, but in his heart poison."

(33) A Suitable Time taught by the Stork.
Jer. viii., 7.

In Denmark the storks are not able to stand the winter; on its approach they congregate and depart in a body, returning in the spring, so do the *cuckow, swallow, tyedchátuk, hargil* in Bengal. Men know the signs of the weather, and when it is time to start on a journey, but not so when the shadows of life's evening are coming, people do not see the signs of death's approach. The Italians say, "time is an inaudible file," which destroys gradually without its being noticed. Christ reproached the people that though knowing the signs of bad weather, they did not know the bulk of spiritual things, so God in Jeremiah reproaches the people for not, like the birds, looking into the future; the wicked are like the ostrich which, when pursued, hides its head between its legs, fancying because it does not see the coming danger that it will not ensue.

(34) Christ the Sun of Righteousness.
Mal. iv., 2.

The sun shines on all, penetrates deeply, exhales the noxious vapors from the earth, cheers by its light: veiled sometimes by clouds, it soon disperses them, and the light of the stars grows pale before it.

The sun is the source of light and beauty; without it all is gloom and dullness. David calls it God's tabernacle; in Chaldea they worshipped the sun; we are to use it, however, to lead us unto God as our rock, as an emblem of God's unchangeableness, and of his being the foundation of inexhaustible, over flowing benevolence. As the sun is a type of God's Effulgence and Energy, so the term Sun of Righteousness is peculiarly applicable to Christ.

1. *The sun is the centre of the planets,* his attraction is an adamantine chain which, hanging on nothing, keeps the planets in their place, so Christ is the head of the church, Eph v., 23. Look not to yourselves but to Christ. Thirty planets, with orbits millions of miles in diameter, some performing their revolution in a century, move round this sun; so Christ is the head of all principalities of angels, Eph. i., 21.

2. *The sun shines by its own light, not so the planets;* the light though 95 millions of miles distant comes in eight minutes. David compares his rising to a bridegroom; so is Christ the brightness of the Father's glory, his eyes penetrate like the sun's rays, his light is the same yesterday to-day and for ever,—but the sun has spots, in Christ there is no darkness, Jer. i., 5. The sun, however, shall wax old as a garment, not so Christ, Heb. i., 12. The sun was stopped by Joshua, not so the Sun of Righteousness; various rays from the sun concentrate in the rainbow, so God's attributes blended in Christ's,—righteousness and peace have kissed each other, Ps. lxxxv., 10. Christ seen of angels received into glory the gaze of Intelligences in other regions of creation.

3. *The sun is the source of light, heat, beauty:* in Christ is the true light, Ju. i., 7, the day spring from

on high; light reveals things as a ray does particles of dust, so the *publican* found when he smote his breast, Lk. xviii., 13. The Sun's light awakens life in the spring, so in Ezekiel's valley of dry bones, Ez. xxxvii. The heat of the sun melts the ice of winter, and brings round the joy of spring, when the birds sing, and the flowers blossom giving life and energy, so with the disciples going to Emaus, whose hearts burned within them talking to Jesus, the Sun newly risen from the grave.

4. *The sun rising is gradual, but punctual*, at dawn a faint streak, the fields have its illumination, then it becomes reddish; so Christ was born in the fullness of time. The sun is seen before his rising owing to refraction, and the sun's rising is known years before, so Christ's rising on men and angels, who knew of this and like the three *wise men* hailed the rising, as, travellers go to a mountain to see the sunrise; the sun's progress is steady, so Christ first illuminated the Jews, then the heathen. The sun enlightens only half the globe, but Christ the whole of the earth, which will ultimately be filled with his glory, Ps. xlii., 19, Rev. xxi., 25.

The spiritual Sun knows no setting, Is. lx., 20, so the believer's Sun shall no more go down; no need of the material sun in the new Jerusalem, Rev. xxi., 4.

---

(35) FAITH THE BODY, BUT WORKS THE SOUL.

Jas. ii., 26.

Faith is the root, works are the fruit: to try to do works without faith is like the Bengali proverb, "cutting away the root and watering the branches." The *Egyptians* painted a tongue with a hand under it, to show that knowledge and speech are efficacious and good, when that which is known and said is done. We must be golden-handed as well as golden-mouthed. Blessed are they that *do* his commandments, that they may have right to the Tree of Life, Rev. xxii, 14. Knowledge without action is a man without arms; it is wine shut up in the vessel that does good to none, and will corrupt at last and mar the vessel. Such knowledge will be like the poison that lies long in the body and at last kills without remedy.

Chanakya says, *learning placed only in books, and wealth in the hands of others, are of no use as not available in the time of action.* A Sanskrit proverb says, *Patitā Nihatā Stryā, a fallen woman, is dead,* so she that liveth in pleasure, 1 Tim. v., 6.

In *rain* not mere water fructifies, but a secret spirit or nitre that descends with it. Doing is the noblest improvement of being. The soul's essence is *action.* Religion, if confined to the heart, is not so much entertained as imprisoned, that indeed is to be its *fountain* but not its *channel;* fountains would not be so much valued if they did not produce rivers. God planted religion among men as a tree of life, which though it was to spring *upward* directly to himself, yet it was to spread its branches to the benefit of *all below;* like incense, which, while it ascends to heaven, it perfumes all about it. Not like the man who tells me his heart is right with God when his hand is in my pocket.

---

(36) THE WICKED AS A DEAF ADDER OR POISONOUS SERPENT.

Ps. lviii., 3‑8.

Absalom had, by his insinuating address and beauty of person, so alienated the hearts of his subjects from David his father that he even seduced Ahitophel, David's bosom friend; and they promised redress to the poor and oppressed, but it was all pretence.

Corrupt doctrine like Dragon's wine, Deut. xxxii, 33.
The wicked like poison—
1. *Inflames;* so the passion, envy, and wrath.
2. *Spreads very quick;* so did Adam's sin.

3. *Sting not painful;* but effects evil, Deut. xxxii., 33, Job xx., 12, "no dining with the devil, and supping with Abraham."

4. *Kills eventually if medicine be not taken.*

---

(37) No Discharge in Death's War.
Eccl. viii., 8.

The Turks say, death is a black camel which kneels at every man's gate, *i.e.*, for the corpse. The English say every door may be shut, but death's door. The Bengalis, you may anoint yourself with ghi at Gaya, but you will not escape death.

Christ, however, has abolished death, 2 Tim. i., 10, by taking away its sting, sin, and by his own rising from the tomb.

The wicked are driven away by death—the righteous desire to depart and to be with Christ; death ends all the joys of the wicked and all the sorrows of the righteous—the one sleeps, and the other is in flames.

---

(38) God refines his People like Silver.
Mat. iii., 2.

This simile is taken from the refiners who in their crucible separate the dross from the ore, so believers have the fiery trial of trouble, 1 Cor. iii., 13.

1. *Refiner's work is to try and refine metals;* so God tries his people's graces, Sam. iv., 2,.

2. The metal before refinement is full of dross, Mat xv., 19, Job. xxv., 4, so we are naturally sinners.

3. *Fire* is used to purify, so the furnace of affliction, Is. xlviii., 10, Ps. xvii., 3.

4. *The silver is not pliable before refinement,* so our will is stubborn; Job said, God makes my heart soft, Job xxiii., 16, Jer. ix., 7.

5. *More fire required to hasten the work;* so in heaviness through manifold temptation, 1 Pt. iv., 12.

6. The dross removed makes the metal, though less in quantity, yet of more value, more, Is. xiii., 12.

7. Refining required several times, so silver seven times refined; God has many modes of refining fires, floods, storm, disease, Ps. xxxvii., 20.

8. The fire is not for washing the metal but for purifying it, chastened for our profit, Heb. xii., 2.

9. Fine vessels made by this process, 2 Tim. ii., 20, in a great house vessels.

10. The refiner refines but a little at a time; God refines a kingdom. Alloy is put in to make metal pliable, but the Holy Spirit is the hammer of God's word.

11. The metal is not left in the fire after purifying, Is. xxvii., 78.

12. The refiner uses *fuel*, so the wicked are God's fuel as Pharoah, so Babylon made a burnt mountain, Jer. li., 25, the great captains, Rev. vi., 17, so the sellers in the temple, Jer. ii., 14, 17.

(39) Life a Vapor.
Jas. iv., 13, 14.

The *Shánti Shatak* states "human existence is like a bottomless gulph, and human life like the fleeting cum of its rolling waves." The *Maha Mudgar* writes, "life is quivering like a drop of water on a lotus leaf."

Firdusi writes :—

" Look at the heavens, how they roll on,
And look at man, how soon he's gone !
A breath of wind and then no more—
A world like this should man deplore."

The Bengali proverb, "That employ is the shadow of a cloud."

The *Lalita Vistara* compares life to the view of a dance—the lightening—a torrent rushing from the mountain,—so said Sakhya Muni when tempted to remain in his father's palace.

If life is a vapor what are its comforts? Great if God is an everlasting dwelling place, Ps. xci. Christians are not troubled for *evil tidings*, their heart is fixed, Ps. cxii. The passage in Romans. xiii., 11, converted St. Augustine.

(40) MAN A WILD ASS'S COLT.
Job. xi., 15, 17.

Vain means in Hebrew hollow, empty, insincere.

The wild asses commonly inhabit the deserts of *Great Tartary*, they migrate to feed in summer to the North and East of the Aral Sea, in winter they retreat towards India, they go also to Persia. They were abundant once in Arabia and Mesopotamia. Like wild horses they assemble under a leader, are very shy; they will suffer the approach of man for an instant, and will then dart off with the utmost rapidity, fleet as the wind. The vast salt desert is their home, they scorn the multitude of the city, Jer. ii., 24, the wild ass *snuffeth up the wind* at her pleasure. The European ass is an emblem of obstinacy and immobility, not so the wild one, but the further from Tartary the more degenerate the ass is. The Tartar asses exceed horses in speed, and are never caught alive.

Ishmael is called a wild ass, Gen. xvi., 12. *Ephraim* is compared to a wild ass, Heb. viii., 9, as he traversed the desert as earnestly in pursuit of idols as the wild untamed ass did in search of his mate, Jer. xiv., 6, the asses snuff up the wind like dragons, *i.e.*, seek the air for want of water to cool their internal heat, Job xxiv., 5; *robbers* called wild asses, so the Bedouins the desolate city rejoiced, Is. xxxii., 14, so *Nebuchadnezzar* lived among them, Dan. v., 21.

(41) MAN REVIVES NOT AS A TREE.
Job. xiv., 7, 12.

The *Romans* made trees a symbol of death, planted those in burial places, from whose roots no germs arise such as the pine, cyprus. Man does not revive to return from death to the scenes of his Earthly occupations, not so a tree, night comes, but so does the *Morning* with fresh fragrance glittering with dew. *Winter* ravages but the Embryan blossom survives and spring comes. When the *trunk* of the tree is cut down, it dies not altogether, life remains within, but man cut down does not spring up again.

---

(42) This World a Dark Glass.
1 *Cor.* xiii., 11.

The eastern mirrors were made of *polished steel*, or brass, hence the *sky* is compared in Job. xxxvii., 18, to a molten looking-glass. The Moorish women in Barbary hang looking-glasses on their breasts.

There were in Paul's time no glass windows, but talc or horn such as was used in Calcutta a century ago, through these people saw very dimly, such is our vision now of God's attributes, and of the mysteries of Christianity.

---

(43) Providence as a Hen sheltering her Chickens.
Mat. xxiii., 27.

A hen on seeing the hawk that is hovering over her young, hastens forward to meet her frightened brood. Fearless in that defence she places herself in front of the danger. She gathers her chickens under her wings. Not one of them is denied admission to that hiding-place, which they all so fondly seek, under a sense of their own utter helplessness. How beautiful in so lowly and timid a creature is such an instance of tenderness; such forgetfulness of her own danger, and her own feebleness in the defence of her more helpless progeny! How wonderful an endowment is the *gift of instinct;* less exalted indeed than reason in its capacities; but more true and faultless in exercising them, so far as they extend! But above all how wonderful that so lowly a creature should be capable of feeling and conduct which admit of comparison with the mercy shown by the most high towards the children of men. Yet how faint is even the maternal instinct, when compared with His Divine compassion! "Can a woman forget her sucking child that she should not have compassion on the son of her womb. Yea, they may forget, yet will I not forget thee," Is. xlix., 15. Christ knew our danger. He thought not of his own suffering; He did not keep himself from shame and from the cross; He placed himself in the very front of the danger; and on His side, and hands, and feet are the wounds received in that conflict with the powers of darkness which, for our sake, He underwent.

Christ had previously called the Pharisees the Gurus of that day, hypocrites, blind guides, serpents; in this text all is love to the people of Jerusalem.

Man is more inconsiderate than animals, than an ox, Is. i., 3, or the ass, Is. i., 3.

1. *A hen is very compassionate to her young;* so Christ wept over Jerusalem, Mat. xxiii. 13. The hen even flies at a dog approaching to her young; so Christ resisted the devil, Mat. iv., 6, 8.

2. *A hen becomes weak from nourishing her young;* so Christ sweat great drops of blood, Mat. xxvi., 30, He bore the heavy cross, Lk. xxiii., 14.

3. A hen *clucks* to warn her young of danger; so God pleads—why will you die, Ez. xviii., 11.

4. *A hen's wings receive her young,* Ps. xci., 3, lxiii., 7. God says I have spread out my hands, Is. lxv., 2, come all that labor, Mat. xi., 28, 29.

A hen *scratches* to get meat for her young, so God says—Ho every one that thirsts, Is. lv., 1; she fasts herself to give meat to them. A hen soon forgets *her young* when grown; not so Chirst—Can a woman forget her sucking child? Is. xlviii., 6. A hen loses her young in spite of herself, God's people never perish, John x., 28.

(44) THE DISEASE OF SIN.
Is. i., 6.

David was a man after God's own "heart;" though living in a palace of cedar, he could not prevent disease, the fruit of sin, from entering; "his loins were filled with a loathsome disease," Ps. xxxviii., 7; no soundness in his flesh, no rest in his bones, an emblem of sin; this was the man once so lively who danced before the ark.

Sin is like a sore disease.

1. *This disease causes pain.* Pain is often useful in warning of danger to the body; thus fire warns, but to the conscience there is often an opiate, the absence of mental pain; thus Cain did not feel at first that he was guilty of murder; he said, am I my brother's keeper? So when David committed murder and adultery, he slept well. On another occasion, however, he states the arrows of the Almighty are within him. A pain often points out the seat of disease; opiates are not good in such a case. The pain of everlasting burnings should be anticipated like as in the case of the men that heard Peter who were pricked to the heart, Acts. ii., 37.

2. *This disease wastes the body and beauty.* His beauty consumes like a moth, Ps. xxxix., 11. The Nazarites, whiter than snow, became black as a coal, Lam. iv., 8. God saw once every thing he made was good, even man's body, but sin has dimmed the fine gold. "They are altogether become filthy." The jaundiced eye does not always see its own ugliness; so with the sinner.

3. *This disease impairs the strength of the limbs.* The strong becomes very weak, so the sinner—"sin revived I died." The sick man tries to walk, but falls; he has the will, not the power. The law in the members warring against the law of the mind, Rom. vii., 23.

4. *This disease spoils the appetite.* Food is necessary, yet there is no relish, hence death ensues; the manna of

God's word is despised; the honeycomb of the promises is loathed; the wine and milk of Gospel truth are rejected; he turns as a dog to his vomit, and eats husks, Job. xxxiii., 21. Behold he prayeth was the sign of Saul's spiritual appetite, Acts. ix., 11.

5. *This disease blasts the comforts of life.* The Ear enjoys not music; Job when a leper said, my soul chooseth strangling rather than life, Job. vii., 15. Vanity of vanities, says Solomon; as vinegar upon nitre, so songs to a heavy heart, Pr. xxv., 20.

6. *This diseas unchinges the whole body.* The Heart and limbs feel local complaints. I am poured out like water, Ps. xxii., 14; so the conscience calls bitter sweet, the whole head is sick. The Imagination is only evil.

7. *This disease terminates in death.* The Blood is affected, and then the dust returns to dust; he that liveth in pleasure is dead, 1 Tim. v., 6. How fearful are plagues, such as small-pox, cholera, yet how much more so the disease of sin.

8. *This disease is deeply seated.* Not skin deep, but affecting the vital parts of the blood and the heart which is deceitful above all things.

9. *This disease is widely spread* since Adam's time; small-pox, leprosy are spread to every part of the body, so man's members are made instruments of unrighteousness; "his tongue, a world of iniquity;" his eyes full of adultery; his hands defiled with bribes; his feet swift to shed blood.

10. *This disease extremely complicated.* Now the fever of agitated passion, the palsy of want of natural affection, the decay of spiritual affection—a complication of disorders, so that what is a remedy, in one case is a poison in another.

11. *This disease is hereditary.* "What is born of the flesh is flesh." "In sin did my mother conceive me," Ps. li., 5. By one man sin entered into the world Rom. v., 12; so Gehazi's family inherited from him the leprosy.

12. *This disease is most infectious.* The atmosphere of the earth is charged with it; disease is caught from the air of a room or from clothes, but sin from a glance, or a word as in David's case. Evil communications corrupt good manners. Only Christ was exempt from this infection; like a sunbeam He could penetrate impurity without being soiled.

13. *This disease is very loathsome and malignant.* The body as in leprosy is often a putrid mass, so that friends cannot come near. Paul says, "who shall deliver me from the (putrid) body of this death."

14. *This disease is shameful and criminal.* So the drunkard's and libertine's complaints.

15. *This disease is incurable by human means;* sin when it hath conceived, brought forth death. Quack doctors will not do. No doctors can cure this leprosy.

---

(45) THE RIGHTEOUS ARE GOD'S HUSBANDRY.
1 *Cor.* iii., 9.

The relation of Christ to His Church is pointed out in the Bible under a variety of pleasing images, such as of a *building, jewels, friends;* here it is under that of a well-managed farm.

1. *Christians are God's special property.* Ground in commonage is not well cultivated, it must become the property of some person to be attended to; so the Lord's portion is his people, purchased from the waste of this world by his own blood. "A purchased people," of a price if not according to the intrinsic value, yet according to the interest taken by the purchaser.

2. *Christians are meted out, separated.* Boundaries for farms are necessary, so the boundaries of the visible and invisible church, of the church and the world—"I have chosen you out of the world."

3. *Christians are fenced and protected.* A stone may be a landmark, or a furrow may be a line of division, but a fence is necessary to prevent trespass. "My

beloved had a garden, he fenced it." Church discipline and laws are a fence to Christians ? so is God's providence. "Hast thou not set a fence around Job ?" "a garden enclosed is my sister." Come out from among them, and be separate.

4. *Christians are subject to a spiritual cultivation.* The fruits of righteousness are the great object. Many improvements of late have been made in English agriculture; so it is necessary to improve in spiritual husbandry. God says, "what could I have done more for vineyard than I have done ?"

5. *An adequate band of labourers as instruments is provided.* Labourers are necessary for a farm, among the Jews, a whole tribe was set apart for this spiritual work; in Christianity he gave some Apostles and some prophets; he finds labourers idle in the market; sees and thrusts them out; "he that puts his hand to the plough and looks back is not fit for the kingdom of God."

6. *Suitable instruments are furnished.* Man's hand could do little without the spade and plough. God's word is the plough to root out weeds. The fallow ground of the heart must be ploughed up, Heb. x., 12, Is. v., 6. Weeds must be destroyed, and the light must enter; "the word of God is sharper than a two-edged sword;" the plough-share of conviction breaks up the fallow soil; such were those who were pricked to the heart when Peter preached, Acts. ii., 37. "The peaceable fruits of righteousness,"—rending the heart not the garment. The Mattock of the law from Sinai will break very hard soil, Is. vii., 25; so the hammer of God's word, Jer. xxiii., 29. Affliction destroys the weeds of corruption.

7. *The soil is improved and enriched.* Drainage for some, manure for other soils is necessary; so God gives a heart of flesh, as the field becomes fertile from blood and bones, so the blood of atonement purges the conscience from dead works."

8. *The soil must be sown with heavenly seed.* Without this seed vice will spring up; sowing requires good seed, good soil and a good season, Rom. vii., 4; no good seed of itself, Jn. iii., 6, Hos. xx., 12.

9. *The crop must be watched and dressed.* Seed must be pressed into the soil, and protected from vermin and cattle; the crop is sometimes over luxuriant.

10. *The soil must be watered.* Egypt was watered by the foot to convey water in rivulets. Blessed are they that sow beside all waters "floods on the dry ground."

12. *Fruit is expected;* hence the waiting for the latter rain. "The harvest of the earth will be gathered" in by God, then the joy of harvest home, Heb. xi., 9.

13. *Low lands are more fertile than high.* Rain descends on the valley and remains, Jer. xvii., 8.

Fruit was sought on the fig-tree three years, Lk. xiii., 7, hence Christ cursed it. The husbandmen that would not cultivate were destroyed, Mark xii., 9. The seven Churches of Asia had their hedges broken down. God is the sole proprietor, and cannot be dispossessed, He is never weary, and never grows old, Is. xl., 28, he can make bad trees good and sends rain..

---

(46) THE SEED OF GOD'S WORD.
Lk. viii., 11.

The Bible, as the Word of God, is compared in Scripture to *a key,* to open out the treasures of Divine Wisdom, as *milk* to nourish the feeble minded, as *fire* to consume or enliven and to *gold* for its value and use, here it is compared to a seed on account of its hidden qualities, its power of spreading from a small beginning. There is a tree in New Zealand, 400 feet high and 50 feet in circumference, yet this has sprung from a small seed.

1. *Seed is small, compared with its future produce;* as the seed is small, compared with the tree's spreading branches, so faith is like a grain of mustard seed or leaven which leaveneth the whole lump;

the seeds of faith, in the 11th chapter of Hebrews, "yield plentiful fruit," "do not despise day of small things."

2. *Seed must be sown.* Industry and forethought are required; bad seed springs up of itself. God cursed the ground, so that it gave of itself thorns and thistles. The seeds of faith spring up as the gift of God as the radicle from the kernel; when God sows in the wilderness an oasis springs up.

3 *A good seed requires good soil.* The application of the plough is, however, necessary as weeds grow anywhere; Christ in his parable mentions three soils as unproductive; our heart is the soil, and conviction the plough, we must be moistened by the tears of Godly sorrow, saturated by the dews of God's grace, like the 3,000 pricked to the heart who were baptized, Acts ii., 40, 41.

4. *Seed must be buried,* Jer. xii., 26. Some seeds, though thrown on the surface, however strike their roots deep, and require soil above them, Mat. xiii., 6, Lk. ix., 44, but in other cases the root and stem soon wither; so Lydias' heart was opened, Acts xvi., 14, believers are rooted and grounded in love, Eph. iii., 17.

5. *Seed lies for a time in the earth in darkness.* Sometimes a very short time, so the thief on the cross. Egyptian mummy seed after being buried 3,000 years springs up, so the *Prodigal's son* came to himself after he had spent all in riotous living, and was feeding swine; so *Manasseh* after many years sought in affliction his father's God, 2 Chr. xxxiii., 3, cast thy bread on the waters, Eccl. xi., 1; one soweth, another reapeth.

6. *Seed once sown makes steady progress.* Christ speaks of the blade, the ear and the full corn, Mark iv., 27, 28; grow in grace. They shall bring forth fruit in old age, Ps. xcii., 14. The righteous shall grow like a cedar of Lebanon, Ps. xcii., 11.

7. *Seed depends on the influence of heavy rain, which waters the earth.* Light, soil and moisture are necessary; we must wait for the latter rain; so Paul

plants, Apollos waters, but God gives the increase, Is. xliv., 3. God will pour floods on the dry ground.

8. *Seed matured yields a rich return.* God's word is compared to rain that returns not again, Is. lv., 10. You shall reap if you faint not, Gal. vi., 9, and have 100 fold more in this present time.

9. *Produce is as the seed sown.* There is a great variety of seeds, but the generic distinction remains as figs come not of thistles, Mat. vii., 16. He that sows to the flesh, reaps corruption, Gal. v., 8; he sowing the wind reaps the whirlwind, Hos. viii., 7. Haman sowed pride, reaped defeat; so the wine-bibber, Pro. xxiii., 29; so the rich man drowned in destruction, 1 Tim. vi., 9; so war from lust Jas. iv., 1, Ephesus John's seat, is now a Mussalman city.

10. *Water is required;* hence the thorny ground allows none; so the dews of the Spirit, early rain necessary after the seed is sown and the latter rain when the corn is ripe, Jer. v., 24.

11. *The Seed dies,* Jer. xii., 24, *i.e.,* the albumen dissolves an emblem of the resurrection, 1 Cor. xv., 36, Is. vi., 63.

12. *If sown too deeply no air comes;* hence ploughing brings the seeds up, for malting barley heat, moisture, and air are neccessary thereby the starch is changed into sugar, the seed to sow is reserved from the choicest grain by the husbandman, Ps. cxix.

13. *A Skilful sower required;* such was Christ.

14. Seeds must be covered from the birds, so David, Ps. 119, 9, Col. 3, 11.

15. The sooner the seed is sown the better the crop, 1 Tim. 3, 15.

16. Diligence needed, 1 Cr. xv., 8, winds, storm, thunder hinder not the sower.

17. *They must be widely scattered,* 1 Cor. i., 16, seed must be sent from land to land, and handed down to others, some seed bad, some not successful.

When the corn is fully ripe it bends down the ear; so the Christian is to be clothed with humility, 1 Pet. v., 5.

(47) CHRISTIANS TO BE AS LITTLE CHILDREN.
Mat. xviii., 2.

Christ the Lord of Glory became an infant wrapped in swaddling clothes, He carried the lambs of the flock in His own bosom. When His disciples repelled them He took the little children up in His arms and blessed them. He has used children as an emblem, He was a teacher of babes, and has taught us humility by babes, and particularly when the disciples disputed about pre-eminence He set a child in the midst.

1. *Docile* a child is; no prejudice; no habit to prevent its receiving impressions, "train up a child in the way he should go, Pr., xxii., 6, so believers made new men by the Spirit, the mind of a child is compared to a sheet of white paper on which you can write any thing. David calls himself a weaned child, Ps. cxxxi., 2.

2. *Confiding*; the young of animals are not so dependent in reference to the world as are infants. This, however, causes more love. The mother's smile and breast are everything to the helpless babe; so the believer depends entirely on God for many years; the father's house is its home. "Ask and ye shall receive; so Abraham went forth, not knowing whither he went." Jacob in the same spirit went down to Egypt. Moses forsook Egypt not fearing the king. Paul said, I know in whom I have believed.

3. *Humble and contented with little things.* Christ said, I am meek and lowly in heart. Paul said, in whatever state I am, I have learned to be content; submissive obedience is easily taught to a child; so with the Christian every high thing is cast down; whom the Lord loveth He chasteneth.

4. *Simple-minded* a child tells its meaning at once, its desires and aversions; so the Christian has God's

glory as his sole guide. "Behold an Israelite in deed, in whom is no guile," still to prevent imposition in the world the wisdom of the serpent is to be united to the harmlessness of the dove. Gentle love to be without dissimulation, anger endures only for a little. The Christian does good unto all, especially to those of the household of faith.

5. *Detached from the world*, 1 Cor. xiv., 20, to it business, ambition, wealth pleasures are nothing, on the Exchange it would find no pleasure, "not a grey head upon green shoulders;" so the Christian is not conformed to the world; his joys a stranger intermeddles not with, buying as though they bought not.

6. *Attached to its father's house.* Early recollections lead him to it as a bird to its nest; so Jacob domesticated in Padan-Aram, longed for his father's house; so Joseph when he saw his brethren; so the Christian longs for heaven, as the hart after the water brooks, for Jerusalem above his home, we in this tabernacle groan.

(48) THE HOLY SPIRIT LIKE WATER.
Rev. xxii., 1.

The Gospel is the ministration of the Spirit; hence the Spirit with his gifts is often compared to water, as Christ said to the woman of Samaria, Jn. iv., 14.

1. *Water comes from the ocean* and returns to it; so the Holy Spirit the Comforter comes from the Father the Ocean of Being, Jn. xv., 26.

2. *Cleanses* the soul from sin, 1 Cor. vi., 11; so Christ's blood through the Eternal Spirit, Heb. xiii., 14, 1 Pet. i., 22.

3. *Cools;* (so evil desires cooled by the Holy Spirit, Dives begged water to cool his tongue, Lk. xvi., 24.)

4. *Fructifies;* man naturally as the wild heath in the desert from draught not like grass kept green.

Zaccheus the publican on his conversion cried out the half of my goods, I give to the poor, Lk. xix., 8; so those who laid their money at the Apostles' feet, Acts iv., 37.

5. *Softens*, Ps. lxv., 10. Water softens and prepares the earth for the plough. Saul so fierce, cried out what wilt thou have me to do, Acts ix., 6. 3,000 were pricked to the heart, Acts ii., 37.

6. *Quenches* thirst. The desires of the soul are only satisfied by the Holy Spirit, Jer. iv., 14.

7. *Accessible to all*, cheap, Is. lv., 1. Ho! every one athirst come to the river of water of life, Rev. xxii., 7.

8. *Extinguishes* fire; so the fire of passion and of pride is extinguished. Too much earthy water may surfeit; it may become muddy. The Romans symbolised diseases by muddy waters. One of their punishments was to throw a criminal into a lake of muddy water Many go long distances to get good water, but the Spiritual Water is in the reach of all. The water of purification among the Jews was mingled with the ashes of the red heifer being sprinkled by a branch of hyssop on the unclean party and he was purified, Ex. xxxvi., 26. God will sprinkle clean water on the wicked.

9. *Penetrates easily*; so the Spirit, poured out, Joel. ii., 28, Is. xliv 3, floods on the dry ground.

---

(49) DOING GOOD IS BREAD CAST ON THE WATERS.
Eccl. xi., 1.

Rice is sown upon the waters, but before sowing the ground, while still covered with water, is trodden by oxen which go mid-leg deep. This is the best way for preparing the ground for sowing; and as the rice is sown on the water so it springs up through the water, and the height of its stem is generally in proportion to the depth of the water on the surface of the soil.

It is in reference to this practice of the rice in the rains being formed into balls, and sunk in water, Is. xxxii., 20, that the passage in Is. xxxii., 20, is to be explained, "blessed are ye that sow beside all waters." In six months in Egypt a rice crop comes up.

The relief given in secret to a stranger, who may never be seen again, shall be blessed not only to him, but still more surely to the donor; it shall be found after many days; so Abraham entertained angels who afterwards requited him. And the same may be said of the word of good advice, given "in season" to some one at a period of brief intercourse; nor shall any effort fail of due fruit, by which persons have shown forth their love to Christ their Saviour.

The Turkish proverb says: "*Do good, throw bread into the water, even if the fish does not know, yet the Creator knows.*" All the promises are yea to those in Christ, 2 Cor. i., 20.

The corn-seed throwing into the mud, at the subsidence of the Nile, seems lost, but nothing is lost that is done for God, Is. xxxii., 20. The fruit will be found at the resurrection of the just, Lk. xiv., 24, so also is the case with instruction, Is. lv., 10.

(50) THE WICKED LIKE THE TROUBLED SEA.
Is. lvii., 20.

The sea is generally considered as terrible, men do not reflect on the wonders and blessings which it presents to us in so visible a manner, it conveys ships, cools the air, yields plenty of fish, supplies water to the clouds and salt, the saltness of the sea is such that a pound of its water contains two ounces of salt. The sea-salt appears to be lighter than that which we use in common; yet it is not drawn into the air by evaporation, nor does the salt diminish by the continual pouring in of fresh water from all the rivers flowing into it, yet not filling it; this saltness is necessary for certain purposes; it prevents the water from corrupting, and contributes to make it so heavy that the greatest ships may be transported from one place to another. The colour of the sea-water also deserves our attention, it is not the same everywhere; as in all water, the colour of the bottom, and of the sky appears in it, so the different insects, marine plants, the mixture of many things which the rivers carry, into the sea, also vary its colours here and there. When calm it sometimes appears strewed with brilliant stars; the track of a ship, which cuts the waves, is often luminous, and seems a river of fire. These phenomena ought to be attributed, partly to the sulphurous particles, oily, and other inflammable substances in the sea, and partly to shining insects. The creatures of which the sea is full, ought also to excite our wonder and admiration, as well as its depth, in some places as much as five miles.

The quiet spirit of a good man is like the clear water of the fountain; but the restless mind of the wicked is like the dirty waves of the sea, when the mire of the bottom is stirred up by their motions. Such were *Sampson*, Jud. xvi., 16. *Saul* 1, Sam. xvi., 14. Our wicked passions, such as pride, wrath, and envy, disturb our hearts, like the winds which blow upon the sea, and nothing can quiet them but the word and grace of Jesus Christ, who spoke to the raging waves, and commanded them to be still, so can He now command our restless spirits, and restore them to peace; so that there shall be a calm within us.

The *Lalita Vistara* states: "Men consumed by desire can gain as little repose as fire can be extracted from rubbing two pieces of green-wood under the water."

The wicked are like the sea, (1) a collection of *many waters;* so the wicked from many nations, Jer. li., 42, the sea in scripture sometimes means numerous armies.

2. *Sometimes roars* and *swells*, the waves rise in great storms 60 feet; such are persecutors swollen with pride, Ps. lxv., 7.

3. *Bounds* set by God, Job. xxxviii., 8. The sea shut up by doors, hitherto shall thou come, so God stilleth the tumult of the people, Ps. lxviii., 7, Jer. v., 22. God set the sand as the ocean's boundary, Jer. v., 22, the clouds as its garment, Job. xxxviii., 9, and darkness as its swaddling bands, Job. xxxviii., 9.

4. *Still at God's* commands; so God quietens the wicked. The winds and seas obeyed Jesus, Mat. viii. 26.

5. *Monsters* in it, Job. xli., 31; so Daniel's four beasts of the sea or monarchs. Dan. 7, 3, the Roman beast had great teeth; such was the emperor Nero who killed his own mother. Great monsters live in it, some are 80 feet in length.

6. *Restless* tides, currents, winds always agitate it; such was Haman against Mordecai; *i.e.*, the sea is always in motion even in a calm; hence the peace of heaven is represented as there being no more sea, Rev. xxi., 1. No more trouble; mud and dust are cast out; so from the wicked heart arise envy and malice, the filthy waves of passion.

So men change from restlessness. Ahasuerus turns off Vashti his queen, and entertains Esther, a Jewish maiden. *Reuben* is unstable as water, Gen. xlix., 4. *Pharaoh* now on the throne, anon in the bottom of the sea. *Hezekiah* healthy, now anon hears, set thy house in order for thou shalt die. *Jerusalem* besieged and freed in one night. In youth we are for pleasure, in manhood for fame, in age for riches, as if thick clay must be a provision for heaven. There is no constancy in health or wealth.

7. *Deceitful;* the sea allures by its calmness, then heavy storms arise; so the world promises content, but that cluster never grew on the world's thorns; it gives an hour's pleasure and eternal torture. *Dives'* dainties

now bite like a serpent. *Achan's* wedge of gold purchased the stones that beat out his brains. *Judas's* thirty pieces bought the halter that hanged him. *Sechem's* lust brought the sword upon himself and the city; like a man in the sea with his pockets full of gold which hastens his drowning. *Job* presented kindness to Amasa, but it is cruelty, he kissed and killed him, 2 Sam. xx. *Agag* is hewn in pieces, and *Jezebel* was eaten by dogs like a piece of carrion. *Jael* began with milk and butter, but ended with a hammer; so *Adonija*, 1 Kng i., 50.

8. The *sea-water* is *unsatisfying*. A *Persian* proverb states: "He who covets this world's goods, is like one who drink sea-water; the more he drinks, the more he increases thirst, nor does he cease to drink until he dies." The Bible compares the tranquillity of heaven to a sea of glass, *i.e.*, still without storms.

We all have to pass over this worldly sea, but we have the Bible as our chart. Christ is the Pilot and the winds from heaven waft us on; hope is our anchor—we can thus escape the hidden rocks and whirlpools which abound in this sea.

---

(51) LET THE DEAD BURY THEIR DEAD.
Mat. viii., 22.

One of Christ's disciples asked Him leave of absence to go and bury his father. He replied, your business is to preach my religion, and let those who are dead to God attend to burying the dead. A man in England, who lived to the age of 84, but was converted when 80 years old, had the inscription on his tomb:—"died, aged 4 years"—*i.e*, he reckoned that he was only really alive when he served God.

What could Christ mean. How can one dead man bury another? This can never be, unless the word dead be taken in two different senses; for then a man who is dead in one sense may be buried by another, who in a different sense is as dead as he; that is, dead in trespasses and sin. To be carnally minded is death, saith St. Paul and the poor *Prodigal's son* in the parable, having lived in that state of mind till his conversion, the father says of him: "This thy brother was dead, and is alive again." Man has a soul and body, each of which dies in its own way; and so either of them may be alive while the other is dead. There is a sense in which *Adam* died on the day when he sinned; and there is another sense in which Adam lived nine hundred and thirty years. Adam delivered down a natural life to all us that are born of him: but the only inheritance he could leave to our spirits was that death to which he was fallen. It is this death of the spirit which make it necessary for every man to be born again.

There are multitudes of people who seem to live but are no better than dead; and they might as well be in their graves; they are, properly speaking, unburied dead. They have in them nothing of the life of the Gospel, nor any symptoms of it, no sight, no sense of spiritual things, no appetite, no affection for them. We may preach to them all day long, and do no more good by it than if we were to preach to a man in his coffin. If we were to cry into their ears, or blow a trumpet to give them warning of the fire of judgment, and of eternal damnation, they would hear nothing. If we offer to them the bread of life, they want it not; for a dead man hath no appetite. Were the souls of men as visible as their bodies, we should see as much difference betwixt devout Christians and the children of the world, as betwixt a living, healthy body and a corpse. They are twice dead, as St. James saith, dead once by nature, and dead again unto grace. The pleasures of this world will extinguish the life of a Christian; she that liveth unto this world is dead while she liveth. All heavenly affections will die.

---

(52) GOD WILL NOT BREAK THE BRUISED REED.
Mat. xii., 20.

This illustrates God's kindness to the humble and penitent.

The bruised reed, which has been crushed by some weight that has passed over it, and appears to be bowed hopelessly to the ground, is the emblem of one who has been crushed under the burthen of his sins, and of all that sorrow and remorse which are sure to follow in their train. Judas was so weighed down with remorse that he went and hanged himself.

"The smoking flax" is another emblem of the same case; and with this additional resemblance. If the flax which has been lighted will not burn, its smoke is so offensive, that all cry out impatiently to have it quenched as soon as possible. And this fact is elsewhere used to show how abominable are the wicked in the sight of their Holy Maker; for He says of them, and especially of such as say to their fellow-sinners: "Stand by thyself, for I am holier than thou." "These are a smoke in my nostrils, Is. lxv., 5, a fire that burneth all the day," that is, not a quick and pleasant flame, but a mere smouldering fire; such as lingers in flax when too damp for any flame to break out, and emitting only a noxious smoke. Christ will not rashly snap asunder the last thread by which a spiritual life keeps its hold on the soul of one who has fallen. It is far better to be as a bruised reed (of a contrite and humble spirit) than to be as the cedars of Lebanon that are exalted and lifted up, or as the oaks of Bashan, on which the day of the Lord of Hosts shall be.

(53) RICHES HAVE WINGS LIKE AN EAGLE.
Pro. xxiii., 5.

The Lalita Visara says: "Everything composed is soon dissolved, frail as a vessel of earth or a city of sand; thus the *Eleusina Indica* is by the effect of art changed into a rope by having the support of the herb Sachharum Munja." The eagle is the king of birds; he has long wings; he can carry off a sheep in his talons, and fly high above the storms and lightning; so Haman had great wealth, yet in one day he was hung on a gallows 60 feet high, and thus his riches fled. Wings mark speed; hence the expression wings of the wind, Ps. civ., 3, and ships are said to have wings, Job ix., 25, 26, *i. e.*, their sails. The four wings of riches are, water, fire, debts, thieves. The Bengali proverb states: "Riches are like a tree on a river bank." "The boat is now carried on the cart, and the cart on the boat." A Hindi proverb states "fleeting as the sunshine of noon." The Mahamudgar writes: "Boast not of wealth, family, youth; fortune takes them all away in the twinkling of an eye." If Nebuchadnezzar be in the palace among his nobles anon, he is soon in the park among the beasts. Adonijah was one day on the throne, on another seeking refuge for his life at the horns of the altar. Zedekiah, on Jerusalem being taken, saw his sons slain before his eyes, then his own eyes being put out, he was bound in fetters and sent to Babylon, Is. xiii., 17. Josiah goes forth to battle; he is slain. Ahab goes forth against the Assyrians, he is slain. Judah got 30 pieces of silver for betraying Christ, but he went out and hanged himself.

(54) God's Providence as Dew.
Hos. xiv., 5.

The dew arising from the moisture evaporated, by the sun in the day, falling by night, refreshes the parched earth, and often supplies the want of rain. The short-lived character of the form of Godliness, without the power, is compared to early dew exhaled soon by the sun, Hos. vi., 4. The love of brethren is compared to the dew, Ps. cxxxiii., 3. God's word is said to drop as rain, and distil as dew, Deut. xxxii., 2. God's influences are likened to a cloud of dew in the heat of harvest, Jer. xviii., 4. The refreshing, vivyfying influence of God's spirit is in this text is compared to the silent but powerful dew as the dew of herbs, Jer. xxvi., 19.

1. *Dew comes from above*, from the air, not from the clouds; "drops down;" so Christ promised to send from above the Comforter, John. xiv., 16. Every good gift is

from above (Jas.) I will pour water on him that is thirsty, Mic. v., 7, so the dew of influence from Jehovah.

2. *Dew is the result of the sun's influence.* The sun evaporates the water which the cold makes to descend, the brighter the day the more dewy the night; so Christ shed down the Spirit. The sun must withdraw for the dew to fall; so Christ said, John. xv., 20, but the Spirit will abide. The sun comes again not like the natural dew, Is. lix., 2.

3. *Dew falls from a calm unclouded sky.* Wind or a cloud will dissipate it, but Christ, the Sun of Righteousness, dispels the clouds of unbelief. If we walk in the light we have fellowship with God; so when the mind is so clouded by passion, the dew of the Holy Spirit does not fall.

4. *The dew's descent* is silent and imperceptible; rain falls in torrents. Dew is seen only by its crystal drops, 2 Sam. xvii., 12. The Kingdom of God cometh not by observation. The still small voice alone is heard, 1 Kng. xix., 11, 12. Conversion is a change taking place in the mind; the dew like gravitation is known by its effects; hence the Spirit's influence is compared to the wind, Jon. iii., 2, Sam. xvii., 12. We cannot see it or tell whence it comes, but we know it by its effects.

5. *The dew's influence is allpervading.* Where dashing rain will not enter dew will; it rests on blades of grass; the travellers head is filled with dew; so in Christ's influence all things are become new; the dry bones live Ezek. xxxvii., 3. All partake, it pervades each.

6. Dew often *copious*, always seasonable. In Israel once for $3\frac{1}{2}$ years there were no dews—how lamentable were things, 2 Sam. i., 21. The Spirit in the latter day is to be poured on young and old. When the weather is hottest, the dew is heaviest; so Stephen, when stoned, saw heaven opened, Acts vii., 55; so John in Patmos was in the Spirit and saw wonderful visions, Rev. i., 10. Innumerable are the drops of dew; such are God's graces.

7. *The dew's effects are most obvious and salutary.* When the ground is parched the dew gives new life; so the letter killeth, 2 Cor. iii., 6. The sun hardens the soil, but the wilderness becomes a fruitful field, the times of refreshing arrive, eating their bread with gladness, Acts ii., 46. The growth of plants from the dew is often wonderful; so the Christian strikes his roots deep in the Rock of Ages, and in humility bends towards the dust, but the refreshing, sheltering branches shoot up in beauty, the flowers and leaves from the dew drops look as pearls, so beautiful are they, so the robes of Christ's righteousness. A fragrant smell arises in the morning from the dew on flowers; so Christ is the savor of sweet ointment, "Awake O north wind," dead souls are nauseous. Fruitfulness and moisture are necessary to the growth of plants, the dew of heaven, and fatness of the earth are conjoined to the fruits of the Spirit, the righteous bring forth fruit in old age; are we withered, God is no niggard with gifts, Mat. vii., 11; Heb. ii., 22. God will open the windows of heaven, Mat. iii., 11. Dew contains sulphur in it good for the earth. Egypt would be almost uninhabitable, were it not for the dews—the dew of heaven was promised to Ishmael.

---

(55) THE NIGHT OF LIFE AND DAY OF ETERNITY.
Rom. xiii., 12.

The *Shánti Shatak* states, "Nature is as a bottomless gulph and man's life like the fleeting foam of its billows which remain but a moment." An impenitent sinner is said both to be "asleep" and also to be "dead." He is "dead," because his soul is destitute of spiritual life; as, however, it has a capacity for receiving spiritual life, he is compared also to one who is "asleep," but who can wake again.

A man who is buried in sleep is unconscious of all that is going on around him. His mind is entertained, indeed, with dreams, which for the time he takes for realities, while the real and important business of life is totally unheeded and neglected by him. Matters which affect his interest, or even his life, may be transacted around him, while he is dreaming on; and when he awakes, he will find how material it would have been to him to have resisted the drowsiness in which his faculties for the time were lost. The ship was on the point of being engulphed in the raging waves, when *Jonah* was fast asleep! The building may be in flames, or the thief may have broken through the house, but the owner sleeps on in total ignorance of his danger or his loss, until it is too late to escape the one, or to prevent the other.

Angels are rejoicing over penitents, souls are being quickened from the death of sin, the Spirit of God is changing many a desert into a garden of the Lord, the church is coming up out of the wilderness—while the poor foolish sinner is buried in a deep sleep, following with eager desire the merest vanities and shadows, and knowing nothing of the danger which is ever hanging over him, or of the bright inheritance which he is forfeiting, for want of taking the necessary pains to gain it. The *Shánti Shatak* compares the careless sinner to a moth, unaware of approaching evil, hovering over a lighted lamp until consumed by it, or to a fish falling into the hands of the angler.

In sleeping the fancy is led about by dreams—we are disturbed by vain hopes and fears; on awaking they are all gone. In dreams we run away when there is no danger, and are delighted with that which is nothing but a shadow. We think we are flying through the air, while we are motionless in our bed; we think we have found great treasures, but we awake and are as poor as ever. Of that which is real we have no knowledge, while our mind is thus filled with shadows: but, perhaps, we dream that we are sailing on the water, while the chamber in which we sleep has taken fire; and we know it not till the flames reach our body and awaken us; then we start up, but it is too late to escape.

Are not we who are thus deceived in our sleep, in danger of being deceived when we are awake? If our fancy is filled with such things as will have no substance, when we awake in the morning of the resurrection, then will our whole life be no better than a dream: and of that which is real we shall have no knowledge or sense. When we are told of God or of the wrath to come, these things will not effect us because we are in a sort of sleep, and our heart is filled with things of no substance. The rich man in the parable was lulled to sleep by his fine clothing and his sumptuous living, and he never awoke till he died. Then he lifted up his eyes, and found himself in a place of torment, calling for a drop of water to cool his tongue.

The World like Night.

The *Shánti Shatak* says, " the world is like a wild desert, the house of our body is full of holes, our fancies are a night which throws the veil of illusion over us, be watchful and defend yourself with the sword of knowledge, the shield of resignation, and the armor of caution."

1. A state of intellectual darkness, whereas light implies knowledge, Is. viii., 20; Holiness, 1 Jn. i., 7; Comfort, Ps. xcvii., 11; and Glory, Col. i., 2.

2. The time of *sleep*, 1 Th. v., 7, hence sleep is called the son of night. Half our days we pass in the shadow of the earth, and the brother of death (sleep) extracts a third part of our lives.

3. Time of *darkness*, beasts and thiefs prowl, Is. xxi., 12, Heaven is light, "the inheritance of the Saints in light."

4. *Inactivity*, ignorance, Luk. i., 79, night an emblem of death, Jon. ix., 4. The Arabs say he who has done justice in the night has built himself a house for the next day.

Morning comes after night, so the morning of eternity, Ps. xlix., 14; morning longed for, Ps. cxxx., 6;

morning makes things manifest, 1 Cor. iv., 5 ; morning brings joy, birds sing, flowers are fresh, Is. xxvi., 19 ; morning foreshows the king of day.

(56) The Christian a Soldier.
2 Tim. ii., 3, 4.

A soldier is one employed in Military affairs bearing arms under Military command, Mat. viii., 9. Every true Christian is a soldier to fight the good fight of faith against the world, the flesh and the devil, Is. li., 9, Col. ii., 15 ; 2 Tim. iv., 7.

He is like a soldier.

1. Christ is the Captain of our salvation, Heb. ii., 10, there is a covenant in Baptism.

2. *Leaves all other worldly affairs.* Reuben, however, abode among the sheepfolds, for this Debora rebuked him, Judges v., 16; so the Christian forsakes all as did the apostles, their heart was set on things above, they minded not the things of the flesh, Rom. viii., 5 ; they were crucified with Christ, Col. iii., 1, *i. e.*, a painful separation from the world like crucifying.

3. *When enlisted is armed,* so the Christian has armor, Eph. vi., 10, 12, but only one offensive the sword.

4. *Uniform worn to distinguish him,* so the garment of love and humility, 1 Pet. v., 5.

5. *Clad at the King's expense.* The Christian's white raiment an emblem of purity was purchased with Christ's blood, Rev. vii., 14.

6. *Enemies fixed for him.* The world, the flesh, and the devil, John. ii., 16. Paul writes, that the Christian is more than a conqueror, Rom. viii., 37.

7. *Obedience in everything,* Mat. viii., 9, so Paul, Acts xxvi., 19.

8. *Order and discipline,* 1 Cor. xiv., 33.

9. *Acquainted* with devices of the enemy ; wise as serpents, 2 Cor. ii., 11.

10. *Courage* necessary, no turning back, Hb. xi., 38, the cause good, Is. xli., 10, a good conscience, Pt. iii., 16, sure of victory, Rev. xii., 11, to endure hardness, Mat. x., 22, Heb. xi., 38, Acts xxvi., 24, David watered his couch with his tears.

(57) The Fickle like the Morning Cloud and Early Dew. *Hos.* vi., 4.

The *Lalita Vistara* compares life to an autumnal cloud. The *Shánti Shatak* says, "as the lightning by its flashes merely drives away the darkness for an instant, so are those who decide for a while to root out sensual desires from their minds." The morning cloud is very beautiful with its golden hues, and colors shifting and changing every minute. Early in the morning every blade is glistening with the early dew, and the light clouds are painted with all those gorgeous colors by which they seem to prepare themselves for the return of their absent king the sun ! But how soon do those hues and those jewels of the early morning pass away. Long before the sun has attained his meridian height, the sky has become cloudless, and the parched land seems in vain to thirst for the refreshing dew, and the kindly shower.

Thus beautiful is early piety as in Samuel's, and Timothy's case. Thus engaging and full of promise are the fresh feelings of youth, before the withering chill of the world has passed upon them. How easily is the heart then touched with tenderness or pity; how the eye glistens at the tale of sorrow ; how the cheek shows that the sense of shame may be awakened by the gentlest admonition ! But before some few short years are passed the character, in too many instances, is fatally changed ; mere profession is like the dew that is soon dried up, but true principle is like a *well of water*, springing up perpetually—the wicked are said to be clouds without water. While in Egypt it rains sometimes only once in two years, were it not for the dews of night and inundations of the river, all vegetation would perish. Peter's resolution not to deny Christ passed away as a morning cloud before the sun of temptation, so did Judas's before the sun of gold.

(58) THE WATERER WATERED OR FATNESS FOR THE LIBERAL. *Proverbs* xi., 25.

Abraham was no loser by his liberality to Lot. (Gen. xiii., 9, 14, 15,) nor by his hospitality to the three Men. (Gen. xiii., 2.) He thereby entertained angels unawares; in the care he took of the religious instruction of his servants, (Gen. xiii., 19,) he was rewarded by their fidelity to him, as appears from the conduct of his eldest servant, Gen. xxiv. The widow's oil increased not in the vessel, but by pouring it out, 2 Kings iv. 1, 7. The *barley bread* in the Gospel multiplied by breaking and distributing it; the grain brings increase not by the lying in a heap in the garner, but by scattering it upon the land, so with the graces of faith, hope, and love; the talent gathereth nothing in the napkin but canker and rust.

(59) MAN A WORM. *Job.* xxv., 6.

The *Shánti Shatak* compares the wicked to dogs who delight in swallowing human bones filled with worms and moisture, eagerly licking the putrid juice as if it were palatable. Man is compared in the Bible to earth, dust, grass, a lie, vanity, in this text to a worm.

The butterfly spreads its wings, and the sun shines upon its plumes! The wisdom of the Creator has adorned it with beautiful lines, and painted it with glorious colours! It flies about and finds the plant which is proper to feed its brood of caterpillars: and there it lays its eggs to be hatched by the sun. In their infant state it crawls about as a helpless worm and feeds upon green leaves. Then it folds itself up in a case like a coffin, where it lies, as it were, asleep, till the time of its change: when it breaks this covering, and comes forth with wings and feathers like painted birds, to fly about the air, and the dew of the fields and meadows, and visit every sweet and pleasant flower; the white-ant in India also has its change when it gets wings.

We are now like the infant worms crawling about upon this earth. But if we go on in the ways of God, we shall at length be changed from a worm into an angel. But first we must be shut up in the grave, and hide ourselves in the state of death till the resurrection. Then we shall be raised to life and liberty, and put on a spiritual body, and be able to visit and enjoy all the wonders of God's works, such as poor helpless mortals cannot now see or understand. O! let us not forfeit this expectation for the sake of such low enjoyments as caterpillars are capable of—grovelling on the earth!

The worm of the text means that kind which breeds in flesh such as the worms that came out of the manna reserved contrary to God's commands, Ex. xvi., 24.

A Worm is

1. *Earth sprung*, from corruption and putrifaction, so man was made of clay, Am. ii., 7; hence he loves earthly things, and feeds like swine on the dunghill of vice.

2. *Mean looking*, so is man by sin, though once in God's image and very beautiful.

3. *Frail*, trod on easily: so man's life is sometimes ended by a fly or a bit of bread; a worm cannot easily escape from dangers, it becomes like seed a prey to fowls, Mat. xiii., 4; Herod was eaten up of worms, Act xii., 22; great men like glowworms at night may seem great, but in the morning they are like others.

4. *Various kinds*, but all are worms, so the silk-worm which spins its dress out of its own bowels, the muckworm, also the glowworm, the caterpillar, Joel, i., 4, the palmerworm, Am. iv., 9.

5. *Abode* mean suitable to those who dwell in it. Job calls the grave his house, Job xvii., 13; yet God says, fear not, thou worm, Jacob, Is. xli., 14; though man is a worm yet he will nestle above the clouds.

(60) CHRIST THE MORNING STAR.
Rev. xxii., 16.

Angels called morning stars, as being made in the morning of creation. The dawn said in The Vedas " to be born in the eastern quarter of the firmament, displaying a banner of light bringing health to human habitations, many tinted," Ib. xxxviii., 7; angels as the morning star beautiful, so Stephen's face when dying like an angel's, Acts vi., 15; Satan was called Lucifer, *i. e.*, an angel of light.

The morning star, called the day star, arising in your hearts, 2 Pt. i., 9; the King of Assyria is so called, Is. xiv., 12, as Babylon was the first of kingdoms.

The Morning Star is

1. *Solid light*, twinkles not, fixed in its orb, so no intermission in Christ, his spiritual light the same yesterday, to-day and for ever, Hb. xiii., 8; so Christ will never leave, Hb. xiii., 5; Mat. xxviii., 20.

2. *Harbinger of the sun*, so when the day-spring came, people that sat in darkness saw the light, Mat. iv., 16; forerunner of the morning of the resurrection, Ps. xlix., 14; the night of life is far spent the day of resurrection is at hand, Rom. xiii., 11, 12.

3. *Ornaments the heavens*, beautiful to see, so is Christ above Moses, Ps. xlvii., 1; David in his day said I shall be satisfied when I awake after his likeness, Ps. xvii., 15; Paul said I have a desire to depart, Ph. i., 23.

4. *Guides mariners*, when they have lost the polar star, so Christ, the light of life, warns against the rocks and shoals of the world the flesh and the devil in the ocean of life.

5. *A star of the first magnitude*, John, Peter James were stars, but Christ, though the offspring of David, was the brightness of the Father's glory, Heb. i., 3.

6. *Terrible to thieves*, indicating the departure of darkness, so Satan at the dawn of redemption attempted Christ's destruction in the temple, Mat. iv., 5; Jews said, let us kill the heir, Mat. xxi., 38; the Nazarines led Christ to the brow of the hill, Lk. iv., 29; so the devils thought he was come to torment them before the time, Mat. viii., 29.

7. *Gives most light before the break of the day*, so when the angel with the everlasting Gospel shall fly through heaven, Rev. xiv., 6; the day of salvation is nigh, Heb. ii., 14.

8. *Most useful in wintry darkness*, so are Christ's offices, now of prophet, priest and king.

9. *The name honorable*, son of the morning, so Christ called Emanuel, Anointed, Prince of Peace, Heb. i., 4.

10. *The same as the evening star*, so Christ is the Alpha and Omega, the author and finisher of our salvation, Rev. i., 8; Heb. xii., 2.

11. *Clouds hinder not its course*, so Christ will come and will not tarry, Heb. x., 37; so *Galileo* said, men may imprison me for believing the Earth moves, but it moves. It is hard to kick against the pricks, Act ix., 5; the blood of the martyrs was the seed of the church. *Julian*, a Roman Emperor, dying, said of Christ whom he opposed, O! Galilean, thou hast overcome.

The Morning Star is created; but a fiery red, Christ is meek a mild light, Christ made the heavens, Ps. cii., 25; The Morning Star and Sun are different; Christ is both; The Morning Star gives light only by *night*, Christ is an everlasting light, Is. lx., 20; The Morning Star enlightens only this world,

Christ this world, and the heavenly Jerusalem, Heb. xii.; The Morning Star shall be dissolved, Christ never, Heb. xiii., 8.

(61) THE WORLD A WILDERNESS.
CANT. viii., 5.

The *Shánti Shatak* states "our mortal bodies are liable to decay—our earthly friends are like passengers on a journey whom we meet casually and from whom we soon separate." In the wilderness the sun smites by day and the cold by night, serpents infest the rocks while sand-storms often overwhelm the traveller, or the Simoon destroys thousands of men and camels, or they perish by thirst; like this is the world which Solomon, the wisest and richest of men, called vanity of vanities, and Paul called dung, Ph. iii., 8. People hasten through a desert looking for rest at the end, Hb. iv., 1, like Lot, they must not linger in Sodom, all creation is groaning under the curse, Rom. viii., 22.

In reading of the journey of the Hebrews from Egypt to Canaan by the way of the wilderness, we see a pattern of our own life, and of all the trials we are to undergo as Christians in our progress through this world to the kingdom of heaven. The Jews' journey began with baptism in the Red Sea, a deliverance from Pharaòh and his host, so is our baptism, with which our Christian life begins is an escape from the Spiritual Pharaòh. As they were supported by manna, and the waters of the rock, so must we live by bread from heaven, and our thirst must be satisfied by the waters of life. The end of this our pilgrimage upon earth is the possession of the heavenly land, which God hath promised to us, but in the way to it, we must undergo trials and temptations of every sort, and die in this wilderness, as Moses and his people did, before we can obtain it. As they proceeded by encampments, and wandered many years in the wilderness, so is our life a pilgrimage, and their example assures us that we have here no abiding place, no fixed habitation.

A wilderness

1. Is a *waste* wild place, no planting, Zch. ii., 5 ; so the Earth in spiritual matters.

2. Abounds in *thorns* the wicked are briars destined to be burnt, Heb. xi., 36, 38.

3. *Dangerous*, wild beasts numerous, the wicked are compared to wolves, bears, lions, dogs, Cant. iv., 8 ; Dt. viii., 15 ; Jer. ii., 6 ; Mat. xii., 43 ; hence is God a wall of fire to keep off beasts, Heb. xi., 38, or as a great city, Is. xxvii., 10, 3.5, 1; people travel in caravans composed of persons of different countries, this keeps off robbers, so is Christian communion necessary.

4. *No path*, Is. xxxv., 8 ; liable to wander, hence a guide necessary through the sands, so Job felt, xxiii., 8, 9.

5. *Lonely*. Christ compares the world to a field Mat. xiii., 38 ; as wheat and tares grow together and harvest is expected ; good plants are injured by wild beasts, Is. xli., 19, 32, 16.

6. *The Sand is burning* ; the sky is as brass ; water and shade wanting. So in spiritual matters.

7. *Storms* frequent; the Simoon buries thousands of men and animals.

8. Though *barren*, oasis are found, *i.e.*, cultivated spots for a short rest, so for the Christian are ordinances.

9. *Thieves* abound, Acts xxi., 38 ; Job was robbed in Arabia.

10. *Foggy and misty*, so Satan raises heresies to hide sin, (misleads travellers.)

11. *Food* little, so the husks of this world, Luk. xv., 16 ; the believer gets manna from heaven.

(62) THE PRISON OF HELL.
Rev. xx., 7.

The Prisons in former days with their bolts, cells, darkness, fetters, dungeons, scowling prisoners were a gloomy scene, showing human degradation, a picture of slavery.

A Prison is

1. The *abode of the guilty;* all men are sinners before God who sees, without the aid of police, their guilt. Innocent people in prison have been cheerful as Paul and Silas, not so the criminal, who says with Cain, my punishment is greater than I can bear. Hell contains all the unpardoned criminals since Cain's time.

2. A place of *condemnation;* the wages of sin is death, Rom. vi., 23; the condemned cell a gloomy one, stone walls, little light.

3. A place of *degradation!* jail birds lose their character, rude companions, who corrupt each other.

4. A place of *confinement;* fetters and high walls, with guards; the iron of Joseph's fetters entered into his soul. Yet Paul and Silas sang in jail with their feet in the stocks. Bunyan the tinker wrote his "Pilgrim's Progress" in jail, giving glorious visions of the celestial city, his mind was not confined.

5. A place of *discomfort;* old prisons were dangerous as Jeremiah's horrible with mud, snakes, rats, lice, Sampson's eyes were put out in his prison house, Judg. xvi., 21.

6. Without means of *escape;* high walls, gates, keepers, no escape from God's prison; Jonah could not escape from vengeance in his ship, but those washed in Christ's blood in white robes have come out of the prison of corruption; whither shall I flee, Ps. cxxxix., 7.

1. *The prison of Hell has* no *alleviation;* not a drop of water, Lk. xvi., 21; they drink the wine of the wrath of God, Rom. xi., 10; Is. xxx., 13. 2. Infinite *power* there to inflict acute torment. 3. The worm of *conscience* is gnawing; the fire of remorse never extinguished; a meditation on hell ought to be a bridle to curb us from sin, and a spur to incite us to all godliness.

(63) CHRISTIANS TO WATCH.
Mat. xxiv., 42, 43.

The *Shánti Shatak* compares man to "one in a ferry-boat crossing the whirling gulph of this world, which he must do with watchfulness so as not to be drowned in the abyss." David says, his soul watched for the Lord more than they that wait for the dawn, Ps. cxxx., 6; an allusion to the watchmen on the city wall or the watchers of the temple who passed the night there in devotional exercises, anxious to catch the first beams of the morning sun on the hallowed day of atonement.

Watchmen were set on high towers to give notice of fire, or the invasion of an enemy's approach, hence called seers, 1 Sam. ix., 9; Is. xxi., 8; watchman what of the night, Is. xxi., 12; the night far spent, Rom. xiii., 10.

Watchmen

1. Must have *sharp* eyes to be overseers, see to a distance, Ez. xxxiii., 6; if the blind lead the blind both fall into the ditch, Mat. xv., 14, ignorance or mental blindness leads to destruction, Is. ix., 16.

2. Must be *active*, not drowsy, Is. lvi., 10; otherwise wolves come in, Acts xx., 29; while men slept the enemy sowed tares, Mat. xiii., 25.

3. Must endure *hardship*, the heat of the day, cold of night, Is. xxi., 11, 12; sentinels are out in all weathers, so Paul, 2 Cor. xi., 23, 30; the Apostles were beat Acts xvi., 22.

4. Consult not their own *interest*, Paul sought not theirs but them, 2 Cor. xii., 14; Ph. ii., 21; cry aloud, spare not, lift up the voice as a trumpet, Is. lviii., 1.

5. Charged with the *care* of others, Heb. xiii., 17; Ps. xci., 12; death the punishment of sleeping on their post.

6. *Appointed* to the duty, Ez. xxxiii., 7.

7. Prevent evils by *forewarning* of fire, Deu. viii., 16; Num. xxii., 26; so angels watchmen to Lot in Sodom, Gn. xix.

Angels called watchers, Dn. iv., 17; hence represented full of eyes, Ez. i., 18; said to have wings to move about, Zch. i., 11; 1 Kings xxii., 19; 2 Kings vi., 17; gave warning to Lot, observant, Lk. xv., 20; Zch. i., 11.

Ministers are watchers of the word, 1 Tm. vi., 13; preach 2 Tm. ii., 1; of Ordinances Mat. xxviii., 19; of the flock, Acts xx., 27; all men have to set a watch on the door of their lips, Ps. cxli., 3.

(64) SIN BLOTTED OUT AS A DEBT.
Acts iii., 19.

Chanakya "writes to extinguish fire, remove disease, and pay debts are of use as they increase if they remain." Sinners are Debtors, the money duty, Gl. v., 3; Rom. viii., 12, 15, 27.

Sinners are

1. *Unconcerned* about the debt, so Cain who slew his brother, Gn. iv., 7; Mat. xviii., 24; Luk. xvi., 2.

2. *Wasteful* about saving up; so the prodigal son, Luk. xv., 16.

3. *Love not to see the creditor* or settle accounts Zch. xi., 8; Jb. xxi., 14, 15; who is God, say the wicked, Mat. xviii., 24; Lk. xvi., 2.

4. *Afraid of the bailiff*, so Cain afraid of every one he met, Gn. iv., 13, 14; Adam hid himself, Gen. iii., 8; so Felix, Acts xxiv., 25.

5. *Dilatory*, so the debtor who ask a suspense, Mat. xviii., 29; so excuses for the supper, Luk. xiv. 18.

6. *Estimate* their debts, Mat. iii., 5, 13.

7. *Unable to pay*, Rom. iii., 19; Mat. xviii., 29; hence punishment, Ex. xxi., 7; 2 King iv., 1.

8. *Death* will arrest, Eccl. viii., 8.

9. *The Creditor* judge in the case, Rom. v., 12; Rom. xiv., 12; Eccl. xi., 9, 12, 14.

10. *Hell* the prison, Mat. xviii., 34: tormentors, the rack; eyes taken out.

God forgives the Debt, now by

1. Staying the process, Jb. xxxiii., 19, 21, 24.
2. Cancelling the bond, Col. ii., 14; the handwriting against us, abolishes the old covenant, Heb. viii., 13.
3. Acquittance written on conscience, Rom. viii, 6.

Forgiveness obtained by

1. Confessing the debt, Ps. xxviii., 13; God's mercy procured from confession. 2. Ascribing it to Christ, Mat. xx., 28; who gave his life a ransom. 3. Contract no more debts. 4. Forgive others, Mat. vi., 14, 15. A spirit of forgiveness to others necessary—as we are, liable to many injuries in our own persons, Acts xii., 2; the Apostles were imprisoned; in the line of *duty*, so Moses suffered from his brother and sister, Num. xii., 2; in our *relations*; so Herod destroyed the infants, Mat. ii., 16; in our property, 1 King xxi., 15; so Jezebel took away Naboth's property; in our character, vengeance is Gods, Rom. xii., 19.

Reparation, however, is required in thefts, so Moses law required restitution in important crimes.

Sinners are debtors to God as the *servant*, Mat. xviii., 24, who owed 10,000, Luk. xvi. 1. The wasteful servant, Gl. v., 3; Rom. viii., 12. 2. As *tenants*, Mat. xxi., 33, 34; see parable of householder and vineyard. 3. *Borrower*, 2 Chr. xxxii., 25; Hezekiah. 4. *Covenant makers*, Dt. xxvi., 17. 5. *Malefactors*, Gal. iii., 10; sin as a debt takes what is not its own. Some debts very great, make a man anxious, Mat. v., 25, xviii., 29. The Jews punished debt with slavery, Ex. xxi., 2, 7, 2 Kings iv., 1; natural debts only affect the body—may be forgiven without payment; worldly debts have only a temporal punishment, Rom. xiv., 10; Mat. xiii., 50, and debtors may escape, not so the spiritual.

(65) BRAYING A FOOL IN A MORTAR.
Proverbs xxvii., 22.

Vemana compares the trying to produce good qualities in a crooked heart to pouring milk and sugar over bramble berries, and boiling them, which will give no flavor. In Turkey great criminals were beaten to pieces in huge mortars of iron in which they usually pounded their rice. The Jews were in Babylon under captivity, yet were their proud hearts not humbled, 2 Chr. xxvi., 15, 17; God sent them messengers, but they ill-treated them, the Chaldeans came, yet they bound the Prophet Hezekiah Ezek. The plough breaks the earth in many places, but does not better it if nothing is put in, if nothing be sown, thorns and thistles will come up so, afflictions may break our estate, yet if God do not sanctify these afflictions they yield only the harvest of tares. Mere affliction changes not the disposition as the fire softens not a stone; pour vinegar from vessel to vessel it never becomes wine, Is. i., 5.

(66) THE LAMP OF THE WICKED PUT OUT.
Proverbs xiii., 9.

Lamps were used by the Jews at weddings and on festive occasions, a man in prosperity is compared to a blazing lamp, he is ready to slip with his feet, Jb. xii., 5; as a lamp extinguished, *i.e.*, adversity. The lamp of the wicked gradually fails of oil, Mat. xxv., 3, 8; in its extinction a stench from the wick arises, so the memory of the wicked rots.

(67) TRUTH A GIRDLE.
Is. xi., 3.

Some girdles are made of gold or fine linen yet are perishable, but truth is immortal, as the *Russian* proverb has it, *truth is not drowned in water, nor burned in fire*, or the *Bengali* proverb "false words and sprinkled water remains not long. Better totter in our bodies than in our words." Truth means the unleavened bread of sincerity, 1. Cr. v., 8.

Truth or Sincerity is like a Girdle.

1. A *belt* used by soldiers to preserve the stomach and vital parts. We are told to gird up the loins of our mind, 1 Pet. i., 13.

2. *Cleaves close* all round ; therefore the clothes not easily loosed. Christians should turn not to the right hand or the left, 1 Kings xiii., 21, as the Bengali proverb, "one foot on land, another on water."

3. *Strenghtens the loins*, gird up thy loins, 2 Sm. xxii., 40; God girds the loins of kings, Jb. xii., 18; sincerity strengthens, 1 King xx., 11; so sincerity the girdle to faith, hope, love, Mat. vi., 22.

4. A *preparation for battle*, Ps. lxv., 3; a war of words necessary to contend for the faith as the Christian is a soldier.

5. A *preparation for travelling*, as the garments were long; so Elisha's, 2 Kings iv., 29; so Christians are pilgrims, have to travel far, and the storms of persecution will blow away loose garments.

6. *Preparatory to serving*, so the servant ploughed with loins girt, Lk. xii., 35.

7. An *ornament*, covers the joints of the armor, hides seams, sincerity covers low birth even in one of low descent, Is. xliii., 4; covers poverty, all are yours, 1 Cr. iii., 22.

(68) THE STORM OF GOD'S WRATH.
Is. xxv., 4.

The wrath of God called in the Hebrew fire, Dt. xxviii., 22; Heaven is represented as our Father's house, a Marriage Feast, the House-hold of God; Earth is stormy but Christ is a hiding-place from the wind, Is. xxxii., 2; Earthquakes have destroyed cities, as Lisbon, so the Blast of the Prince of the Power of the Air blew down Eden, hence David wished for the wings of a dove, when assailed by storm of calumny, Ps. lv., 6; so many make shipwreck of faith.

God's wrath a Storm.

1. Of *God's sending* so, with Jonah, i., 4; *hail showers* destroyed the Amorites, *wind* buried the

Egyptians like lead in the sea, so *brimstone* rained on Sodom, so Tophet ordained of old, Is. xxx., 33.

2. The *sinner first raised it*, Is. xvii., 15.

3. *Of fearful violence*, Ps. cxvii., 23; in it ships mount up to heaven and stagger like a drunken man; hell a storm of brimstone raising fiery waves that destroy the soul.

4. *Everlasting*; in earth storms are fierce but short; everlasting burning in hell, Is. xxxv., 14.

5. Of *extensive* range; most storms are local, this is universal.

6. *No shelter*; the hail storm fell in Egypt not on those who were in the house sheltered, the sea gives no shelter as it shall give up its dead, Rev. xx., 13; rocks and hills will not cover the wicked, Rev. vi., 16.

7. *Controlled by God*; to the sea it is said hitherto shalt thou come, Job. xxxviii., 11, but Heaven and Earth shall pass away before God's storm, Rev. vi., 14.

---

(69) GOD'S POWER THE EVERLASTING ARMS.
Dt. xxxiii., 27.

God's strength is denoted by his arm. A stretched-out arm anttributed to him, Jr. xxvii., 5; so man's strength in labor and fighting is shown by it, Ex. xxv., 14.

1. *The arm an essential part of man*, so is the power of God to protect us from three enemies, the flesh, the devil, and the world, Ps. lxxvii., 15; Is., liii., 10; God lays bare his holy arm, *i.e.*, as servants strip up their sleeves and make their arms ready for service.

2. *Holds things*; so God led the Jews through the wilderness by His glorious arm, Is. lxiii., 12.

3. Sign of *love*; young lambs come in arms, Is. xl., 11; outstretched by father to call back his child, Is. lxv., 2. Thus Laban embraced Jacob, Gn. xxix., 13; and on meeting them Jacob embraced

his sons, Gn. xlviii., 13; so Esau embraced Jacob at meeting, Gn. xxxiii., 4.

4. Sign of *strength,* so Sampson broke with his arm the cords like flax, and slew 1,000 men with the jawbone of an ass, Judg. xv., 13, and overthrew the house of the Philistines, so God's arm brought salvation, Is. lxiiii., 5.

Man's arm is of flesh, God's of Spirit, Job. xi., 9; man's arm short, God's long, Jr. lx., 1; man's arm for a time, God's always; no king saved by the multitude of an host.

---

(70) CHRIST A ROSE OR LILY AMONG THORNS.
Canticles ii., 2.
The wicked are compared to thorns.

1. *Little use or value* except for hedges or fuel, Jer. xv., 19; Pr. x., 20; Is. x., 17; Jr. xxii., 28; so Antiochus, Dn. xi., 21; men gather not grapes from thorns, Mat. vii., 16; Jud. ix., 15; Job xxx., 8.

2. *Change not their nature,* the same in the garden as in the Jangal, so Pharoah changed not by miracles nor Saul by being made king, so Jeroboam worshipped a calf notwithstanding God's promises, 1 Kings xi., 27, 38; Mic. vii., 4.

3. *Encumber the earth;* draw away its moisture so the Canaanites, Num. xxxiii., 55; Josh. xxiii., 13; Abimelch the bramble was made king, killed his 70 brethren, plagued the Shechemites, Judge ix., 1; so the barren fig-tree, Lk. xiii., 7; when the wicked perish there is shouting, Pr. xi., 10; but when Josiah died great mourning, 2 Chron. xxiii., 24.

4. *Low things;* mount not as the cedar; they overrun fields, so in the Church of Galatia, Gal. v., 12; so David resolved to cut off the sons of Belial, 2 Sm. xxiii., 6; they when high are burnt, Heb. viii., 68; Is. xxvii., 4; Is. xiv., 9; Jr. vi., 18, xxii., 19.

5. *Dangerous by their pricking;* so the Canaanites were thorns in the Jews' sides, Num. iii., 55; Josh.

xxiii., 9; Nabal was churlish to David; so the Samaritans to the Jews, Neh. vi., 6; scoffing at the Jewish sabbaths and sacrifices, Neh. iv., 2, 3; so the Priests threatened the apostles, Acts iv., 17; so Saul breathed out slaughter, Acts ix., 1; Christ was called a wine bibber, a Samaritan or devil. Paul was called a pestilent fellow, Acts xxiv., 5; so Amaziah, 2 Chr. xxv., 17, 25. Ahab said to Elijah, are thou the troubeller of Issrael? 1 King xviii., 17; Lot's righteous soul was vexed in Sodom, 2 Pt. ii., 7, 8; Delilah vexed Samson, Jud. xx., 16; Josh. xxiii., 12, 13; so the daughters of Heth to Rebekka, Gen. xxvii., 46; so the Jews in Babylon, Ps. lxxix., 4.

6. *Care needful in walking among them*, otherwise one gets entangled and scratched; Christ warned us to be wise as serpents, Mat. x., 16; David, Jeremiah found thorns, Jer. xxxviii., 6; Paul was scratched by thorns, owing to thorns speed in walking is not often great, thorns hindered the growth of good seed, Mat. xiii., 22; so was Achan at Ai; Tobiahs, and Sanballat in the building up the temple, Neh. vi., 17.

7. *Thorns will not* always vex; the fir-tree shall come up, Is. lxv., 13; so the Jews were delivered from Egypt and its thorns.

8. *Thorns came in with the curse*, Gn. iii., 18; so the wicked with the fall.

9. *Sometimes useful* as hedges, so the Earth helped the woman, Rev. xii., 16.

10. *Hard and knotty*, 2 Sm. xxiii., 6.

11. *Thorns thrown into the fire*, Is. x., 17; Ps. ix., 17; Is. xxx., 33; so Saul and his family, the Jews.

(71) Christ the Rock of Ages.
Mat. vii., 24, 25.

1. *A Rock firm*; hence good for a foundation, 1 Cr. iii., 11; other foundation can no man lay, 1 Cr. iii., 11; who shall separate us, Rom. viii., 1; 31 Pt. 1., 25;

a hard heart compared to a rock from its firmness; in India bridges not built on a rock are soon swept away.

2. *Habitations in;* hence formerly in them, Is. xxii., 16; so the Christian like the dove has his nest in the clefts of the rock, Ps. xci., 7; xci., 1; 1 John iv., 16. The Buddhist caves in India were in rocks inhabited by monks.

3. *High;* yet their foundation low; so Christ's human nature was low though high in his Divinity. Believers dwell in heavenly places.

4. *Prospect* from fine; Balaam said from the tops of the rocks I see him, Nm. xxiii., 9; so Moses saw Canaan from Pisgah; so the Christian sees heaven by faith from the rock Christ.

5. *Strong;* David fled for security to one Christ, 1 Sm. xiii., 6; so the Saints find, Ps. xciv., 22.

6. *Durable;* Christ the rock of ages, Is. xxvi., 4. Houses made in the rocks of Palmyra 3,000 years ago are still standing, so the Buddhist caves in Orissa, Nasik, Ellora.

7. *Honey* from the rock flowed to the Jews, Dt. xxxii., 13, and oil, Job. xix., 7.

8. *Pure water* from it; so water of life from the throne of God and the lamb, Rev. xxii., 1.

9. *Diamonds* and minerals found in; so in Christ all the treasures of wisdom hid, Col. ii., 3.

10. *A Shade* to travellers, shadow of a great rock in a weary land; to keep off the scorching heat.

Earthly rocks, however, sometimes moulder, always are barren, and of earth; not so Christ. The iceberg shifts with the wind, tide, or current, and is melted by the sun; it has no place in the chart, appears deep, high, and dazzling, but being carried to the tropics, it melts and changes its appearance; it is bright but cold. Not so Christ the rock, 1 Pt. i., 25.

(72) Cast not Holy Things to Dogs.

Mat. vii., 6; *Rev.* xxii., 15.

Chanakyea states, what use of science to a man without sense or a looking-glass to a blind man? The *Telegus* say, what does a bullock know of the taste of parched grain? What does an ass know of the smell of perfume? The Bengalis use the proverbs, "Krishna's name in a crow's mouth," "feeding a dog with pulse." The Arabs have a proverb, the world is a carcase, and they who seek it are dogs.

Sacrificial remains were not to be given to dogs, as they were counted so unclean.

Dogs resemble the wicked.

1. *Differ in disposition and size*, yet all are dogs. The young man that Jesus loved was a sinner as well as Judas; the Pharisee as well as the publican.

2. *Vile, beastly*, eat dead bodies in the river, licked Ahab's blood, 1 Kings xxix., 38; Ex. xxii., 31. So men enslaved to diverse lusts, so Nebuchadnezzar, Ps. xxxvii., 12.

3. *Churlish, snappish*, bay at the moon, so the Jews gnashed on Stephen with their teeth, Acts vii., 4.

4. *Bite and tear*, so do bloodhounds, bulldogs, Jer. xv., 3; such was Paul before his conversion. Some bark and bite not; others bite, but bark not, so some injure secretly, while chains are necessary for very fierce ones, Ps. iii., 7.

5. Some used as *Hunters*, so the Devil uses Persecutors.

6. *Bite each other*, so the Egyptians destroyed each other as well as the Jews; so in the case of Babylon and the Jews.

7. *Greedy*, Is. lvi., 11; never satisfied.

8. *Become sometimes mad*, then great mischief arises, Ph. iii., 2.

9. *Lazy*, hence the proverb, a dog's life, hunger and ease; the prodigal son fed on husks.

10. *Shut out* of doors. Without are dogs, Rev. xxii., 15. The Bengalis say the thief and hog have one road, *i. e.*, impurity.

Some dogs watchful, loving, and protecting, yet all dogs throw up when sick a loathsome vomit and swallow it again, so those who turn back to sin, Pr. xxvi., 11, 2; Ps. ii., 22; applied to the Gentiles by Jews, Mat. xv., 26.

Beware of dogs, Phl. iii., 2. A false teacher, so called, 1 Sm. xxiv., 14; so the Sodomites, Gen. xiv., 14; Pharoah.

(73) GOD OUR FATHER.
Heb. xii., 9.

Authority and dignity belong to a father, hence the rulers of Israel were called fathers. Abraham commanded his children, and was called the father of the faithful.

God like a Father.

1 *Compassionate* to children, so were the Apostles, 1 Thes. ii., 11; hence Paul calls Timothy his son, Tit. iii., 4; John iii., 16; Ps. ciii., 13; God treats them as lambs, Is. xl., 11.

2. *Reverenced* by children and not rebuked.

3. *Governs* with wisdom.

4. *Gives being*, so Jacob to the twelve Patriarchs, so Abraham to the Jews numerous as the sand of the sea, Acts vii., 8; so believers begotten by the word of truth, Jas. i., 18; 1 Cr. iv., 15; God is the Eternal Father of Christ, Ep. i., 3; of all men, Lk. iii., 38; especially of all regenerate, Gl. iv., 6; Ep. iv., 6.

5. *Nourishes*, believers as new-born babes receive the milk of the word, 1 Pt. ii, 2; a father gives a fish not a serpent, Mat. vii., 9; Ps. xxxiv., 8—10.

6. *Clothes*, so Jacob made for Joseph a coat of many colors, God clothes the grass, so will He us, Mat. vi., 30; He gives the robe of salvation, Is. lxi., 10.

7. *Protects*, covers them with His *wings*, so David, 1 Chr. xvi., 21, 22.

8. *Delights* even in their lisping, so prayer the language of a sigh, Rom. viii., 26; though they chatter like a crane, Is. xxxviii., 14; the publican only smote on his breast, yet God delighted in his humility, Luk. xviii., 13.

9. Sets a *good example*, so to be perfect as God, Mat. v., 48; merciful, Lk. vi., 36; patient, Col. i., 11.

10. *Loves* best those most like Him, so *Daniel* was greatly beloved, Dn. ix., 2; so David a man after God's own heart, Acts xiii., 22; John the beloved disciple.

11. *Educates*; God's word makes wise unto salvation, 2 Tim. iii., 15; sends Prophets, Eph. iv., 11; in Christ hid treasures of wisdom, Col. ii., 3.

12. Ready to *hear requests*, 2 Cor. vi., 3; grants not injurious things, Jas. i., 5,6; but takes away hurtful things, so hedges their way with thorns, Hos. ii., 6.

13. Regards them even *at a distance*, so Ephraim, Jer. xxxi., 20; so in the parable of the prodigal son, Luk xv., 20.

14. *Patient*; values sincerity, Jer. iii., 7; the children have rebelled, Is. i., 2—5.

15. *Chastises*, Pr. xxii., 15; He rebukes transgression with a rod, sometimes He only remonstrates, Mic. vi.; 13, to be without chastisement a note of bastards, Heb. xii., 8; punishment a mark of love, Rev. iii., 19; for our profit, Heb. xii., 10; even then He is pained, Is. lxii., 9; this chastisement is in measure, Heb. xi., 4.

16. Makes *provision* for, 2 Cr. xii., 14; Jr. xxxi., 3; Earthly fathers often passionate, though they be kings, yet of poor dignity; often know not the condition of their distant children who may become poor, Is. liv., 10; cannot convert, Heb. ii., 14; Ez., xxxvi., 26; estate divided or only given to one, Lm. iii., 23; are mortal.

The wickedness of a child does not estrange the heart of a parent, so God remembers we are but dust, Ps. ciii. 14; pities as Christ our High Priest is touched with a feeling of our infirmities.

(74) Sowing to the Flesh—Reaping Corruption.
Gal. vi., 17.

The principles of ruin in ourselves, like iron breed rust or like filthy garments they produce moths, or ill-humours in the body from a fever.

The Buddhists of Ceylon say—"If any one speak or act from a corrupt mind, suffering will follow the action, as the wheel follows the lifted foot of the ox." An English proverb—"He has made his bed, and he must lie in it," Job iv., 8; they that plough iniquity reap the same, they sowing the wind reap the whirl-wind, Hos. viii., 7. A Persian proverb is, he that plants thorns shall not gather roses; the field of wrong brings forth death as its fruits, Pro. v., 28; he is holden with the cords of his own sin, so fire in his lips, Pro. xvi., 27; Job v., 2; Por. i., 32; Heb. xiii., 9.

The Burmese, while denying a God, say suffering is the necessary consequence of sin, just as when you eat a sour fruit a bowel complaint ensues, or as the wheel follows the lifted foot of the ox.

The *Shanti Shatak* states, to wherever you roam in sky or ocean, yet your actions from birth up will follow up before the Judge as the shadow the substance.

The *Telegus* say a man's shadow remains in himself. If you expect much fruit from few offerings, will it be obtained? The Bengalis say from the jack do you get the mango juice.

The Danes say, whoever will eat the kernel must crack the nut. The Bengalis as the sin, so the atonement. The ant's wings produce its own death.

The husbandman's labours are often blasted, not so the Christians, Heb. vi., 10; God will not forget the labour of love. Husbandmen have to reap every year, the Christian all at once.

The harvest is the sabbath, the fulfilment of God's promise to Noah that harvest should not cease, Gn. viii., 21; when joy arises on remembering dangers past in regarding the success of harvest.

Adonizebek was paid in his own coin, Jud. i., 7; Ahab's blood was licked up; and Haman was hung on his own gallows. David sowed adultery, reaped the sword, 2 Sam. xii., 9, 11; Joseph's brethren sowed envy, Gn. xlii., 21; Judas sowed covetousness, reaped a halter, Mat. xxvii., 5.

(75) SINS LIKE SCARLET MADE WHITE AS SNOW.
Is. i., 18.

Scarlet being bright is used for clothing, *Saul's* daughters wore it, 2 Sm. i., 24; it is obtained from the eggs of an insect found on the leaves of the oak in Spain.

Crimson was used in dying wool, Lk. xiv., 19; hence white as wool referred to its natural state; a scarlet thread was fastened to the scapegoat on the day of atonement; neither dew, rain, washing, nor long wear can remove the scarlet die; it is the fastest color, so with sin the stain is not removed by ordinary means; white was the emblem of purity, Rev. i., 14; hence the Nazarenes, a sect of the Jews, were said to be purer than snow, Lam. iv., 7.

(76) THE RIGHTEOUS AS SHEEP.
Mat. x., 16.

The Righteous resemble Sheep in—

1. *Cleanliness*, not like swine, dogs, wolves, they come out of the wilderness of sin, 1 Cor. vi., 11; yet subject to *filth* need washing, 1 Cor. vi., 11; Ps. li., 7; hence they love still water, Ps. xxiii., 3.

2. *Harmless*, innocent as doves, Mat. x., 16; not crafty as foxes or devouring as a lion, 1 Cor. xiv., 20.

3. *Meek*, so Christ was led as a lamb to the slaughter, Is. liiii., 7; so Stephen and Job; so David, Ps. xxxix., 9; and Aron when his sons were killed.

4. *Profitable*, in life by fleece, in death by their flesh, so the blood of the martyrs was the seed of the Church, so saints are lights; ten saints would have saved Sodom, Gn. xviii., 32; being dead they yet speak; so Jacob proved to Joseph and Joseph to Potiphar.

5. *Obedient*, follow the shepherd, John. x., 4,27; Mat. xi., 29; Ph. ii., 5,11; Ruth. i., 14,16; Nm. xiv., 24; the shepherd knows their name; calling them they follow him.

6. *Feeble*, Gn. xxxiii., 13; God will deliver from temptation, they are apt to go astray, 1 Cor. x., 13; 1 Sam. xvii., 20; Ez. xxxiv., 6; Ps. cxix.; they have many enemies—wolves, dogs, Rm. viii., 36; nourished for slaughter, Ps. lxiv., 22; subject to many diseases, Jer. vii., 28.

7. Love *union*, saints are like David and Jonathan; scattered by dogs they soon unite, Acts iv., 23.

8. *Live on little*, often on barren commons, so Christian's content, 1 Tim. vi., 8.

9. *Fruitful*, the blood of the martyrs was the seed of the Church, though butchers kill them, yet they multiply.

10. *Need a shepherd*, Acts x., to select pasture, 1 Pt. v., 1; to select shade, Is. xxxii., 3; sheep may be lost, not so Christians, Jer. x., 27.

11. Love green *pastures*, Cant. i., 7.

12. *Silly*, not so jackals, Jer. v., 21; Dt. xxxii., 28; when one strays, the others follow, 2 Sam. xx., 1, 2; Acts v., 36, 37. Sheep may return of themselves, the spiritual sheep never.

---

(77) Faith more Precious than Gold.
1 Pet., i., 7.

In Rev. iii., 18, Divine grace which stands the fiery trial is called Gold. Faith here is not mere knowledge as the devils have, or as King Agrippa had, Acts xxvi., 27; it is reliance on Christ's merits for salvation.

Gold like Faith.

1. *Scarce,* so the grace of God in those days no open vision, Dt. xxxii. 9; Is. xliv., 4.

2. *Desirable,* men go to deep mines for it, or to California; so search the Scriptures, John v., 39.

3. *Tried in fire,* to distinguish it from false metal, sometimes a touchstone used, so God's word like faith tried by fire, so Abraham three times, Job six times, Job xxiii., 10; Rev. iii., 18.

4. *Precious,* in its nature, hence faith called lively, effectual, 1 Thes. i., 3; unfeigned working by love, Gl. 5, 6; holy, procured by Christ's blood, Cl. ii., 12; its fruits, Mat. xiv., 30; made a river go back, caused a man to give half of his goods to the poor, Lk. xix., 1; and people to burn bad books, Acts xix., 19.

5. *Chief metal.* Babylon had a head of gold, Dn. iv., 42; called the golden city, Is. xiv., 4; the skull called the golden bowl, Ecc. xii., 2.

6. *Much in little,* compared with brass, so the Bible is a little book, but great truths in it.

7. *Weighty* and firm, so faith in adversity.

8. *Splendid,* used as ornament; the locusts had it, Rev. ix., 7; hence given by the father of the Prodigal used in crowns; Babylon had a golden cup, Rev. xvii., 4.

9. *Forms fine vessels.* So saints are golden candlesticks, Rev. i., 20; so the vessels in Solomon's temple.

10. *Durable,* wastes not in fire, so the three Hebrew children, Dan. iii.

Faith not taken away, not corruptible, Is. v., 3; profits the soul, refined in the heat.

Faith precious as bought with Christ's blood, wrought by God's spirit. Object of is Christ; unites to God, Eye of the soul.

(78.) THE RIGHTEOUS BOLD AS A LION.
Proverbs xxviii., 1.

The roaring of a lion in quest of his prey resembles the sound of distant thunder, and being re-echoed by the rocks and mountains, appals the whole race of animals, and puts them instantly to flight. So great are the terror and dismay which his roaring produces that many animals, which by their swiftness might escape his fury, astonished and petrified by the sound of his voice, are rendered incapable of exertion. This noble animal has been considered as the most perfect model of boldness and courage in every age, and among every people acquainted with his history. He never flies from the hunters, nor is frightened by their onset. But if their numbers force him to yield, he retires slowly, step by step, frequently turning upon his pursuers. He has been known to attack a whole caravan, and when obliged to retire, he always retires fighting and with his face to his enemies.

A lion was the symbol of a king, hence Ali Muhammad's son-in-law was called the lion of God; as the lion sleeps with his eyes open; the Egyptians represented a brave person by a lion; Judah is called, from its brave character, a lion's whelp, Gn. xlix., 9; Babylon is called a lion on the eagle's wings of conquest, Dn. i., 4; Paul was delivered out of the lion's mouth, *i. e.*, from the wicked, 2 Tim. iv., 17; Nebuchadnezzar called a lion, Jer. iv., 7.

A Lion is

1. *Courageous*, such was David, Ps. xxvii., 3; so Nehemiah said, shall such a man as I flee, Neh. vi., 11; so Paul boldly avowed his doctrine to be what the governor called heresy, Acts xxiv., 14; so he fought with beasts, 1 Cr. xv., 32; so the Apostles said they must speak of the things they had seen, Acts iv., 20; so Elijah, 1 Kings x., 15, 19; Is. iv., 14; Is. xli., 14; so the priests, 2 Ch. vii., 1, xxvi., 17, 2. The lion called the king of beasts, so

Christians are more than conquerors, Rom. viii., 3; other beasts fear it, so Herod feared John, Mat. xv., 5; Christ called the lion of the tribe of Judah, Rev. v., 5.

2. *Majestic in* look, hence the saying an army of deer with the lion as leader is more terrible than an army of lions with a deer as leader; Christ is the Captain of our salvation.

3. *Strong,* Sampson says out of the strong lion came forth sweetness, Jud. xiv., 14; Christ as a lion is mighty to save, Is. ix., 6; at times he is still when he crouches down before his spring, Christ now a lamb, but afterwards a lion, so the Lord shall do on the last day, Am. iii., 8.

4. *Revenges* injury, so was Amalek punished, 1 Sm. xv., 2, 3; God resists the proud, but gives grace, Jas. iv., 6, Pro. xxii., 22; God's messengers to the Samaritans, 2 Kings xvii., 25, 26.

5. *Mild,* to these submissive, yet firm; so John before Herod; Paul before Felix; so Moses, Heb xi., 27, Ps. xxix., 25.

---

(79) THE WICKED ARE DROSS.
Ps. cxix., 119.

The wicked of the earth are made of it and return to it; they prosper in the earth, Ps. lxxv. 12; not so the righteous; nettles grow in any soil, Ps. xxxvii, 1, 2; not so flowers.

Dross.

1. Like the metal, but only in *appearance*; so the wicked, Ps. lxvi., 10, have a name to live, Rev. iii., 1.

2. To be *burnt* and consumed in the fire, not so silver which is only refined; wicked like a house on the sand, Mat. vii., 27, Ez. xxii., 20.

3. Mixed with pure metal only *temporary*, so wheat and chaff, Mat. xiii., 27; the sheep and goats are only together for a time.

4. *Unprofitable*, the good are gold or diamonds, though esteemed in the world, the offscouring, 1 Cor. iv. 13.

5. Dross more *abundant*, Zch. xiii., 8; Luk. xiii., 23, 24; God takes away the dross by judgment, Mat. iii., 12, Is. iv., 4; by church censures, 1 Cor. v., 5.

5. Not *improved* by fire as silver or gold are; Jerusalem was compared to a pot, Ez. xxiv., 6.

---

(80) THE TONGUE LIKE A FIRE.
Jas. iii., 6.

Solomon writes, a soft tongue breaketh the bone, Pr. xxv., 15; so a gentle answer softens the heart; the Bengalis say, " Quiet water splits a stone," Gen. xxxii., 49, 1 Sam. xxv., 24, 35.

1. *Fire* gives heat which makes (passion) boils over, while a man of understanding is of a cool spirit, Pr. xvii., 27, Numb. xvi., 4, 1 Sam. viii., 6—21; so Christ, Mat. xxvii., 12—14.

2. Kindles *great* things, hence fire called a good servant, but a bad master, Pr. xxvi., 18, 19.

3. *Scorches* and gives pain, so wicked compared to coals of Juniper, Ps. cxx., 4; burn hot and long.

The fire of the tongue is kindled from hell; not so the zeal of the Christian compared to a live-coal, Is. vi., 6; the cloven tongues of fire were harmless, Acts ii., 3.

---

(81) DEATH OF RIGHTEOUS AS A SHOCK OF CORN.
Job. v., 26.

The wicked are compared to weeds to be burned, but the righteous to corn in the harvest. Autumn after the hot season is pleasant, a time of the joy of harvest, Is. ix., 3; the righteous in death is compared in the text to the cutting of grain and to harvest home.

Corn is

1. *Sown* in order to be reaped again; at first the leaf is fresh, and the stalk firm, but not so beautiful as when the stalk is thin, and the leaf sere, but grain yellow, so the body must die to be raised at the Resurrection.

2. *Require preparatory agency*, so showers of grace to nourish the sun of God's favor and harden the grain, the dews of the Spirit to refresh, and the winds of affliction to keep the roots loose. Jacob, not knowing the preparatory agency, said all things are against me, Gen. xlii., 36, when he was on the eve of great prosperity; God's chastening gives the peaceable fruits of righteousness.

3. *Only cut when fully ripe*, if cut too soon the ear is watery, if too late dried up; the sower waits for the early and latter rain, Pr. xiv., 32; the wicked are driven away, but the righteous are always prepared by hope; Abijah and Josiah had their harvest in early youth; Noah and Abraham in advanced years.

4. *The ripe corn is handled with care*, the scythe of death is put to the roots, but the sheaves are bound up with care. Lazarus was nursed by dogs in life, but angels took charge of him in death, Luk. xvi., 21; many grains in the natural harvest are lost, but not so with Christ's people, John x., 28.

5. *When ripe housed in safety*, there may be anxiety about the weather, but harvest home is a time of joy, the grain is lodged in the granary, no more tears for the Christian; Christ is gone to prepare a place.

6. *When ripening hang its head*, so with increasing humility the Christian sees more of his sin and of God's goodness; Job repented in dust and ashes, Job xlii., 6; so Peter took off his coat at first through zeal, but finally *waits* to put off his tabernacle, 2 Pr. i., 14, so Paul at first calls himself the least of the Apostles, next less than the least of all saints, finally chief of sinners, a blasphemer.

7. *Ripening becomes weighty,* the Christian, a father in grace, has a zeal and love with a steadier flame, his graces are complete; hope makes not ashamed with joy. Paul says the time of my departure is at hand.

8. Ripening corn becomes gradually *looser* less needs the earth, so Paul learned to be in all things content; the worldling is attached to a shadow, but Paul thinks the world only dung.

9. Ripening easily distinguished from *tares* by smell and fruit; the righteous bring forth fruit in old age, Ps. xcii., 14; tares are then distinguished from wheat.

10. Ripened corn more *susceptible of injury,* as showers or wind may lay it level, so Jacob on his bed said, my soul, come not thou into their secret, Gn. xlix., 6; David wished for wings like a dove to flee away.

11. Ripened corn apt to *fall* of its own accord, so Paul wished to depart. They sought a heavenly country, Heb. xi., 16; hence no tears for them, Rev. vii., 14; they are clad in white robes.

---

(82) CHRIST A RAINBOW ROUND THE THRONE.
Rev. iv., 3.

God teaches by signs, thus Ezekiel drew on a tile the siege of Jerusalem, Ez. iv., 3; so Jeremiah's seething pot to denote Nebuchadnezzar's fury; the potter's vessel, Jer. xix., 1; the basket of figs, Jer. xxiv., 1—8; so Christ when He took a little child, Mat. xviii., 1—6.

The Peruvians paid great honor to the rainbow on account of its beauty of color and its proceeding from the sun.

The promises of God are a spiritual boat to prevent our being drowned in the waters of affliction. The schoolboy tries to catch the rainbow by running after it; the shepherd judges of the weather by it; the man of science admires it as the natural effect of the light refracted in the drops of rain, but the Christian views it as the token of God's covenant, Gen. ix., 12—19.

Christ like the Rainbow.

1. This painted arch *not seen* in every tempest, but when it is, it becomes the sign of fair weather; no rainbow in the tempest of God's wrath on the *impenitent*, Ps. xi., 6.

2. *The sun* must shine to produce the rainbow; so Christ must shine on the rain of God's wrath.

3. In a direction opposite to the cloud; the cloud of vengeance rains blood, brimstone, Ez. xvi., 19.

4. The sun necessary to pierce the rain; the rain then not injurious.

5. Sun's *rays* refracted, so God's covenant is from Christ, the Sun of Righteousness.

6. This bow, turned away from earth, has no marks of war, has no arrows or string, Rev. vi., 2; unites heaven and earth, broken on earth, but complete in the sky.

7. The *colors* of the rainbow make the purest white, so God's seven attributes, gracious, long-suffering, abundant in goodness, mercy, and truth, keeping mercy for thousands, forgiving iniquity, transgression, and sin; so in the Old Testament prophecies ceremonies were seals, signs, tokens, and types, but all united in the Spirit.

8. Three main colors in the rainbow—blue, red, yellow—all unite in one; hence called the daughter of wonder; so in the Trinity three persons in one.

9. Like an emerald *green* denoting that God's covenant is perpetual.

10. Appointed by God, Is. lv., 3; as a sign of the earth no more being destroyed by water, Gen. ix., 13, 17, Is. liv., 9.

11. Set after the sacrifice of Noah, Gen. viii., 20; so God's covenant after Christ's promised sacrifice, Is. liv., 8,4.

12. Appears amidst *rain*, so Christ's grace in trouble.

13. Only half the bow seen, so in this world only part of God's goodness visible to us, the rainbow (mercy) on Christ's head, Rev. iv., 3; rain before (severity), Ez. xxxviii., 22.

14. Though the arch be high, yet the extremities touch the earth, so Christ's two natures, Rom. xi., 6—8.

15. *Embraces* much space, so Christ's mercy.

The promises of God are a plank to swim to heaven, the saints' legacies, Heb. vi., 17. The presumptuous snatch at promises as the spider sucks poison out of good things, and make them a cradle to rock their souls to sleep.

(83) A Good Man as a Tree known by its Fruits.
Mat. xii., 33, 34.

The unripe fruit has little beauty, little flavour; is plucked with difficulty from the tree. But let the air and light, the warm sun and the fruitful showers, unite to swell it, and to ripen it; it is beautiful, it is sweet, falling from the bough into the hand of him that touches it.

Such is the young Christian, with little yet of the glories of holiness, little of the sweet and mellow charities of the Gospel, crude, and yet clinging closely to this lower life. But the fuller warmth of the love of Jesus, the richer influences of the Holy Spirit, shall mature his graces; and ere long he shall assume a deeper glow, and diffuse his fragrancy in the garden of his God, shall hang loosely on this nether world, waiting, but the touch of the messenger of the Lord, to drop off, and be no more seen below.

In Gal. v., 22, 23; the fruits which the righteous ought to bear are described; the barren fig-tree was cut down, Luk. xiii., 7.

Sadi says :—

> Though the water of life from the clouds fell in billows,
> And the ground were strewn over with paradise loam.
> Yet in vain would you seek from a garden of willows,
> To collect any fruit, as beneath them you roam.

An Oriental proverb compares expecting good fruits from the wicked to draining *swallow's milk*, plucking a *hog's soft wool* sands yielding pomegranates. The *Bengali* proverb says one knows the horse by his ears; the generous by his gifts. The *Tamul*—will the tiger's young be without claws?

(84) SINNERS MORE UNGRATEFUL THAN THE OX OR ASS.

Is. i., 2, 3.

Menu says an ignorant man, even by a small gift, may become helpless as a *cow* in a bog.

Ingratitude is represented by an English proverb—put a *snake* in your bosom when warm he will sting you; by a Spanish—bring up a *raven*, it will pick out your eyes; eaten *bread* is soon forgotten.

The ass is of a patient, laborious, and stupid nature. *Issachar* is called, Gn. xlix., 14, a *strong ass* in reference to his descendants who, being agriculturists, cultivated their own territory with patient labour; of *Jehoiakim*, it is said, Jer. xxii., 19; he shall be buried with the *burial of an ass*, for Nebuchadnezzar, having taken Jerusalem, put the king at once to death, and flung his unburied corpse over the walls. *Christ* is represented, Zch. ix., 9, Mat. xxi., 5, as *sitting on an ass*—a triumph of peace. The ass was an emblem of peace, as the horse was of war; the former required a whip, the latter only a *bridle*, Pr. xxvi., 3.

The Jews prohibited using horses, asses were large, temperate, used by nobles, Jud. x., 4, xii., 4; ox and ass not to be drawn together as unequally yoked, 2 Cr. vi., 14; asses were unclean, hence eaten in Samaria only in famine, 2 Kings vi., 25.

(85)   THE CHURCH COMPARED TO THE MOON.
Canticles vi., 10.

The moon receives her brightness from the sun. She is dark herself, and reflects his light. One-half of her orb is always illuminated therewith—a circle of beautiful splendour; but the whole of that circle is not always visible, sometimes but a thread-like portion thereof, and sometimes it is entirely hidden from the eyes. The moon is not in darkness, when we see not her light; her face still looks towards the sun, and is bright with his brightness; but we are so placed not to have the full view thereof.

Such is the Christian; he is dark himself, but reflects the light of his Lord. For the graces of Christ beheld by faith produce like graces in the soul.

Christians are like the moon : (1) *Receive light* from the sun ; Christ is the Sun of Righteousness, Mat. iv., 2 ; (2) *Dispense* what they receive, Mat. v., 14 ; (3) Give light at *night*, so Christians in this dark world ; (4) Though fair have *spots*, Jud. 12 ; (5) Sometimes full, sometimes *winning* ; the Church now in prosperity, again persecuted, but the wicked have reserved for them the blackness of darkness, Pet. ii., 17 ; (6) *Above* the earth, so Christians, Ph. iii., 20 ; (7) The Church acts by *unseen* influence, like the moon on the tides and weather.

---

(86)   SIN AS POISON OF SERPENTS.
Ps. lviii., 4, 5.

The poison of serpents is like sin—(1) *Inflames* so the fire of passion ; (2) *Spreads* very quickly ; there are Indian cobras whose poison kills in 20 minutes ; like lightning the poison goes through the body. Adam's sin has spread through the world ; (3) *Small* in the beginning, the wound of the cobra scarcely visible, as the Bengali proverb—it goes in a needle, comes out a ploughshare. Eve ate an apple, but it poisoned the whole human race; (4) Bite not *painful*, but the effect deadly; so the pleasures of sin for a season; (5) The serpent has a *beautiful* skin, such was Absalom beautiful, but disobedient to his father David; he raised a rebellion against him.

---

(87) GOD'S INFLUENCE LIKE RAIN ON THE MOWN GRASS.

Ps. lxxii., 6.

The heart of man is often compared in Holy Scripture to the hard ground, which must be ploughed or softened before it can either receive the good seed, or can bring forth such herbs as the sower looks for in their season. The heart is sometimes called a "stony heart;" and the doctrine is then spoken of as "a hammer that breaketh the rock in pieces;" and elsewhere it is compared to "a two-edged sword, piercing, even to the dividing asunder of soul and spirit, and of the joints and marrow." Its gentler influence is alluded to, when it is likened to rain or dew; more gentle, but not less powerful, than when it acts as a sword, or "as a fire," or as a hammer that breaketh the rock in pieces.

The ground is sometimes so hard and parched in summer in India that it might almost be taken for rock. It can be broken only by the most violent effort. Yet, when "a gracious rain" is sent upon it, by degrees the hardness gives way. "He maketh it soft with the drops of rain;" and it is again such as to receive into its bosom the seeds which shall bear fruit in due season. And thus has many and many a heart, which seemed "as hard as a piece of the nether millstone," been softened and penetrated by the heavenly doctrine in due time.

Rain deserves to be called a present from heaven. As the consequences of a continued drought would be fatal to us as seen in Bengal in the great drought, so the advantages, which, the refreshing showers afford, are equally precious. The heat of the sun acts without interruption on the different bodies on earth, and continually draws thin particles from them, which fill the atmosphere in the form of vapours. We should breathe those dangerous exhalations with the air, if now and then they were not carried off by the rain, which precipitates them upon the earth, and thus clears and purifies the air. It is not less useful in moderating the burning heat of the atmosphere, as we see in the rainy time in India. The rain, which falls from a higher region, brings to the lower a refreshing coolness, of which we always feel the agreeable effects when it has rained. It is also to the rain we must partly attribute the origin of fountains, wells, lakes, brooks, and consequently rivers as seen in Bengal. The Amazon is 180 miles wide at its mouth. Everybody knows in what abundance we are supplied with those sources of water in the wet and rainy seasons, whereas they evaporate during a long drought. But, to feel how useful and necessary rain is, we need only observe, how the earth and vegetables languish for want of these fruitful showers, without which every thing would perish. Rain is, in many respects, the food of vegetables; it circulates in their finer veins, and in the vessels of plants and trees, and conveys to them those beneficial juices which preserve their life, and give them growth. When it pours on mountains, it sweeps from them a soft, rich, and fruitful earth, which it deposits in the valleys where it falls, and which it fertilizes. The valley of the Ganges has been thus formed.

Among the Egyptians the prophet carried in his hand a pitcher, as a symbol of his dispensing the water of learning. In the *Lalita Vistara* it is said that Sakhya Muni will render calm and cool by the rain of the law those who are devoured by the fire of envy and passion.

God's Influence like Rain—
1. Comes *irresistibly*, Is. lv., 10, 11.

2. Sometimes in torrents, at other times in showers; the feast of Pentecost, when 3,000 were converted, was a torrent. Lydia's case was the gentle shower, Acts xvi., 14; so Timothy's case.

3. Falls in drops in *succession*, so line upon line, Is. xxviii., 10; Christians, like narrow-mouthed vessels, cannot receive much at a time.

4. At God's *pleasure*; Darjeeling and Assam have the rain in torrents; in Egypt scarcely any falls; so the Gospel was known in England 1,800 years ago; in New Zealand, only 50 years ago.

(88) CHRISTIANS PILGRIMS ON EARTH.
Heb. xi., 11, 13.

Moses gave his son the name Gershom, (the stranger) to signify he was not in his own land, though it gave him shelter when treated with neglect by his own countrymen, and driven away from a Royal Court.

The Jews' journey in the desert—a type of the Christian pilgrimage:—

1. A journey from a house of *Bondage*; the Jews worked in hot weather in a land like a furnace, deprived of their children, so the Christian was a slave to Satan, and his offspring were heirs to misery, serving divers' lusts, Tit. iii., 3. God says to them as the Angel did to Lot, "Escape for thy life, look not back," Gen. xix., 17.

2. A journey to a land of *Promise*; the Jews saw this not yet they had God's word for it. They sent two spies who said, Dt. viii., 8, the stones were iron, a land of fountains flowing with milk and honey; so the Patriarchs were not mindful of that country from whence they came out, Heb. xi., 15.

3. A journey through a dangerous desolate *wilderness*, hunger, fiery serpents, burning sand, flinty rock, a land of drought, of the shadow of death, Dt. viii., 15; so is this world; no food for the soul, temptations for the trial of faith, storms, quicksands of affliction,

the enemies of the Christian are fear, Pr. xxii., 13, Num. vi., 14; unbelief, 1 Sam. xvi., 1; sloth, 1 Tim. v., 13, covetousness, Mat. xvi., 24; presumption.

4. A *long* and crooked *journey*. The Jews might have reached Canaan in one month instead of 40 years, but their trial and punishment were intended, Dt. viii., 2; so Christians have a variety of experience, joy, and sorrow; rest will be, therefore, more sweet.

5. A journey under *Divine Government;* the Jews were few in Egypt, yet kings were reproved for their sake; they multiplied in slavery; in Babylon, God was with the Jews, but in the desert, there was the pillar of cloud by day, of fire by night; they had Angels' food; their garments and shoes waxed not old; so Christ is with His Church to the end of the world. Mat. xxviii., 20; as an eagle over her young ones, Dt, xxxii., 11; they mount up with wings as eagles, Is. xlvi., 13; there are various pretended ways, but Christ is the true one.

6. A journey with a *happy termination;* Jordan crossed, each sat under his vine and fig-tree, so a rest for God's people; all journeys in this world not certain of success, Is. xxxv., 10.

7. Enter by the *straight* way the sea of religious conviction, their foot on the flesh, their eye on the cross.

8. They use the *Provision* on the way bread from heaven; they pass the valley of Baca.

9. Rely on a heavenly *guide* coming up from the wilderness leaning on the beloved, Cant. iii., 8.

10. *Perseverance*—of all that come out of Egypt few entered Canaan, so Lot's wife; the man putting his hand to the plough looking back, Mat. ix., 62; underneath are the everlasting arms, Dt. xxxiii., 27.

11. In *motion* always, but towards home, Gen. xlvii., 9.

12. *Lightly equipped* to travel easier, Heb. xii., 1; the covetous man loads himself with thick clay, Heb. ii., 5, 6.

13. A *varied route*—mud, good roads, desert, green fields, slough of despond, valley of humiliation mountains of opposition, the rock of ages.

14. A *strange* country passed through, Heb. xi., 13; Ps. xxxix., 12; Is. xv., 19—22; stay only a day or so in each place, Heb. xiii., 14.

15. Like *companions* and fellow-travellers dividing griefs and doubling joys, Ps. cxix., 74, Ecc. xi., 9-10; relieves the tedium of the way.

---

(89) A LIVING DOG BETTER THAN A DEAD LION.
Ecc. ix., 4—10.

"*Half a loaf* is better than no bread."
"He with *one eye* sees the better for it."
"A *standing thistle* better than the falling cedar."
"A *living sheep* better than the dead camel."
"A *living headman* better than the dead Emperor."

This text points out the value of life representing it by the dog the meanest of animals, Mat. xv., 26, and the lion the noblest, Pr. xxx., 30.

---

(90) BAGS WAXING NOT OLD.
Luk. xii., 33.

Men count up their money, put it into bags, seal them up that they may be safe, and reserved for a long time.

God seals up the sins of his people in His bag, Job xiv., 17, Dt. xxxii., 34; thus *Israel's defection* remembered after 390 years, Ps. xxv., 7; his *bones* are full of the sins of his youth, Job. xx., 11; *Saul* was dead, but his sin was alive, there was a triennial famine on account of Saul having slain the Gibeonites. God brought the sin of *Joseph's brethren* committed 20 years before to their mind, Gen. xlii., 21; old sins will be old serpents, and sting unto death, Num. xxxii., 23.

(91) Christ knocks at the Door of the Heart.
Rev. iii., 20.

God's ways are not as our ways; with man the inferior waits on the superior, here the great God waits on the lukewarm Laodiceans. The door is the heart; this is barred by nature against Christ by vile lusts and passions by unbelief.

Christ continues to *knock* by his *word*, Heb. iv., 12, his Spirit, his *Providence*.

---

(92) The Fool eats his own Flesh.
Pr. vi., 10.

Solomon refers to those who, seeing that under despotism what they get, may be easily taken away, or is the subject of envy to others, sit still.

The *English* Proverb.—No *pains*, no gains; no *sweet*, no sweat; no *mills*, no meal. *Spanish*.—Where wilt thou have to go ox, that thou wilt not have to plough; sloth the key of poverty. *Turkish*.—It is not with saying honey, honey, that sweetness will come into the mouth.

---

(93) Eye of the Just sheds Rivers of Water.
Lamen. iii., 48.

The righteous comply not with wickedness; so *Joseph*, Gen. xxxix., 9; *Noah*, Gen. vi., 9; so *Zechariah* and *Elizabeth*.

Lament at sin, Lot ii., Pt. ii., 7; so *Christ* over Jerusalem, Luk. xix., 36—38, Mk. iii., 5; so *Ninevites* in sackloth, Jer. iv., 19, ix., 1; Ezrah *plucked his* beard, so Micah, i., 8; seeing Jerusalem's sins, Job xxx., 29, a *companion* of owls. *Elijah* wished to die, 1 Kings xix., 4, so *oses*, Ps. clxvi., 23; David has no power to weep any more, 1 Sam. xxx., 4.

One person's sin produces much evil, so the famine in David's time, 2 Sam. xxi., 1—3.

A blessing on mourners, Mat. v., 4; *marked* out for mercy, Ez. ix., 4. David *watered his couch* for his own sin, Ps. vi., 6; now for others in rivers as *Jeremiah*, Lm. ii., 18, Jer. xiii., 17.

Who to mourn ministers, Zch. iii., 1; responsible as for the ox, Ex. xxii., 10; between the porch and altar, Joel. ii., 17; remember their own experience, Gl. vi., 1, Tit. ii., 3.

How to mourn grief mixed with anger, so *Samuel* spared not Saul in his sin, yet mourned for him. Moses, the *meekest* man on earth, yet broke the tables of the law, so Paul, 2 Cor. xii., 21, so Elijah, 2 Kings viii., 11.

(94) GOD CHASTISES HIS SPIRITUAL SONS.
Heb. xii., 6, 8—11.

In Jer. xxxi., 18, Ephraim is represented chastised by God as a *bullock* unaccustomed to the yoke; the bullock then *rebels* against the will of his master, though nourished and supported by him; it will not *subserve* his interests; when chastised, it rebels the more; *repeated strokes* only serve to inflame its rage; nor will it ever submit until it be wearied out, and unable to maintain its opposition; thus the sinner generally fights against God.

God chastised Solomon and David, 2 Sam. vii., 15; but he punished Saul with death for his offering sacrifice, 1 Sam., and sparing Agag, 1 Sam. xv.; *Peter's* denial of Christ was worse than Ananiah's denial of a portion of his goods; yet how different the punishment.

Christ learnt obedience from suffering, Heb. v., 8; so the Prodigal, Luk. xv., 17; and we are silly *sheep*; prosperity makes us stray the more, as sunshine on the dunghill only produces more stinks, so Jas. i., 2; chastisement as a *fan*, Mk. iii., 12; a *pruning* hook, Jon. xv., 2; plough, Jer. iv., 3; a *Furnace*, Is. xlviii., 10; *cords*, Job xxxvi., 8.

The Germans say a child may have too much of it mother's blessing. Better the child *weep* than the father. The Spaniards say more springs in the garden than the gardener ever sowed. Did God *hate* his people, he would suffer them to go merrily to hell. Calm weather lets Christ sleep. The storm rouses him.

Fruits of Chastisement:

1. *Tests reality* as Solomon's *sword* did the true mother, as the *storm* did Peter's faith, Mat. xiv., 30, 31; a *painted faith* no more avails than a painted helmet.

2. *Fructifies* as the palm-tree by pressure, so prayer as with Mananeh in fetters, 2 Ch. xxxiii., 13, 18, 19; so Paul blind, Acts ix., 19; the hammer of chastisement squares the stones for the heavenly temple.

3. Not a mark of vengeance as sin, Job xlii., 7, Paul's Acts xxviii., 4; Siloam tower, Luk. xiii., 4, 5; Saint *Ambrose* would not stop a night in the house of a man who had never seen chastisement, lest some judgment should seize him.

4. *Peaceable fruits:* the Prodigal happier among *swine* than he had been in his father's house.

Unsanctified affliction *parboils* a wicked man for hell, to a Christian affliction is not a fiery, but a brazen, serpent. God beats his children as we do our *clothes* in the sun only to beat out the moths. *Manasseh* got more good by his iron chain than by his golden chain.

---

(95) THE VALLEY OF THE SHADOW OF DEATH.
Ps. xxiii., 4.

Life is a journey through a waste howling wilderness, the dark valley of the mountain of death forms its close, bounded by the river of death.

The Valley of Death is—

1. *Dark;* the sun beams enter not, so no natural light illumines the grave's path; it is like a dark tunnel. Satan wraps it often in clouds of doubt and darkness—

a darkness that may be felt; so the Jews, when entering the dark cleft of the Red Sea, found it "a land of darkness," Job xviii., 14; the righteous in death, however, has no sting, 1 Cor. xv., 57; the Sun of Righteousness illumines the gloom.

2. *Lonely;* mountain passes are solitary—all pass through this, but none meet even though they die together; Angels, however, are present, but as a matter of faith more than of consciousness. Jacob said of the desert, " How dreadful is this place ?" Moses, entering the cloud, exclaimed, " I exceedingly quake, the Jews crossed the Red Sea at night when quite dark."

3. *Painful;* thorns, stones, and briers abound ; so death is the wrenching of soul and body; even Christ prayed that the cup might pass from him.

4. *Dangerous* ; robbers, wild beasts in the dark possess the domain of death, the king of terrors. Some have passed through this valley amid showers of stones, others wrapped in flames, others knee-deep in blood.

5. *Leads to a strange land.* Separates temporal and seen from eternal things ; no correspondence with friends ; in a moment, millions of miles distant from earth.

6. *A route never retraced ;* the great *gulph* between ; this tree sprouts not again, Job xiv., 7 ; no work, no device in the grave, Ecc. xiv., 7.

7. *Has two terminations ;* the gate of life, the gate of death, the land of rest, and that where the worm never dies, like Pharoah's butler and baker, who looked forward to the third day, but with very different feelings.

All have to pass this valley, 1 Cor. xxix., 15 ; it is the house appointed for all living, Job xxxix., 23 ; the righteous walk in the valley implying calmness, Pr. xiv., 32 ; as to them the shadow of death is like the shadow of a sword harmless. Death is even counted a treasure,

1 Cor. iii., 22; while the wicked shall have brimstone rained on them, Ps. xi., 6, 1 Sam. ii., 9. God's presence cheered the Jews even in the wilderness, Ex. xxiii., 15; and Balaam wished the death of the righteous, Num. xxiii., 10.

Death is naturally a dark, gloomy object that obstructs all light, throws a baleful shadow afar, that over the regions of the dead, Job xvi., 16, on my eyelids the shadow of death. The valley of Hinnom was filthy, Jer. xxxi., 40.

(96) False Peace like Untempered Mortar.
Ez. xiii., 10.

In Persia, proper mortar is made of plaster, earth, and chopped straw well kneeded together, but often to save expense; they put much water to a little plaster which looks as well, but is not plaster.

No cement in a house so built; it is like the house on the sand, Mat. vii., 27, which the whirlwind or flood blows down, or like some of the bridges in India, cemented by rubbish, not by mortar.

Such is all false peace without repentance and faith in the atonement of Christ, Luk. xii., 19.

(97) The Fool as a Bear robbed of her Whelps.
Proverbs xvii., 12.

The female bear is eminent for intense affection to her young, and dreadfully furious when deprived of them. Disregarding every consideration of danger to herself, she attacks, with intense ferocity, every animal that comes in her way, and, in the bitterness of her heart, will attack even a band of armed men. The Russians of Kamtschatka never venture to fire on a young bear when the mother is near; for, if the cub drop, she becomes enraged to a degree little short of madness, and, if she get sight of the enemy, will only quit her revenge with her life.

These considerations give great energy to this proverb, descriptive of the danger of meeting "a fool in his folly," *i. e.*, a furious, revengeful man, under the influence of his impetuous passions, and his heart determined on their immediate gratification, of which Saul, 1 Sam. xx., 30, and Herod, Mat., ii., 16, are striking examples.

The Bengalis say scratching the itch only produces a wound. The *Telegus* illustrate the text by pouring ghee on fire.

A she-bear destroyed the 42 children who mocked the prophet, 2 Kings ii., 24. God's fury with the idolatrous Jews is compared to a bear bereaved, Hos. xiii., 8; David had to defend himself against a bear, 1 Sam. xvii., 34—36. In the Millennium, however, the bear shall feed with the cow, Is. xi., 7.

Jacob's sons, like a bear for one man's faults, destroyed a whole city, Gen. xxiv. Saul similarly destroyed the innocent priests, 1 Sam. xxii., 11—18; so Nebuchadnezzar when he heated the furnace seven times, Dan. iii., 13—19.

---

(98) PURITY OF MIND AS A SINGLE EYE.
Mat. vi., 32, 33.

The *Shanti Shatak* says praise to the stomach which is satisfied with little food, but shame to the heart, which, though it has a hundred desires satisfied, is pursuing after more. The *Telegus* compare a double-minded man to a post in the mud swinging to and fro, or to one who wakes the master, and gives the thief a stick.

The eye enables us not only to see God's works, but to judge the intentions of another by his countenance. The conscience is to the soul what the eye is to the body. It is the faculty by which we discern the difference between good and evil, and by which we orm our judgment, both as to the end at which we ught to aim, and as to the means by which we should pursue it. It is at once a witness and a judge within us; and it fulfils its purpose when it shows us the glory of God, as the end to be set before us, and when it warns us to seek steadfastly and singly that blessed end in each particular action. But as the eye is affected by the diseased humours of the body, and then conveys to the mind only a dim and misty notion of outward things, so the benefit to be derived from the conscience depends on the pains, we take to keep it in a sound and healthful state. By another figure of speech, the wicked are said to "sear the conscience as with a hot iron," so that it is no longer sensitive and tender, but becomes dead and hard. As the eye can not bear in itself the very least speck of dust, and knows no rest until it has wiped it out, so the conscience should be sensitive to the very least stain or spot of sin, and not suffer us to be at peace, until we have washed it out with the tears of penitence; or rather, until it be taken away by the blood of Christ.

The Bible represents the motions of the soul by those of the body; the *feet* to walk in God's commandments, Ps. cxix., 105; the hands to work out our salvation; the knees to bow at Jesus's name, Ph. ii., 12; the ear to hear God's word; a mouth to eat the flesh of Christ; and eyes to see the mysteries of God's kingdom.

There are eyes full of adultery, 2 Pet. ii., 14; the eyes of the fool are in the ends of the earth, Pr. xvii., 24; the proud eye is a lofty one, Ps. cxxxi., 1. Eve was deceived by the eye, Gen. iii., 6; so Achan's eye by the garment, Jos. vii., 21; so Sampson's eye by Delilah, Jud. xvi., 1; so Ahab, 1 Kings xxi., 2; so Nebuchadnezzar, Dan. iv., 27—33.

(99) LIFE PASSES AS A FLOWER.
1 *Pet.* i., 24.

Though the flowers are clad with a raiment superior in beauty to Solomon's, yet the scythe of death, sunshine, storm, rain, or worms sweep them away. The

Prabodh Chandrodaya says the society even of friends is a flash of lightning which is dazzling, but momentary. The Christian, like a plant, may lose his flower which will be a seed behind on earth, but he will be transplanted to the Gardens of Paradise.

(100) Brotherly Unity—a Threefold Cord.
Ecc. iv., 9—12.

The Bengalis say, " With men of one mind even the sea might be dried up." Love like a creeper withers and dies, if it has nothing to embrace; the Ramsanehis, a sect of Western India, say regarding society, " A solitary lamp, however brilliant, casteth a shadow beneath it, place another lamp in the apartment, and the darkness of both is dissipated." The live coal left alone soon loses its vital heat; iron sharpeneth iron, Acts xxviii. 15; God said it was not good for man to be alone even in Paradise, Gen. ii., 18; and Christ sent out the Apostles by twos, Luk. x., 1—3.

(101) Intermeddlers like One taking a Dog by the Ears.
Proverbs xxvi., 17.

From an idle whim or a fool-hardy venture, a man thinks to show his prowess, fancying that he is able to master the dog which others scarcely dare come near. When he has taken it by the ears, he finds his folly, for, if he continues to hold it, his time is lost, and if he lets it go, it will fly at him before he can get beyond its reach. He has exposed himself both to pain and ridicule by a foolish attempt to get credit for courage and dexterity.

The Bengalis say oil your own wheel first; and the English, he that intermeddles with all things, may go shoe the goslings. Of the eleven Apostles, as Peter spoke most, he erred most, Mat. xvi., 22, xxvi., 74. Paul condemns tattling women, 1 Tim. v., 13.

(102) Prayer as Incense.
Rev. v., 8.

Incense was made from the gum obtained from the bark of a tree; being used in sacrifices, it was brought as a present to the Infant Saviour, Mat. ii., 11. It was a symbol of prayer as it *ascended*, so did Cornelius's prayer, Acts x., 4, Ps. cxli., 2; was made *pure* from the gum of a tree in Arabia; was *purifying*, removing the smell from the burning flesh and blood of the sacrifices; was *fragrant*, Ex. xxx., 34; *pleasant*, so when Hannah prayed she was no more sad, 1 Sam. i., 6.

(103) Bread of Deceit fills the Mouth with Gravel.
Proverbs xx., 17.

The *Lalita Vistara* says desires are regarded by the wise as the edge of a sword covered with honey, or as the head of a serpent leading to quarrels, as a corpse among dogs.

Jacob deceived his father with a kid, *Gen.* xxvii., 9, 14, &c.; more than forty years after, his children deceive him with a kid, *Gen.* xxxvii., 31, 32. David artfully contrived the murder of Uriah by the sword, 2 Sam. xi. 14, 15; and the Providence of God so appointed it, that the sword never departed from his house, 2 Sam. xii., 10, Jer ii., 19. So Haman, Esth. vii., 10, *Ps.* ix., 15, the attempt to assassinate Ahasuerus, Esth. ii., 21—23.

The Jews put our Lord to death that the Romans might not come, and take away their place and nation; by that very act they drew down the vengeance of God, which God, as we learn from profane history, appointed the Romans to execute, Jon. xi., 48.

(104) The Fool in the Congregation of the Dead.
Proverbs xxi., 16.

Chanakya says in the dusk we lose our way, and a fallen woman is like a corpse. The marks of fools are—

(1) *Understand* not who will show them any good, Ps. iv., 6; prefer corn to peace; *beasts* in man's form.

(2) *Hurt themselves*; run into a hornet's nest, play with serpents, look on wine, Ps. xxiii., 31, 32; harbour a thief in the house.

(3) *Strive with one stronger;* so the potsherd with its Maker, Ps. xlv., 9, and xxvii., 4; God has frogs, lice, worms, and everything at his disposal.

(4) *Take brass for gold;* so mean things of earth for heaven.

(5) *Feed on ashes, among swine,* Is. xxv., 20, Luk. xv., 16, so Prodigal son; he labors for the wind, Ecc. v., 14.

(6) *Sow when they should reap.* So a deathbed repentance, Gl. v., 6, 7, 8.

(7) *Delight in mischief,* Ps. xxviii., 3.

(8) To save their hat *lose* their head.

Solomon gives the character of a fool—(1) *Meddling*, Pr. ii., 3; (2) *Mischievous*, Pr. x., 23; (3) *Cleaves to sin*, Pr. xxvii., 22; (4) *Full of words*, Ecc. x., 14; (5) *Keeps no secrets*, Pr., xxix., 11; (6) *Destroyed by prosperity*, Pr. i., 32; (7) *Slothful*, Ecc. iv., 5; (8) *Trusts his* own heart, Pr. xxiii., 26.

---

(105) THE MELTING POWER OF LOVE TO ENEMIES.
Proverbs xxv., 21, 22.

The metaphor is taken from founders, who melt the hardest metals by heaping coals of fire upon them. So if an enemy has the least spark of goodness in him, kindness will work a change in his mind, and make him throw off all his enmities; or, if it have the contrary effect, he shall have so much the sorer punishment, and the forgiving man shall not lose the reward which the Lord Himself will give; Saul's hard heart was for a time melted by David's noble spirit of forgiveness, 1 Sam. xxiv, 16—21, and the Lord rewarded David by giving him rest from all his enemies, 2 Sam. vii. 1, and establishing him on the throne of Israel, 2 Sam. vii., 8, 9—12.

The Italians say revenge of a hundred years old has still its sucking teeth, *i.e.*, never grows old.

> The sandal tree, most sacred tree of all,
> Perfumes the very axe which bids it fall.

Forgiveness like fire consumes the dross of passion, purifies the metal of the soul, melts and makes malleable the hardest metal of envy.

---

(106) THE LOVE OF MONEY THE ROOT OF ALL EVIL.
1 *Tim.* vi., 10.

The Bengalis say even iron swims for gain; from covetousness came sin, and from sin came death. St. Paul calls covetousness idolatry, Eph. v., 5; covetousness implies distrust of God, Luk. xii., 29; we ask only for our *daily* bread, Mat. vi., 34—41; hasting to be rich leads to wrong means as with Judas, Balam, Ahab, Ananias, Simon Magus; their root of money-love spread like the banyan, its branches very wide in discontent and carelessness of the poor. Christ said, "Ye cannot serve God and Mammon," or as the Bengalis have it—one foot on land, the other on water. The ostrich cannot fly high because of its wings, and Jacob with his flock had to travel slowly, Gen. xxxiii., 13. He is not rich who possesses much, but who desires little; the evil lies not in the mere acquisition of money—thus Abraham was wealthy, Gen. xiii., 2, xxiv., 2; David, 1 Chron. xxviii., 10, xxix., 1—16.

---

(107) MAN BORN TO TROUBLE AS SPARKS FLY UP.
Job. v., 6.

Sparks, called in Hebrew, the sons of the flame; by God's law they ascend, as bodies that have weight fly downward, or as the seasons succeed each other; but God suits the wind to the shorn lamb.

(108) The Dead sown for the Resurrection.
1 Cor. xv., 42.

Wonderful is the progress of the seed from its first to its second life; for it has two lives. During its first life, it grows, and ripens in the plant which bears it, and then falls away to the earth out of which it grew. But it has a second life after its resurrection from the earth; from whence it springs up with a life of its own, and with a new body. From every seed grows a plant of the same kind with that which bore the seed. *God giveth to every seed its own body.* The word of God teaches us to expect two lives. The one is our present earthly life which we have of our parents; the other is the life which we shall have after we have been buried. For as the seed *is not quickened except it die,* so we cannot obtain eternal life, but by the way of death. The grave is as the furrow of the field in which the seed is sown; and as the sunshine of the spring raises the seed to life, so shall the Sun of Righteousness return to raise all those who are buried in the earth. The time is coming when they, that are in their graves, shall hear his voice, and come forth, as Lazarus came forth from the tomb, when Jesus called him. The good seed of wheat and other grain is gathered for use, and laid up in the barn, as the righteous, when they die, are gathered to their fathers; but the evil seeds of the thistle are blown about by the winds, and scattered over the face of the earth. Such as we are at death, such shall we be at the resurrection. If we are the seed of a thorn or a thistle, when we die, there will be no hope that we shall be found a rose or a lily, when we are risen again, for *every seed* will have *its own body.*

Our bodies every seven years change every particle; so the seed in the darkness of the ground decomposes, drawing its new body from earth, water, and air until it becomes like the banyan or cotton tree; so the body in the grave may be like a worm, but it will become like a butterfly. Seeds in Egyptian Mummies have germinated after a thousand years; we cast our rice seed on the muddy waters it sinks, but soon a plentiful rice harvest appears.

---

(109) God's Name on the Righteous Forehead.
Rev. xxii., 4, 5.

The *Vishnuvites* have the *tiluk* or forehead mark, a longitudinal line marked in vermilion; the *Sivites* a parallel line of a turmeric colour. It was a custom of ancient date in Asia to mark *servants* on the forehead; hence in Ezekiel, ix., 4, the Angel sets a mark on the foreheads of the men who cry for the abominations.

The Jews were forbidden to *brand the forehead*, Lev., xix., 28; only the *High Priest* bore on it a plate of gold, on which the name of God was written. The *Athenians* marked an owl on their captives' forehead; *idolaters* put on such the mark of their god as Jupiter's thunder-bolt, Neptune's trident. Paul says I bear on my body the *marks* of the Lord Jesus, *i.e.*, the scars of the stripes he received, Gl. vi., 17.

Believers have God's mark in regeneration, and sanctification impressed on them, 1 Pt. ii., 9; they shall *serve him* day and night, Rev. vii., 15; the *name* is Jehovah, Ze. xiv., 20; written not with *ink*, but with the Spirit of the Living God, 2 Cor. iii., 3; the *forehead* is the most *conspicuous* part; the countenance is the index of the mind, and implies an *open* confession, as Paul was a chosen vessel to bear Christ's name before the Gentiles, Act. ix., 15, 16.

---

(110) The Hypocrite's Words smoother than Butter.
Ps. lv., 21.

The Bengalis call a hypocrite "*makhal* fruit, *i.e.*, beautiful outside, bitter within; a tiger in a *tulsi* grove, outside smooth and painted, inside only straw like the

Hindu idols stuffed with straw inside. The crow and the cuckow have the same colour, but a very different voice." These words were applied by David to his son, Absalom, who drove him from Jerusalem, 2 Sam. xv., 2, which made the father wish for the wings of a *dove* to fly away, and be at rest, as the dove, sent forth from the ark, found no rest for the sole of her foot. Such a hypocrite was Judas who betrayed Christ by kissing him.

(111) CHRIST THE GREAT PHYSICIAN.

Mat. ix., 12.

Christ went about healing all manner of diseases and spiritual maladies; he said the whole have no need of a physician, but those who are sick.

A good Physician has—

1. *Natural qualifications:* Christ has infinite intelligence; "all things are naked to his eyes," Heb. iv., 13; he has infinite power; we are his workmanship. His heart is tender; a High Priest touched with a feeling of our infirmities. A merry and feeling heart does good like a medicine, particularly so with a physician; but Christ has sympathy as he suffered being tempted; he said to the woman taken in adultery, " Where are thy accusers ?"

2. *Training:* A doctor must know the structure of the body, the symptoms of disorders, and the properties of medicines. Christ partook of flesh and blood; he was wounded for our transgressions.

3. *Authorised* by competent authority: Christ called of God as was Aaron, lifted up as a serpent in the wilderness. The Lord anointed him to bind up the broken-hearted, Is. lxi., 1, Luk. iv., 18; his miracles were his diploma, John v., 36, 37.

4. Efficient *medicines* provided: He sent his word, and healed them, Ps. cvii., 20, to be spiritually minded is life and peace. These medicines are not dear or

difficult to procure; the word can be received into the heart by simple faith; all can come to his dispensary.

5. *Experience:* Christ has had 6,000 years' practice ever since it was said the seed of the woman shall bruise the serpent's head. Age does not impair his skill; he saves to the uttermost, even in Heaven the song is worthy the lamb; cholera baffles doctors, but Christ searches the reins, and checks all diseases; he can make Paul's thorn in the flesh contribute to his humility.

6. *Attentive:* Comes at all times without being asked, and watches the crisis.

7. *Generous to the poor:* Christ takes no fees; says buy without money or price, Is. lv., 1; Christ is the poor man's doctor; he healed the woman who had spent all her money on doctors.

8. *Perseveres:* Christ makes the dry bones live, Ez. xxxvii., 4; he has the brand plucked from the burning.

9. *Successful:* Christ said come all that labor. Adam's rebellion, Noah's drunkenness, Manasseh's tyranny were cured; even death is cured.

10. *Accessible:* Christ is always so; he never sleeps.

Earthly physicians differ from Christ in—(1) sometimes *deceived*, Ps. cxxxix., 4, kill sometimes instead of curing, Hos. xiii., 9; (2) require to be *sent* for, Luk. xix., 10; (3) *charge* for services; (4) make few sacrifices for their patients. Christ gave his blood; (5) cannot raise the *dead;* (6) sometimes *impatient*, Cant. v., 2; (7) visit only *one patient* at a time; (8) subject to *disease* themselves, Heb. ii., 17; (9) their *medicines* lose their virtue by long keeping, 1 Pet. vi., 25; (10) specially attend the rich.

---

(112) An Oppressor like a Crouching Lion.
Ps. x., 9.

A lion is proud, strong, and crafty, lying in wait for the prey; such were Nebuchadnezzar, Dan. iii., Manasseh, 2 Kings xxi., 16, Zachariah, 2 Chron. xxiv.,

21, Rehoboam ; Satan is compared to a roaring lion, 1 Pet. v., 8, 9, active as with Job, knowing his time is short, Rev. xii., 12.

Oppression is an abuse of power, the practice of unjust and uncharitable actions as to a hired servant, Dt. xxiv., 14, or widow, Ex. xxii., 21, 23. Oppression makes a wise man mad, Ecc. vii., 7 ; grinds the face of the poor, Is. iii., 15 ; flays the poor, Mic. iii., 1—3 ; envy one cause of oppression, as in Ahab and Naboth's time ; pride another, as in Jezebel's case.

The *Telegus* say there is no justice in oppression, and no sight in a blind eye. The *Bengalis* say the love of the Mussulman to his fowl is like that of the zemindar to the ryot.

A poor man, oppressing the poor, is compared to a sweeping rain which leaves no food, such a one sells the poor for a pair of shoes, Amos. viii., 4—6.

---

(113) Lip Love as Sounding Brass.
1 Cor. xiii., 1.

The *Bengalis* say by words only the moistened rice is not made into a confection ; a false friendship is like a bank of sand ; now, you, as it were, give me the moon, but shortly you will give me a flogging. In words a tiger in fighting a lizard. My house is your own ; but if you ask for food, you are my enemy. The *English* say great cry and little wool, as the man said when he shaved the pig. The *Telegus* say a barking dog never bites ; does gold ever ring like bell metal ?

---

(114) Sin a Sore as Leprosy.
Is. i., 6.
Sin like Leprosy.

1. *Universal*: the poison affects the judgment, will, memory, and conscience, Tit. i., 5.

2. *Painful*: so remorse of conscience.

3. *Loathsome*: limbs rot off, bad matter oozes out, stinks.

4. *Infectious*: even to walls; so evil company, 2 Kings xv., 4.

---

(115) WOMAN'S ORNAMENT THE HIDDEN MAN OF THE HEART.

1 *Pet. vii.*, 3, 4.

The hidden man of the heart here means a meek and quiet spirit called the inner man, in contrast with the outer man, the body or countenance. Paul states though his outer man perish, his inner man is renewed day by day, 2 Cor. iv., 16; the *Telegus* say the tamarind may be dried, but it loses not its acidity. *Vemun* states look closely at musk, its hue indeed is dark, but its fragrance perfumes all things; thus hidden are the virtues of men of weight.

Chanakya says as the sea defends the earth, a wall the roof, a king the nation, so does modesty a woman. As the voice forms the beauty of the cuckow learning of an ugly man, mercy of an asectic; so is conjugal fidelity—the beauty of a woman. The *English* proverbs are:—Beauty is but skin deep; is but dross if honesty be lost; a woman that paints her face puts up a bill to let. Beauty, without virtue, is a scentless rose; it may have fair leaves, but bitter fruit (like the *makhal*); a contentious woman is compared to a continual dropping, Pr. xxvii., 15; she is a moth to consume her husband's estate.

Ornaments in dress are condemned as exciting the passions, Pr. vii., 10, Rev. xvii., 1—4, encouraging pride, hindering alms, 1 Tim. ii., 10, wasting time Eph. v., 16, the prophets wore rough garments, 2 Kings i., 8; Jezebel painted her face. Herod was arrayed gorgeously, and was eaten up of worms, Acts xii., so the rich man before going to hell, Luk. xvi., so Absalom.

(116) Hearers not Doers—a Looking-glass.
Jas. i., 23, 25.

When we behold our natural face in a glass, let us remember that God has given us a mirror, in which we may see the true character of our soul; in order that we may grow in self-knowledge, and may adorn ourselves, not with what ministers to pride and worldly vanity, but with the ornaments of meekness and holiness, which are of great price in God's sight. This mirror is His holy word, which holds up to us the true lineaments and features of the soul, and shows us how greatly it has lost the beauty of the image and likeness of God, and how it is disgraced and deformed by spots and blemishes of sin. The swellings of pride, the lines of envy and care, the shades of sensuality, sloth, and earthliness appear too plainly, when we look into this faithful mirror, which is not like flattering friends who say smooth things to us, and sometimes puff us up with the notion that we are clothed with various Christian graces; but it tells us the very truth concerning our spiritual state; and no veil of false excuses, or artful cloking and colouring of our faults, will disguise from us our true state, if only we never neglect to consult this mirror in sincerity and with earnest prayer.

Vemana says let the sinner listen to holy texts; he will not relinquish his vile nature, though you wash a coal in milk, will the blackness be removed?

Hearers not doers are also compared to those leading captive silly women ever learning never coming to the truth, 2 Tim. iii., 7, or to those hearing a fine song, Ez. xxxiii., 32; children in the rickets have large heads, but weak joints. God's word was designed as milk to enable persons to grow, 1 Pet. ii., 2. A fresh corpse can have the image of an object painted on the eye, but it reaches not to the heart. Some hearers are like a sponge which suck up every thing, but all goes out again; others like a strainer letting go the good and retaining the bad, while some are like a sieve dropping the chaff, and retaining the good grain.

(117) CHRIST THE LAMB OF GOD.
Is. liii., 7.

Christ was like a lamb—(1) *harmless*, John. xxi., 15, surrounded by wolves; Satan a roaring lion, Herod a fox; (2) *meek*, bore the wrongs of spitting on and scourging when led to the slaughter; (3) *contented*, Christ had not where to lay his head; (4) *Used in sacrifice*, Rev. xii., 11, Christ like the scapegoat bore our sins away into the wilderness, so the *Asvamedh*, or horse-sacrifice of the Hindus, was designed to typify that purpose. An hypocritical power is compared to a lamb with two horns, but speaking as a dragon, Rev. xiii., 11. In the millennium the lamb is to dwell with the wolf, Is. xi., 6.

(118) KEEP THE FEET IN GOD'S HOUSE.
Ecc. v., 1.

This text means take heed to your ways. See that ye walk circumspectly. As in walking we take as much care as we can to keep our feet from stumbling; so in going to the house of God, we must take care about the state of our minds. When Moses saw the Angel of the Lord in the burning bush, the voice of God said to him, "Put of thy shoes from off thy feet, for the place whereon thou standest is holy ground;" and when Joshua saw the same Angel, he said, "Loose thy shoe from off thy foot, for the place whereon thou standest is holy." In both these instances it is believed that the Lord Jesus Christ took human form in appearance, before he really took our nature, and died to redeem us, and, by commanding the removal of the shoe from the foot, he showed that nothing which was defiled could acceptably appear in his presence.

Look before you leap. *Chanakya* says, "A prudent man moves with one foot, but does not move the other till he considers where he goes to." The foot of pride is not to come into the Church, Is. xxxvi., 11. The Philistines and Uzziah were punished for touching the ark; a beast that touched Sinai was to be killed Nebuchadnezzar was chastised for using at a feast; the vessels of the temple. Christ flogged those that bought and sold in the temple. The sacrifice of fools is an offering without obedience.

---

(119) THE HOLY SPIRIT'S INFLUENCE LIKE THE WIND.

John iii., 5—8.

We see not the wind itself, but we see what it does whether when the forest is bowed by some mighty tempest in the Bengal Cyclone, or when the corn waves under the gentle breeze, and the flowers of the garden give out their fragrance, as they tremble at its softest touch.

It is thus with God's Holy Spirit. It is mysterious in its coming and in its influence. Unseen itself, it is seen in its effects. The mighty change which the world has undergone, since first the doctrine of the Cross was preached by peasants of Judea, with no human aid to support them, is the work of the unseen but ever-present Spirit, by which the false philosophies and vain superstitions of heathenism have fallen before the truth, as Dagon before the ark, 1 Sam. v., 3.

The wind is—(1) *invisible*, though its effects are seen in cyclones when it travels at 120 miles an hour, so the Spirit's influence in conversion; (2) comes at *God's command*; He holds the winds in His fist, Pr. xxx.,4; (3) *purifies*, drives bad vapours away; so grace does evil passions; (4) *penetrates*, passes through a large city like Calcutta; (5) *various*, the north wind, piercing, the south wind, warming; so the Holy Spirit rebukes some, comforts others, tempests destroy big ships and large trees; (6) sets in *motion*; we cannot sail across the ocean of life without the wind of the Spirit Providence has his way in the sea, and He walks on the wings of the wind, Pr. cix.

---

(120) IDLENESS MAKES THE HOUSE DROP THROUGH.
Ecc. x., 18.

The aut makes hay when the sun shines; has no guide.

The marks of the sluggard are—(1) loves not *difficulties;* will not plough by reason of cold, Pr. xx., 11; (2) loves not *disturbance*, though death's hand-writing may be on the wall; (3) enjoys not the good *in hand;* roasts not what was taken in hunting, Pr. xvii., 16; (4) his way hedged with *thorns*, Pr. xv., 19, such were the ten tribes too lazy to go up to Jerusalem, 1 Kings xii., 28; so with the servant in the parable of the talents; (5) allows *weeds* on his fields, Pr. xxiv., 30; (6) *desires only*, but makes no efforts; so Balaam wished the death of the righteous, but led not the life of the righteous, Num. xxiii., 10; (7) makes no *progress*, turns as a door on the hinges, Pr. xxvi., 14; (8) makes *excuses;* there is a lion in the way, Pr. xxii., 13.

The *Telegus* say the idle man eats like a bullock, and sleeps like a dog; in a neglected house devils take up their abode. The *Bengalis* say the date fell on his moustaches, he was too lazy to put it into his mouth.

---

(121) THE CHRISTIAN CHURCH A GARDEN ENCLOSED.
Cant. iv., 12.

Paradise means a beautiful garden, to which Christ refers, Luk. xxiii., 43; Babylon had hanging gardens on the roofs of the houses.

As the waste wilderness is the emblem of the world, so a choice garden is set forth in Holy Scripture as an image of God's Church. A garden is a place *enclosed* out of the common *waste* ground, and set apart for special culture and fruitfulness. Its site is *chosen* for advantage of soil and shelter ; and for that abundant supply of *water*, which is so needful for the health and produce of its plants. Care is ever taken to screen it from every rude *blast*, to maintain or improve the natural goodness of the ground, and to make the water flow in such channels as may conduct it most easily to the several plots and borders. In that happy garden which God separated from the world around for our first parents, we read of a river that " went out of Eden to water the garden ;" and that " it was parted, and became into four heads." In laying out a garden, it is divided and arranged, just as in that happy place, according to some well-ordered pattern, so as to bespeak an unity of design; and he, who is set " to dress it and to keep it," is ever careful both to remove whatever is common and unsightly, and to fill every nook and angle with the choicest flowers, and the most useful and delicious fruits. The owner of the garden delights to come into it when the tender shoots are first showing themselves above the ground, or when it is in all the pride of summer beauty or autumnal fruitfulness, Rev. i., 13. Its sunny *stillness* and repose invite him to peaceful meditation. Its exact order, its smooth lawns, its many-coloured borders, cool shades, and clear waters are soothing to the eye that is wearied with the glare and confusion of the crowded marts ; while the soft breeze that whispers among the fruits and flowers, is laden with the most grateful fragrance.

It is thus that God has chosen out of the world a Church or " peculiar people," to be his own portion and inheritance. He *fences* and protects it from the enemies that seek its ruin ; he is a wall of fire, and sets in it the choicest plants, to bear those fruits and flowers which are of price in his sight. So Abraham gave the flower of faith, Moses of meekness, Peter of boldness, Paul of zeal, Gal. v., 22. It is the Paradise of his beloved Son, who is the second Adam, and whose care it is to remove from it the *weeds* of sin and selfishness, and to preserve it in that godly order, and that blessed unity, which makes it the image upon earth, not only of the heavenly peace, but even of the Divine Unity itself. His Holy Spirit is the *fountain* in the midst of the garden which nourishes and refreshes the plants; and is also the gentle *breath* which bears the fragrance of its flowers to Him who is pleased to receive graciously what in itself is unworthy of being offered to him. He sets his *servants* to tend and cherish the various plants on which He is pleased to set such store, and to see, when He shall come into his garden, that there be nothing there to offend those eyes which are too pure to behold iniquity. Whatever resembles the fruits of the evil world must be rooted out; whatever is useful and lovely must be planted and fostered.

---

(122) THE CHRISTIAN THIRSTS FOR GOD LIKE A HART.
Ps. xlii., 1.

The hart was lovely, hence Saul was called the roe of Israel, 2 Sam. 19; delighted like the horse in music, gentle, clear-sighted, quick of hearing.

The deer are accustomed to gather themselves at noon to the cool solitude and refreshing brook, and are often seen reclining in groups upon the mossy bank, or quenching their thirst in the shallow stream. Sometimes the hunters scare them from their nook, and chase them over the open brow above the woods under the sultry sun. Panting with the heat and exertion, they make for their favourite haunt and the quiet brook. From some change of purpose, the pursuers discontinued the chase; and the frightened and exhausted creatures are suffered to plunge into the copses, and find their way to the shades for which they longed. How eager must have been their draught, when they reached the brook!—how grateful and refreshing the plunge into the flood, and the rest amidst the moss and fern! Such is the soul in the desert of this world thirsting for the true *amrita,* or waters of life, flowing from God's throne.

(123) THE CHRISTIAN RUNS A RACE.

Heb. xii., 1, 2,—1 *Cor.* ix., 24—27.

It was the practice in ancient Greece to celebrate once every four years with great solemnity, certain games which were chiefly trials of bodily strength or skill in wrestling, leaping, running the quoit; these were attended by a vast assemblage of people of all ranks. The *prize*, that was contended for, was a crown or chaplet of leaves, with which the victor was crowned, while his name was proclaimed by heralds in the presence of the whole assembly; and there were *judges* appointed to decide on the merits of the candidates, and to see that the several contests were conducted according to the laws that were laid down.

The foot-race was one of the principal of these games; and St. Paul has in many places alluded to it in illustration of the Christian life. He means us to understand that a Christian's life should be a continual strife or contest for victory over our manifold, corrupt, and deceitful lusts; and he encourages us to maintain the conflict by the thought that we are contending for a glorious *prize* in the presence of a great crowd of witnesses. The *crown* for which we contend, he reminds us, is not a chaplet of fading leaves, but a crown of righteousness and glory. "Now, they do it to obtain a corruptible crown, but we are incorruptible." The *witnesses* of our manful efforts are the great company of those cited by the Apostle, who have before us gained this mastery over sin, the world, and the devil, and have now by faith and patience attained the promises. We should also always remind ourselves that we contend for the prize of our high calling in the presence of God and of His Holy Angels.

We are to remember, then, that a man, who was about to contend in a foot-race, would first lay aside every weight that might be about his person, and would disencumber himself of every needless garment. Yet Paul ran his race in Rome, when he was a prisoner in chains.

Thus we are to prepare ourselves for our course by laying aside every weight; and this is explained by what is added, "The sin that doth so easily beset us." The prophet Habakkuk says, "Woe to him that increaseth that which is not his! · · · · and to him that loads himself with thick clay!" He who does not take pains to divest himself of covetousness, sensuality, pride, and other too easily besetting sins, is as one who should lade himself with thick clay when about to start upon a race.

We are to remember, too, that when once they have started on their course, the candidates do not suffer themselves to relax in their *efforts* until they have reached the end. They do not linger on the way, nor stop to look back with satisfaction on the progress which they have made; but they think only of what yet remains to be done; and they keep the eye steadily fixed upon the mark or goal. If they find themselves disposed to give way, they remember the prize which is such an object of desire, and press forward with renewed spirit, Rev. ii., 10. It will not do for us to relax our efforts to obtain the mastery over our own lusts and passions. They will gain upon us if we give them the least advantage.

Thus St. Paul says, "Brethren, I count not myself to have apprehended; but this one thing I do; forgetting those things which are behind, and reaching forth unto those things which are before, I press toward the mark for the prize of the high calling of God in Christ Jesus." We must run the race with faith and patience.

In the Christian race all may be winners; there is no jealousy, the strong are to help the weak; there is joy in running, Rev. xxii., 14; the value of the prize is an exceeding weight of glory; the spectators are Angels, Devils, and God; the Judge is impartial and perfect in knowledge.

(124) Sin a Burthen.
Mat. xi., 28—30.

A burthen presses heavily on the chest as the tenderest part, so sin on the heart provided it be not past feeling, Eph. v., 14; Christ pressed by the weight of the world's sins, sweat, blood, Luk. xxii., 44; a burthen impedes action, so does sin, Heb. xii., 1; Christians are to bear one another's burthens, Gal. vi., 6; not so did the priest who passed by on the other side of the way, Luk. x., 31; the Jewish law ordered one to relieve even the ass of an enemy. Sin is to be carried not as a golden chain round the neck, but as an iron chain round the feet. The devil, when he mocked Eve, did not see sin a burthen, neither did the old world when it ridiculed Noah's building the ark.

(125) A Bottle to hold the Tears of the Righteous.
Ps. lvi., 8.

The tears shed over departed friends were by the Romans collected in *urns*, which were placed by the monument or sarcophagus of the deceased, and held sacred. Here David implores God to have his tears in a perpetual memorial.

(126) The Axe laid at the Root of the Tree.
Mat. iii., 10—12.

Time has been figured as a scythe mowing down the grass; here God's vengeance is compared to an axe. The King of Assyria is so called, Is. x., 15.

The Church of God is often likened to a vineyard or garden of fruit trees, from which the owner looks for fruit in due season, and too often finds none. He is unwilling, however, to relinquish his hope of a return for all his labour, and continues year by year to prune with the greatest skill, as well as patience, the plants which so ill-repay his toil.

However high and stately may be the tree, and however green and luxuriant its foliage, the time comes when the owner is tired with waiting for fruit, and trying the effect of only cutting off branches; he determines that he will lay the axe to the root, and remove the tree itself from the ground which might be so much better filled.

We know how fearfully the event, thus figuratively described, was accomplished, when the temple of Jerusalem was burnt, and the city taken by Titus, the Roman General; and how afterwards, when the nation rebelled against their conquerors, Jerusalem was utterly destroyed by Hadrian; and the miserable people who survived were sold in vast numbers as slaves.

What God wants is fruit, not leaves; however rich may be the foliage, in other words, however high the profession, it is utterly worthless in His sight, if there be not the true fruits of repentance towards God and faith towards our Lord Jesus Christ.

(127) THE WICKED ARE CHAFF.
Mat. iii., 12.

Chaff is *light* and easily carried away by the wind; such are sinners, light in their behavior and easily carried away by the wind of temptation or persecution; of *little value*, and therefore given over to the fire, a seer of wheat is worth a maund of chaff; *mixed* with the wheat for a time, it seems like it, but the flail in threshing separates it; so the Judgment Day will divide the sheep from the goats, Mat. xxv.

(128) THE GLUTTON'S GOD HIS BELLY.
Ph. iii., 18.

The Bengalis call a glutton one all belly. The Egyptians, on embalming a body, threw the belly into the river as the cause of all sin. *Vemana* says why suffer anxiety for the belly, as to having a belly the frog that lives in a rock is thy equal. Meat itself is not sinful, but inordinate desire of it, Mat. xv., 11, longing after delicacies, Num, xi., 4, eating at unseasonable times, Ecc. x., 16, 17, eating too much, Luk. xxi., 34, injures the understanding, Pr. xxvii., 7, xxiii., 21. Solomon says put a knife to thy throat if thou be given to appetite; Isaac's appetite was a snare to him, Gen. xxv., 28, xxvii., 4, so Esau's, Gen. xxv., 30, not so Daniel's, Dan. i., 8—16.

---

(129) BEGINNING OF STRIFE THE LETTING OUT WATER.

Pro. xvii., 14.

It was but a narrow channel which was cut in the dam, to let out the waters from the reservoir, yet how wide a breach have they already made!

Chanakya says to pay off debts, quench a fire, and remove disease is good, for should they increase, they will not be stopped. The *Bengalis* say going in a needle, coming out a ploughshare; one drop of filth from a cow will spoil a vessel of milk. The *Italian* proverb is, if thou suffer a calf to be put on you, they will soon put on the cow. The *Spaniards* say give me to sit down, I shall soon make a place to lie down. Daniel would not take even the king's meat, Dan. i., 8—16; Job made a covenant not to look on a maid, Job xxxi., 1; well, if David had done so in Bathseba's case. Sin is first like the spider's web, but soon becomes like a cart rope.

---

(130) BAD COMPANY THE UNFRUITFUL WORKS

OF DARKNESS.

Eph. v., 11.

The *Shanti Shatak* says, Oh! ye mind like fish swim not in the waters of woman's beauty, for women are like nets. The *Telegus* say unless you had touched garlick, your fingers would not have smelt; among a hundred crows what could one cuckow do; what does a weaver want with a young monkey; bad company is friendship with a snake fencing with a sword. *Vemana* compares entertaining a bad man in your house to a fly entering the stomach; will it not torment you; how should the Saint mingle with men!—when a drop of water is converted into a pearl, will it again unite with its former wave?

Bad company is called the unfruitful works of darkness; they turn God's grace into lasciviousness, Jud. 4, like the soldiers who said, Hail! king yet spat in Christ's face. Fellowship with the wicked is necessary in business, 1 Cor. v., 10, Mat. xxiii., 12; the tares and the wheat are together in the Church; Christ went, however, as a physician, not as an associate; such were Joseph in Egypt, Nehemiah in Persia, Lot in Sodom, Daniel in Babylon.

The *Raghuvansa* states a good woman, beset by evil women, is like the chaste mimosa surrounded by poisonous herbs. The *Bengalis* say he who goes to Ceylon becomes a demon.

(131) THE WICKED ARE CLOUDS WITHOUT WATER.
Jude. 12, 13.

Clouds without water may be of some use in giving shade, but they do not fertilise the land, which full clouds, called the bottles of Heaven, Job. xxxviii., 37, do; they are empty, and easily carried away, as is seen in famines in India arising from droughts; they darken Heaven, hence the day of the Lord is called clouds and darkness, when storms and lightning arise; the clouds are God's chariot, and he holds the winds in his fist. Christ is the bow in this cloud, as he was the pillar of cloud in the wilderness, the guide of his people.

(132) THE RIGHTEOUS SHALL SHINE AS THE STARS.
Dan. xii., 3.

The bodies of the righteous after the resurrection will be bright and dazzling like Christ's body on the mount of transfiguration, Mat. xvii., 1; Paul, on his way to Damascus, saw a light brighter than the sun, the effulgence of which blinded him for three days, Acts xi. The righteous will be like the stars in—(1) being a great *ornament* to the Heavens; (2) they *differ* in brightness, 1 Cor. xv., 40; (3) guide mariners on the ocean and at night, so believers will on the dark ocean of life; (4) though *distant*, they exercise an influence, but many do not, as there are stars so far from this world that their light has not reached the earth from the time of Adam's creation, though travelling like the sun's light at the rate of 12,000,000 miles in a minute; many of them are bigger than the earth, though they seem so small, and are so remote that a cannon ball would take 700,000 years to reach the nearest of them; (5) their *number* is immense; the redeemed in Heaven are a great multitude which no man can number.

(133) ANGELS ENCAMP ROUND CHRISTIANS.
Psalms xxxiv., 7.

Angels are called a host, Gen. xxxii., 1; are commanded by Christ, the Captain of Salvation; they protect the saints; they slumber not like chowkeedars, hence called holy watches, Dan. iv., 13; the figure of Cherubim, an order of Angels, had four faces—that of a *man* representing their majesty, prudence, and beauty; that of a *lion* their strength and courage; that of an *ox* their patience and diligence; and that of an *eagle* their quick vision and continued vigor.

The great Mogul at Agra used to have an encampment several miles in circumference, accommodating many thousand soldiers; it was soon broken up, and removed to another place. The Angels' encampment has many millions of troops in number, Dan. vii., 5—14. Christ on the Cross said, he could call to his aid twelve legions of Angels, or 80,000. Those angels are encamped and are powerful; they broke the iron gates, Acts, xii., 10; caused earthquakes, Mat. xxviii., 2; destroyed 185,000 Assyrians in one night; killed all the first-born of Egypt in one night; they are orderly; there are reckoned seven orders—thrones, dominions, principalities, powers, Cherubim, Seraphim, and Archangel.

(134) OUR DAYS ON EARTH A SHADOW.
Job viii., 9.

The Bengalis speak of a service fleeting as the palm-tree's shade or the cloud's shadow. There is no hand to catch time. The *Sanskrit* says, time is stronger than all things else. Gotthold compares time to an image in the water easily broken, yet the shadow gives shelter for a time, as Jonah found at Nineveh under the gourd, iv., 6. Life like a shadow has little substance, is fleeting; it is compared in Job viii. 11 to a rush springing up in the mud, and drying up before the influence of the sun.

(135) THE BOOK OF LIFE.
Rev. xx., 12.

We often read in Scripture of God's books. Frequent mention is made of "The Book of Life." This may be an allusion to the register book, or books in which the names of all the tribes and families of Israel were entered from generation to generation, so that their claims to property and to the privileges of their fathers could not be disputed. It may also refer to a custom in the courts of princes, of keeping a list of persons in their service, of the officers in their armies, and even of the names of their soldiers. When it is said that any one is "blotted out of the book of life," this signifies erased from the list of God's friends and servants, like as those guilty of treachery, are struck off the roll or list of officers belonging to a prince. When therefore God speaks of any being blotted out from the book of life, it means the same as not being written there. There are also books of *judgment*, which are said to be opened, and the dead judged out of them according to their works, Rev. xx., 12. This may allude to a custom of the Persians, to write down every day what had happened, the services done for the king, and the rewards given to those who had performed them, as we see in the history of Ahasuerus and Mordecai, recorded in the book of Esther.

This book of life is the *oldest* book, Rev. xiii., 8; it is written in Heaven, Heb. xii., 23; time destroys not its writing as it does that on tombs or pillars. The life, it writes of, is spiritual life which differs from natural life in—(1) the *Holy Spirit*, being the parent, 1 Cor. xv., 45, has hidden manna to eat, John vi., 55; (2) *eternal* natural life is common to devils, worms, trees, flies; man dies as the beast, but lives for ever in his soul. Life preserves from corruption, so does spiritual.

(136) The Christian a Spiritual Merchant.
Proverbs iii., 13, 14.

Some supposed in Paul's time that gain was godliness; this is not true, yet godliness with contentment is great gain, 1 Tim. iv., 8. Christ calls the Christian a *merchant*, Mat. xiii., 45, inasmuch as he must be diligent, Heb. vi., 11, punctual, Ecc. xi., 6, regular in correspondence like the importunate widow, Luk. xviii., 1; useful Christians are the salt of the earth, but losses at times occur from storms, robbers. His *articles of trade* are the gold of God's love, Rev. iii., 18; the pearls of Christ's blessings, Mat. xiii., 45; the oil and wine of God's Spirit, Ps. xxiii., 5; arms of defence, Eph. vi., 11; the spices of graces, Cant. iii., 6. His *capital* is Christ's offices, as prophet, priest, and king; the *port he trades* to is a distant one, Is. xxxiii., 17; a rich one, Ph. iv., 19; a royal one all made kings and priests there; a heavenly, Ph. iii., 20; his *profits* are satisfying, Jer. xxxi., 14; enduring, Jas. iv., 13. The Christian deals not in adulterated articles; is sure of his profit.

(137) Believers Sealed by God's Spirit.
2 *Tim.* ii., 19.

The ancient Hebrews wore seals in rings on their fingers, and in bracelets on their arms. The wicked queen Jezebel wrote the condemnation of Naboth, whose death she plotted to get his vineyard for her husband Ahab, and sent it to the elders of Israel, signed with his seal. So the ambitious Haman sealed the decree of king Ahasuerus against the Jews with the king's seal; it is afterwards stated that the king took off his ring, which he had taken from Haman, and gave it to Mordecai. The seal was a mark to prove that things were genuine, as in the above cases it showed that the royal authority was granted for the purposes named within; at other times, it was a pledge for fulfilling terms agreed on between two parties, and also to secure anything by closing it up. So God, when he seals us by his Holy Spirit, marks his image upon us. God is holy; and we cannot be marked with his seal unless we are made holy too. When the Holy Spirit so seals us, he also secures us to the day of redemption, as a thing is shut up from harm by being sealed up; in this way men seal up their writings and treasures, marking them with their own seal, that none may break in, and steal them.

The Jews used to write on the head of a corpse with ink, "May he be in the bundle of life, Jehovah the Lord;" this was called sealing the dead. The *seal* makes impressions like itself, so the believer is changed into the same image, 2 Cor. iii., 18; the *wax* must be soft to receive the impression, Heb. x., 16; so the heart; the wicked have stony hearts; the things are secured, so believers sealed on their forehead, Rev. vii., 3; they are a fountain sealed, *i.e.*, secured against weather, sand, beasts, Cant. iv., 12; the sins of the wicked are sealed up in a bag, *i.e.*, not forgotten, but the seal of the Holy Spirit on the believer is God's image.

---

(138) CHRIST'S BRETHREN THOSE WHO OBEY.
Mat. xii., 50.

Christ declared to those who asked who his mother and brethren were, it was those who did the will of His

Father. The term relations is applied metaphorically; thus Job in his affliction called corruption his father, the worm his mother and sister, dragons his brothers, and owl his companions, Job xxx., 29.

Vemana says, in reference to action it is easy to lay hold on the sword, but hard to become valiant; the *Telegus*—will empty words fill bellies?

---

(139) OLD AGE.
Ecc. xii., 1—7.

In the 12th chapter of *Ecclesiastes*, the Preacher Solomon admonishes us to dedicate our youthful days to the service of our *Creator*, considering the *evil days* of the winter of life which are coming upon us, when the faculties of our minds and bodies often fail us under the infirmities of age. For then, as the preacher beautifully represents it, as in a glass, or mirror, *the sun and the moon and the stars are darkened, i.e.,* the superior powers, which rule in the body of man, as the heavenly luminaries do in the world the understanding and reason, the imagination and the memory, are obscured as when the clouds interpose between us and the lights of the firmament. In the earlier season of life, the clouds of affliction having poured down their *rain,* they pass away, and sunshine succeeds; but now the *clouds return after the rain, i.e.,* old age itself is with the wicked a continual sorrow, and there is no longer any hope of fair weather. *The keepers of the house,* the arms and hands, which are made to guard and defend the body, begin to shake and *tremble;* and the *strong men,* the shoulders, where the strength of the body is placed, and which were once able to bear every weight, begin to stoop and *bow themselves;* the *grinders,* the teeth, begin to fall away, and *cease* to do their work, *because they are few. Also those that look out of the windows are darkened, i.e.,* the eyes, those windows of the soul, through which we look at all things abroad, as we look out from the windows of a house, become dim; and he that uses them is as one who looks out of a window in the night. *The doors are shut in the streets, i.e.,* difficulties and obstructions attend all the passages of the body, and digestion becomes weak when the *grinding is low.* The youthful and healthy sleep soundly, and are apt to transgress by taking too much rest; but the aged sleep with difficulty, and *rise up at the voice of the bird;* they are ready to leave their disturbed rest at the crowing of the cock. *The daughters of music are brought low;* the voice falls, and becomes hoarse; the hearing is dull; and the spirits, now less active than they used to be, are less affected by the powers of harmony; and so the old sit in heaviness, hanging down their heads, as virgins drooping under the sorrow of captivity. Old age, being inactive and helpless, becomes *afraid of that which is high;* it is fearful of climbing, because it is in danger of falling; and, being unfit to endure the hardships of fatigue, and the shocks of a rough journey, the *fears* which are *in the way* discourage the old from setting out. Then the *almond tree flourishes, i.e.,* the hair of the head becomes white as the early almond blossoms in the hard weather of the winter before the snows have left; and even *the grasshopper becomes a burthen, i.e.,* the legs, once light and nimble to leap, as the legs of that insect, and which used with ease to bear the weight of the whole body, are now become a burthen, and can scarcely carry themselves; and, when the faculties thus fail, the *desire fails* along with them, for nothing is desirable when nothing can be enjoyed.

Such are the *evil days* which come upon many when their youth is past in sin, and prepare the way for that last and greatest evil of death, when *man goeth to his long home,* and the *mourners go about the streets,* lamenting his departure. Then the *silver cord,* the nerves, whose coat is white and shining as a cord of silver is loosed, and no longer does its office. The circulation of the blood stops at the heart, the fountain of life, as when a *pitcher,* which draws water, *is broken at the well,* or the watering *wheel,* circulating with its buckets, which it both fills and empties at the same time, *is broken at the cistern.* Thus do the vital motions all cease in death ; and the *dust returns to the earth,* to become such *as it was* before man was made out of it ; and his immortal *spirit returns unto God,* the fountain of immortality from whom it proceeded.

(140) AS BUTTER FROM MILK SO STRIFE FROM WRATH.
Proverbs xxx., 33.

The *Shanti Shatak* compares the soul excited by anger to furious elephants, breaking the cords with which they are bound.

In Arabia and Palestine butter is made from milk, put into a goat's skin, turned inside out-pressed to and fro in one uniform direction, till the unctuous parts are separated, Job xxix., 6. An angry man is compared to a city whose walls are broken down, such were Sampson, Jud. xvi., Saul, 1 Sam. xx., 30—33, the mob at Ephesus, Acts xvi., 28—34; Christ was different, Mat. xxvii., 14, John xx., 11 ; the fool's wrath is heavier than a stone, Pr. xxvii., 3.

(141) GOD A JUDGE.
Rev. xx., 12.

The *Bengalis* say sand sharpens a knife, a stone the axes, good words a good man, a thrashing a rogue.

From God's judgment seat there is no escape by bribery, as the *Bengalis* say before a turning lathe, a thing cannot remain crooked. God spared not the devils, neither Nebuchadnezzar nor Pharaoh. He is the Father of Lights, and knows the law he himself made; He is patient; he spared the world in Noah's time 120 years ; and the world has been spared now 6,000 years.

The eyes of the Lord are in every place, beholding the evil and the good. There is no secret place in which the sinner can hide himself; for God, who is present everywhere, sees in the dark as well as in the light. He hears us when we do not speak, because he hears our thoughts. As the light of the sun reaches to the ends of the world, and to the bottom of the sea, so does the presence of God reach to all places and all times, though we see him not. If his power were not constantly upon us, we should be nothing, for *in him we live and move, and have our being.*

The judge, who punishes sins in a court of justice, receives his information from *others*, and can know only that which the witnesses tell him. But God is both judge and witness, and knows all things. When the judge has condemned a man and he is put to death, he has no more that he can do ; but the power of God reaches *beyond the grave*, for he can destroy both the soul and body in hell. His hand shall find out those whom the grave has hidden from our sight, and they shall be brought forth, and placed before his judgment seat to be judged for their past lives. Thefts, murders, and other sins, which were committed in the *dark*, and were hidden from men so long as the offenders lived, shall then all be discovered, and made known. With the fear of this, the guilty shall tremble when they rise from their graves ; then shall they call upon the mountains to fall upon them, and hide them from the face of their judge ?

That I may not be afraid to meet my God in that great day, let me now set him before me in all my thoughts, words, and actions. Let me live every day as in his sight ; then will he be my friend to save me, and my Father to reward me, not my judge to condemn and punish me ? It is his will that all should repent, and be saved. The fire of hell was not made for men ; it was made for the devil and his Angels. If I come there at last, it will be my own fault, for God has sent his son to seek me, and deliver me from the wrath to come.

---

(142) THE GRAVE A REST TO THE CHRISTIAN.
Job vii., 3, iii., 17—19.

The saints are weary of battling with their three great enemies—the world, the flesh, and the devil like Job, 2

Pet. ii., 8. Paul wished to depart, and be with Christ. On Jewish monuments is this, *ie..*, inscription rest in peace in Eden This rest is not the rest of a stone, but is a change to a better state. How strong was Job's wish for rest when he had to clean his burning boils with a potsherd, ii., 8 ; his flesh was clad with worms, vii., 4, 5 ; his breath was corrupt ; his bones cleaved to his skin ; his friends knew him not, xix., 14.

A Christian ought not to be in death like a child compelled by the rod to give up play; but like one who, tired of play, wishes to go to bed, or like a seaman who only waits for a favorable wind to raise his anchor.

How faithfully does the labourer exert his strength, that he may honestly earn the hire for which he has undertaken to bear the burden and heat of the day ! Now and then he looks wistfully at the lengthening shadows, and notices how far the sun has gone down in the heavens, Job vii., 2. Most welcome to him will be the hour of rest and payment; but he does not suffer himself to suspend his work, until the time agreed upon is come. The time for rest will come, when the time for work is over. Thus is man set upon the earth to work the work of God for an appointed season ; and thus faithfully should he spend himself, and be spent in the service of his gracious Maker. He owes to his Maker every faculty of soul and body ; and that gracious Being has promised to all who serve Him truly a rich reward when the day of life is over. The reward, indeed, will be of grace and not of debt, for at best we are unprofitable servants, who have done only what it was their duty to do. And who of us has done even so much ?

On the other hand, the grave to the *wicked* is a slaughter-house, death like a *rakhas* feeds on them; like sheep they are laid in the grave where their beauty consumes, while the upright shall have dominion over them in the morning of the resurrection, Ps. xlix., 14., Pr. vii., 22.

(143) Believers walk in white Raiment with Christ.

Rev. iii., 4.

White raiment signifies Christ's justifying righteousness, Rev. xix., 8 ; typified by the skins of the sacrifice in which God clad Adam and Eve, as our own righteousness is but filthy rags, Is. lxiv., 6.

Walking refers to religious conduct, thus Enoch walked with God, and he was not, Gen. v., 9 ; Abraham walked before God ; Isaiah after the Lord, 2 Kings xxiii., 3 ; believers walk in the spirit, Gal. v., 25 ; the Churches after Paul's conversion walked in the comforts of the Holy Ghost, Acts ix., 31 ; Nebuchadnezzar condemned those that walked in pride, Dan. iv., 37.

Walking implies—(1) *Life*, the believer has a resurrection from the death of sin, Gal. v., 24 ; (2) *Light*, to see the road, Mat. xxii., 24 ; (3) *Motion*, not mere knowing, but doing, 1 Kings xi., 38 ; (4) *Progress*, steady like an elephant, not by jerks as a goat goes. Paul forgot the things behind in pressing on, Ph. iii., 13 ; (5) *Perseverance*, so Hezekiah on his death bed, 2 Kings xx., 3 ; (6) A *road*, the old path trodden by Abel, and marked out by sacrifices ; (7) An *object*, through the wilderness to the heavenly Canaan.

Walking in noble company is a great privilege for an inferior ; Christians were slaves to Satan ; they now walk with God as their father.

---

(144) Little Sins like Dead Flies in Ointment.

Ecc. x., 1.

The *Telegus* say the remains of a debt, a sore, or a fire should not be left, as they may increase. *Vemana* says a stone in the shoe, a gadfly in the ear, a mote in the eye, a thorn in the foot, and a quarrel in a family, however small in themselves, are unspeakably tormenting. The text refers to the acid salts in insects which dispose syrups to fermentation, and then to putrescence, causing a bad smell and sour taste, and so the whole ointment is spoiled, as a little leaven leavens the whole lump, 1 Cor. v., 6; the tongue is a little fire, and kindles great things, as the little helm of a ship turns a big vessel, Jas. v., 4.

---

(145) THE CHRISTIAN LIKE A DOVE.

David, suffering from the wicked, wished to have the wings of a dove which flies very rapidly, and loves freedom like the dove imprisoned in the ark. The Christian resembles a dove in being—(1) *Harmless*, in the midst of a crooked generation, Ph. ii., 15, yet he is to be wise as a serpent, Mat. x., 16; (2) Hates *impure* things, not like the crow or jackal, the Holy Spirit in the form of a dove descended as John at his baptism, Mat. iii., 16; (3) Shuns birds of prey; its mild eye very different from the hawks; it is mild, but sharp, enabling it to flee from danger; (4) Loves its *home*, if taken hundreds of miles away, it will find its way back, hence it is used to carry letters tied to its legs; the Christian's home is with dove like men in the clefts of the rock of ages, *i.e.*, Christ.

---

(146) FAITH IN GOD—THE STRONGHOLD OF HIS PEOPLE.
Zach. ix., 12.

In times of plunder and war in India property and people were insecure, hence they were taken to strongholds for protection. Oude, in the days of the king, had many of these. Faith is like a stronghold—(1) Built on a *rock* to prevent its being undermined; such were the fortresses of Gwalior, Chunar, Dowlatabad; the Christians dwelling in the munition of rocks, Is. xxxiii., 16; Christ is the rock of ages; (2) Strongly *defended*; yet Babylon, with its walls 300 feet high and gates of brass, was taken. Tyre like Calcutta, a great trading place, is now only a rock for fishermen to dry their nets, though it was once a stronghold. Jerusalem had three walls round it, yet it was ploughed up; not so the heavenly Jerusalem, God is to it a wall of fire; (3) Fully *supplied* with provisions and arms, not like Jerusalem where the women eat their own children, or Carthage where the women cut off their hair to make strings for the bows, by the Christian weakness is God's strength made perfect. Elijah was surrounded by a strong army, but he saw the mountain full of Angels under the form of horses and chariots of fire, 2 Kings vi., 17.

---

(147) THE FURNACE OF AFFLICTION.
Is. xlviii., 10.

There are two furnaces, one of affliction, as Egypt was to the Jews, Dt. iv., 20, 1 Pet. i., 6, 7, the other of hell like Nebuchadnezzar's fiery furnace; the former is like a pruning knife which improves the plant, the latter like a chopper that cuts it off, Mat. xiii., 42—50; the fire of hell is never extinguished, and never consumes the body, but the fiery furnace injured not the three Hebrew children, Dan. iii., 25.

God's afflicted people are compared to silver. The precious metals are first taken out of the earth. They are then impure—mixed with other substances, and in this state they are called ores. In order to refine them, they are put into a furnace, and exposed to great heat. But this does not injure them; it only takes from them what is impure, and leaves the gold, or the silver, bright, beautiful, and clear. The refiner watches the metals all the time they are in the fire; and when he finds that they are so clear and pure that he can see his own face reflected in them, he takes them out of the furnace, and uses them, or the purposes he intended. In Malachi iii. 3, God compares the afflictions with which He tries His people, to the furnace into which the gold and silver are cast to be refined and purified. God loves and values His people. He calls them His "treasure," His "jewels." But, like the gold and silver, they have that in them which is impure—sin. And this sin must be taken away. God's people must be made pure and holy before He can have pleasure in them, and use them for His service, or take them to adorn His glorious home in Heaven. And how does God purify them? Sin must be taken away by Christ, and the heart must be made clean by the Holy Spirit. God has many ways of working all this in His people, and one way is by affliction. Like the refiner, He puts His precious gold and silver into the furnace—the furnace of affliction. He sends sorrow and pain, and sickness upon them. And why? Not to hurt them: no; but just for the same reason that the refiner puts his metals into the fire, to melt, to soften, to purify them. And then, like the refiner, God watches over them. He does not let them suffer more or longer than is right; and when He has made them what He intended by putting them into the furnace, He takes them from it. What God desires is to see His own image, His own likeness, reflected in His people. A silver coin or medal is generally stamped with the image of the sovereign; this can be done only when the metal is soft, and it is made soft by the heat of the fire. So, God's people should bear the likeness of Christ, their King, stamped upon them in their conduct; and God sends affliction to soften their hearts, that they may more easily receive that holy impression, and so become more and more like Jesus.

A *Sanskrit* proverb says a bad man, gold, a drum, a woman, a bad horse, stalks of sugar-cane, sesamum seed, and Sudras should be beaten to improve their qualities. The *Atmabodh* states after mortifying the body, the pure spirit is discerned by reason, as rice is separated from the husk by beating it.

(148) REMEMBRANCE OF FORMER MISERY AS WATERS PASSED AWAY.
Job xi., 16.

In Arabia which was Job's abode as in India, rivers, that are 60 feet deep in the rains, are only a bed of sand in the dry weather. The rough, swollen stream foams and dashes along, threatening to sweep everything away; but it goes swiftly to the sea, and will never come back. So with afflictions the most intense *pain* like that of Job's leprosy quickly subsides; the *man* whose life is a burden will soon die. On the cheeks of the *prisoner* in a dungeon, a mortal paleness will soon settle down. The *rack* of torture checks itself, as the excess of grief makes it soon mortal. The flood of past sorrow comes back no more.

(149) The Wicked are Captives.
2 Tim. ii., 26.

The *Bengalis* compare one at the will of another to an ox with his nose pierced. Christ, in his first sermon which he preached at Nazareth, stated he came as a Redeemer to purchase the captives. Men are captives to—(1) *sin*, Rom. vii., 14—26, ancient tyrants fastened captives to a dead body face to face until they were suffocated by the stench ; (2) *Satan*, 2 Tim. ii., 26 ; (3) the *Law*, Gal. iv., 25 ; (4) *Death*, Heb. ii., 15, is called the king of terrors. The Christian's body may be captive, but his mind is free as in Paul's case.

Captives in war are often stripped naked, and thrown into a dungeon ; their eyes were put out, as Hezekiah's, 2 Kings xxv., 7, or as the Mahrattas gouged out the eyes of the Great Mogul in Delhi ; they were often loaded with chains, fed on bread and water, living among rats

(150) Christ drank the Bitter Cup.
Mat. xxvi., 39.

This cup denoted Christ's intense sufferings, Mat. xx., 22 ; wine mixed with bitter ingredients was given to malefactors before being put to death to render them insensible to the acute pain of hanging on a Cross. Christ refused to drink the cup. Babylon is represented as a golden cup in the hands of Jehovah, *i.e.*, to give pain ; the cup of salvation, Ps. xvi., 13, denoted the joy from the river of God's pleasure, Ps. xxxvi., 8; the cup of the wine of God's wrath, Rev. xiv., 10, was the vengeance of God apportioned to each, as the master of a feast appointed to each of his guests his particular cup, Jer. xxv., 15.

(151) HE SPARING THE ROD HATES HIS SON.
Pr. xiii., 24.

The bee sucks sweet honey out of the bitterest herb! So God will by afflictions teach his children to suck sweet knowledge, sweet obedience, out of all the bitter afflictions and trials he exercises them with; that scouring and rubbing which frets others, shall make them shine the brighter; that weight which crushes and keeps others under, shall but make them, like the palm-tree, grow better and higher. Stars shine brightest in the darkest night; torches give the best light when beaten; grapes yield most wine when most pressed; spices smell sweetest when pounded; vines are the better for bleeding; gold looks the brighter for scouring; and juniper smells sweetest in the fire.

Joseph's advancement might have been fatal to him, had he not been previously prepared for it by a long course of suffering. We should have looked upon him with concern, had we seen him in bonds and known his innocence. But God, who had a far more indulgent and tender compassion for him, left him in a condition from which we would have delivered him, Gen. xxxvii. 23—36, xxxix., 20, xxi., 23. So with the Israelites in the wilderness, and God's love in subjecting them to such trials in it, Dt. viii., 3—6, 15, 19.

So with Jehoshaphat.—God destroyed his fleet to disengage him from his connexion with wicked Ahaziah, 2 Chron. xx., 35—37, and it seems to have had this effect, 1 Kings, xxii., 49. It is a mercy to have that taken from us that takes us from God. The people of Judah were sent into captivity to Babylon for their good, Jer. xxiv., 5—7; and in this, as appears from Ezra, Ezra ix., 10, and from Nehemiah,

Neh. ix., the effect was good. Paul's thorn in the flesh was sent to preserve him from pride, 2 Cor. xii., 7; these examples show that the gem cannot be polished without friction, nor man perfected without adversity. That affliction is an angel of mercy sent to lead us out of Sodom; that the way of the Cross is the royal way to the Crown; and that the waters, which drowned the world, only lifted up the ark.

(152) CHRIST THE ROSE OF SHARON.
Cant. ii., 1.

What the *lotus* is in India, the rose is in Judea, like the lily of the valley, the *queen* of flowers, the only flower that bloomed without a thorn, a worm or canker in it; such was the youth of Christ; it bloomed in the barren desert of Judea as amid the filth of Jerusalem; like the rays of the sun, it could enter dirt without being defiled; the rose is noted for its fragrance, and the name of Christ is like ointment poured forth; like the roses of Ghazipore which, when distilled and pressed, yield the fragrant rose-water used at feasts.

(153) THE DEATH OF THE RIGHTEOUS A SLEEP.
John xi., 11.

Sleep in death is applied in Scripture only to the righteous, as to Lazarus, Solomon, Hezekiah, Jehoshaphat, Stephen. It is like natural sleep—(1) *Calm* in its *commencement;* people know not when they are dropping off to sleep. We gradually become insensible to outward things; such was Moses' death; (2) *Rest* from labor; life is warfare; death is peace; the slave hears not the voice of the oppressor, Job iii., 18; (3) *Awakening* to vigor after sleep, Is. xxvi., 19; Isaiah calls the grave a bed; (4) *Mind active* even in dreams.

(154) CHRIST'S LEGACY TO HIS PEOPLE.
Luk. xxii., 29.

These words were spoken by Christ previous to his Crucifixion, giving to his disciples high honor in the next world: his legacy. A legacy is a proof of friendship, a sign that death does not dissolve it, so Christ 1,840 years ago in an upper-room, eating His last Supper gave this proof; the next day He was to hang on a Cross; He sealed this legacy by breaking bread, and drinking wine.

This Legacy is—(1) in the *Bible;* we are to search the Scriptures as the miner searches for gold, or as people examine a will immediately after the death of the testator; (2) *Eternal;* some are left things acquired by fraud or force, and therefore disputed; this property does not corrupt the possessor, 1 Pet. i., 4; (3) The legatees are *ruined* sinners; blessed are the poor in spirit, Mat. v.; (4) *Ratified* by a seal; baptism and the Lord's Supper; the Sunday is the memorial of it; (5) *Unconditional;* no debt or mortgages entailed; Boaz kinsman wished Naomi's property, but not without the condition of marrying Ruth; so Moses rejected the treasures of Egypt, when the condition implied forfeiting the reproach of Christ; (6) *Enough for all;* when the division is small quarrels are apt to arise, as in Abraham's, Isaac's, and David's families, but this kingdom is boundless; many mansions in the Father's House.

---

(155) THE EARTH WAXES OLD AS A GARMENT.
Psalms cii., 26.

The earth itself is millions of years old, and has changed its garment, *i.e.*, the surface many times. The Himalayas were once islands in an ocean which covered all India, and the Bay of Bengal washed the foot of the Himalayas. England itself was then in a tropical climate; sharks, alligators, and elephants lived there, though it is now too cold for them. India was once not a Continent, but an archipelago; its present mountains were then islands, while the valley of the Ganges was formed from the earth brought down from the mountains.

The heavens will be folded up as a scroll Is. xxxiv. 4, Rev. vi., 14.

(156) Christ the Way to Heaven.
John xiv., 6.

The Hindus call *panth* or way the line of doctrine of any sect followed, in order to attain to *mukti* or deliverance from sin. Way signifies the chief means to an end, and is applied to the Bible, Ps. cxix., 1, to God's counsels, Rev. xi., 33, to God's works, Job. xli., 19. This spiritual way is—(1) *easy* to find, Is., 35 ; (2) *clean*, no mud of sin ; (3) never out of *repair*. Christ the same now as 6,000 years ago ; (4) no *lion* or wild beasts on ; (5) *costly*, the blood of Christ made it ; (6) not *lonely*, many believers on it, Heb. xii., 1 ; (7) no *toll*, all may come ; (8) *wide*, Christ sends out to the highways and hedges, Mat. xxii., 9. The way to the cities of refuge was 48 feet wide. The map of the Bible shows this path ; (9) the *end* pleasant—Heaven.

The veil that was hung before the Holy of Holies, and which none might pass through, but the high Priest once a year, signified to us that there was no direct way to Heaven under the law. "By the law is the knowledge of sin," not the means of deliverance from the power or punishment of sin. And by the rending of the veil at the time of our Saviour's death, was signified that a way was henceforth opened to the penitent unto life eternal, even by the blood of Jesus Christ. In the passage—" I am the way, the truth, and the life," our Lord meant, " I am the way to Heaven." He had just before told his disciples that he was soon going to leave them, and to prepare a place for them, meaning that he was going to Heaven, and there they should follow, and be happy with him for ever. But his disciples did not quite understand him, and when he said, " Whither I go ye know, and the way ye know." Thomas replied, " Lord, we know not whither thou goest ; and how can we know the way ?" Christ meant, that he was going to Heaven, and that there was no getting there but through him, just as a way leads to a place, or, in other words, we must follow him, and he will show us the way ; for like him we must have holy lives, like him we must pass through the grave, like him our bodies must rise again.

---

(157) ANGER RESTS IN THE BOSOM OF FOOLS.

Ecc. vii., 9.

The Bengalis say should the angry man retire even to a forest, there is no peace for him.

The bosom is the seat of love, so Christ carries the lambs of the Church in his bosom, Is. xl., 11. The beggar rested in Abraham's bosom, Luk. xvi., 22.

Christ took on him our natural infirmities; he wept, and was angry, which shews there might be gall in a dove, passion without sin, fire without smoke, and motion without disturbance, for it is not bare agitation, but the sediment at the bottom which troubles and defiles the water, and when we see it windy and dusty, the wind does not make, but only raises a dust; true anger, like the sword of justice, is keen but innocent; it sparkles like the coal on the altar with the fervor of pity. Anger passes through a wise man's heart, but does not rest in it, as it did with Cain, Gen. iv., 5—8, with Jacob's sons, Gen. xxxiv., 7; with Absalom, 2 Sam. xiii., 22, and with Herod. A gust of anger puts holy feelings to flight as with David, 1 Sam. xxv., 21, Elijah, 1 Kings xix., 4, Job. iii., 1, Jonah iv., 19, Paul xxvi., 3.

Abraham, though the elder, waived his right of choice for the sake of peace, and promptly removed all occasion of strife, Gen. xiii., 7—9; God put honour upon him after his disinterestedness, Gen. xiii. 14—17. David took Abigail's advice, 1 Sam. xxx., 32—34, and did not imagine that, because he had entered into contention, a regard to his honour required him to continue it. Let it pass for a kind of sheepishness to be meek. It is a likeness to Him that was as a sheep before the shearers, not opening his mouth, Is. liii., 7; it is a portion of His spirit.

(158) The Husband the Head of the Wife.
Eph. v., 25.

Bartrihari writes this is the fruit of love among married people, one mind among two persons, where there is discord, it is the marriage of two corpses.

The woman is the weaker vessel, 1 Pet. iii., 7. She is to learn at home, 1 Cor. xiv., 25. She is to reverence her husband as Sarah, 1 Pet. iii., 6, Gen. xviii., 6. The man as head implies eminency; woman was created last, and there is an union not as in Nebuchadnezzars' image, Dan., ii., 33. Hence no bitterness is to be shown, Col. iii., 19. The Egyptians represented a man without a woman by a single millstone which alone cannot grind.

The *Mrichhakati* states—

> Look round the garden, mark these stately trees,
> Which duly by the Kings command attended;
> Put forth abundantly their fruits and flowers,
> And clasped by twining creepers; they resemble
> The manly husband, and the tender wife.

---

(159) God the Fountain of Living Waters.
Jer. ii., 13.

As water is one of the most essential requisites for life as well as for health, it is continually applied in Holy Scripture to represent to us the necessity of divine grace; and thus a *well* or *spring* of water becomes an emblem of the eternal source of all spiritual blessings and of salvation itself. The blood of our blessed Saviour, by which his people are washed from the defilements of sin, is called a fountain opened to the house of David and to all the inhabitants of Jerusalem for sin and for uncleanness, Zech. xii., 1. The quickening and refreshening influences of the Holy Spirit are in like manner compared by our Lord Himself to rivers of living water, John vii., 38; and when God by the prophet Jeremiah declares Himself "a fountain of living waters," we may understand that it is God the Father, who thus sets Himself forth to us the source of all temporal and spiritual good.

With what eager longing must the pilgrims crossing the desert look forward to their repose on the favoured spot, where a perpetual spring creates a little island of verdure or oasis in the midst of the burning plain!

God is called "The Fountain of Living Waters," or of waters always moving, flowing, and in action; and in him we have an abundant and constant supply of all the comfort and relief we can possibly need. When Israel sought other ways of happiness, and forsook God to worship idols which are broken cisterns, they left the fountain of living waters, which alone could constantly supply their souls when athirst after happiness.

The sun has not the less light for filling the air with light. A fountain has not the less for filling the lesser vessels. There is in Christ the fulness of a fountain. The overflowing fountain pours out water abundantly, and yet remains full. The Lord Jesus is such an overflowing fountain; he fills all, and yet remains full. Christ has the greatest worth and wealth in him. As the worth and value of many pieces of silver is in one piece of gold, so all the petty excellences scattered abroad in the creature are united in Christ.

God is like a fountain—(1) the *source* of life, natural and spiritual, Rev. xxii., 6; (2) yields *abundantly*: Christ is an ocean of goodness; (3) *pours* into low places: so the founts of the Ganges rising in the snows of Gangotri, flow into the Ganges valley; (4) *free* to all; (5) *clear*: rivers have sediment in them; (6) *pleasant*: refreshes the garden of the Church; water makes vegetation spring up even in the sandy deserts of Rajpootana; (7) *constant*: tanks in India dry up often in hot weather. Abraham's servants dried up the well; but this is a fountain sealed against filth; (8) often *hidden*: yet known by its waters. Christ's fountain was opened on the cross when his side was pierced, and when he sweat blood; the dying thief was a monument of its efficiency.

(160) The Believer Guarded as the Apple of the Eye.
Psalms xvii., 8.

The eyebrows turn aside the perspiration of the forehead from the eye, while dust and insects are kept off by the eyelids; the socket of bone, the eye is placed in, protects the apple or pupil of the eye, which is in the centre of this surrounded by the white of the eye.

Such is God's protection, as the Bengalis say he who has given life will give food.

---

(161) The Christian a Stranger on Earth.
Heb. xi., 9.

David, though a king, acknowledged he was a stranger on earth, 1 Chr. xxix., 15; saints are citizens of the new Jerusalem, Heb. xii., 12, being born from above, they have a new fatherland; they therefore rejoice as though they rejoiced not, 1 Cor. vii., 30; they abstain from fleshly lusts, 2 Pet. x., 11; take joyfully the spoiling of their goods, 2 Cor. iv., 8, 9; fall not out with their companions on the way, Gen. xlv., 24. Abraham left his country, because it was idolatrous, Josh. xxi., 2, 3. The patriarchs lived in tents to show they were strangers. A traveller sat by a well in a wilderness; he had been expelled from his country, because he took the part of slaves against their royal oppressors. He quenched his thirst, and showed his politeness to several maidens, and procuring drink for their flocks; invited to their house, he spent 40 years there in seclusion as a shepherd. A son was born to him, named Gersham or the stranger; the father's name was Moses.

Christians are strangers on earth as to—(1) *place*, heaven is their home, as they are born anew; the earth to them is like a wilderness with its brackish water, burning sands, fierce storms, such as are in Central Asia; (2) the *people*, worldly people have the devil as their father, believers in God bear the image of the heavenly; (3) *employment*, while one does the works of the flesh, the other does those of the Spirit; minding the one thing needful; their God is not their belly; (4) *manners*, believers are clothed with humility, roll not sin as a sweet morsel under their tongue; they have put off the old man; (5) *language*, believers talk of Bible subjects which are sealed to the world, &c., they have little intercourse with worldly people.

Christians as pilgrims or travellers, finding no rest for their soul on earth, carefully consider the cost, the difficulty, the danger, of their journey to Heaven; wisely they put on the light, the new, the defensive, and never worn out garments of salvation, and take to them the whole armour of God, for their safety against foes. Wisely they receive Jesus and his fulness, as their gold, their treasure, to bear their expenses on the way. They receive his Father for their companion; his Spirit to be their guide; his word to be their director and compass; his love, his power, and promises for their supporting staff. Carefully they ask for the good well-beaten old way of holiness, and continue walking therein; sweetly they drink out of its wells of salvation, and refresh themselves, but do not tarry in the inns of ordinances built close at hand! Now, their duty is pleasant and easy; anon it is rugged and difficult. Now, they enjoy the fine weather of peace and prosperity; clear views of Jesus and his countenance, wide prospects of his loveliness and love; clear discoveries of the vanity of this world, of the happiness of their present, and of the glory of their future state; anon, they are distressed with cold winters of trouble, storms of temptation, dark nights of sin and disorder, that they know not what to do, or whither to go. How oft fearfully pinched for provision! How oft the wells of promises seem dry, and inns of ordinances are found empty! How oft exposed to the gazing, ridicule, and malice of carnal men! How oft by Satan and their lusts harassed and robbed of their grace, or its evidence! How oft tempted like Lot's wife to turn back! But, through every tribulation they push forward to the city, the celestial kingdom of God, and with so much more cheerfulness, if they enjoy the company of eminent saints; they go from strength to strength till they appear before God in Zion. They are called strangers and sojourners with God on earth. How strange to carnal men is their state of union and communion with Christ! How strange their birth from above! Their having God their Father! Christ their husband! Glorified saints their principal people! In what strange, what celestial country, are their portion, their inheritance, their hopes, their affections, their thoughts, their desires! With what strange robe of divine righteousness, implanted grace, and Gospel holiness are they decked! What strange armour of God they have put on! How strangely they speak the spiritual language of prayer and praise! Pour out their hearts, behave as becomes the high calling of God! Walk with Father, Son, and Holy Ghost whom the world see and know not! Feed on the strange provision of Jesuss' person, righteousness, and benefits! How employed in the unknown labour of numbering their days; of considering their latter end; of ploughing up the fallow ground of their heart; of sowing to themselves in righteousness; of buying without money and without price; of denying and loathing themselves; of warring with principalities, powers, and spiritual wickedness; of renouncing the profit, pleasure, and honour of this world; of extracting good from evil and sweet out of bitter; of loving their enemies, and rendering them blessing for cursing.

(162) THE CONSCIENCE SEARED AS WITH A HOT IRON.
1 *Tim.* iv., 2.

The *Telegus*, referring to a conscience dead to all moral restraint, say it is a tongue without nerves moving all ways. Reason is compared by Plato to a *charioteer* driving his two horses' concupiscence and anger.

Conscience called God's *vicegerent*, named Luk. xi., 35, the *light* within, as a law also enlightens and directs;

a blind man sees not evil coming, neither do sinners good and evil, life and death. Sin blackens and darkens the light of conscience; holiness, compared to white, shines as crystal, or is transparent, but only when the sun is on it; dirt obstructs the sun's rays.

Conscience is called by Christ the *eye* of the soul which, if single, the body is full of light, so *David's* soul was darkened when his eye was dimmed by adultery. Nathan awoke him; the affections are apt to go to excess, like a balance when one side moves up, and the other moves down, so with the *flesh* and spirit, Gal. v., 7; thus—(*a*) Sensuality blinded Sampson and *Herod*. (*b*) *Intemperance* others, Hs. iv., 11; fumes of meat and drink obscure the upper regions, hence Paul's watching and fasting, 2 Cor. xi., 27; he who comes to make his belly his business will quickly come to have a conscience of as large a swallow as his throat; loads of meat and drink are fit for none but a beast of burthen to bear; and he is much the greater beast of the two, who comes with his burden in his belly than he who comes with it on his back, Pr. xxiii., 29; such as are *best at the barrel* are generally *weakest at the book*. (*c*) *Covetousness* buries the soul underground in darkness, while the body is above it, Dt. xvi., 9, 1 Sam. xii., 3, Ecc. vii., 7. (*d*) *Ambition* looks high, and giddiness from it makes a mist before the eyes. Satan like an expert wrestler usually gives a man a lift before he gives him a throw. Sensuality, covetousness, pride are the devil's trident to strike men's hearts.

The conscience is seared when a man's wounds cease to *smart*, only because he has lost his *feeling*; they are nevertheless *mortal*; he does not see his need of a *chirurgeon*; acquitment before trial can be no security in this case. Great and strong *calms* usually portend, and go before the most violent storms.

Men's conscience is compared to a *candle*, Pr. xx., 27, to lighten us in the darkness of this world, to a *judge*, John iii., 20; a *witness*, Rom. ix., 1; a *worm*, Mat. x., 44.

(156)

(163) THE CUP OF SALVATION AND SUFFERING.
Psalms cxvi., 13.

Joseph's cup was that out of which he drank, and which was taken from Benjamin's sack; and the cup which our Lord gave to his disciples at the last supper was one out of which they drank the wine. "The cup of salvation" is an expression taken from the custom of the Jews, of making a feast after presenting their thank-offerings, when the priests and offerers ate and drank together. Among other rites, the master of the feast took a cup of wine in his hand, and solemnly blessed God for it, and for the mercy which was at that time acknowledged, and then gave it to all the guests, of which every one drank in his turn Christ, suffering on behalf of sinners in the hour of his agony, prayed, "O! my Father, if it be possible let this cup pass from me." When afflictions are the result of God's vindictive justice, then "cup" has a more awful sense, and the wicked are often threatened with the dregs, which is the most unpleasant part of the liquor, Is., lvii., 17

(164) CHRISTIANS BURIED WITH CHRIST.
Rom. vi., 4.

The old man, *i.e.*, our corrupt nature, derived from the first man, dies by the painful lingering death of spiritual crucifixion to the world; it becomes dead to sin, but alive to righteousness, Rom. vi., 11, and is buried with Christ a great honor not like Jehoiakim said to have had the burial of an ass, Jer. xxiii., 19.

(165) THE HYPOCRITE'S HOPE A RUSH IN THE MIRE.
Job viii., 11—15.

The *Mahamudgar* states day and night, evening and morning, the seasons come and go, time plays with our passing age, yet the false winds of hope forsake us not, though the limbs be dissolved, the hair heavy, the jaws toothless, the hands tremble. The

Telegus compare visionary hopes to a bag of money seen in a looking-glass. Worldly hope is compared by Job to a web spun by the spider beautiful, but frail spun out of its own bowels, so with the rush it springs out of the mire, and its growth is as rapid as its greenness is bright "before the sun." While the bed in which it grows is filled with the season rains, it flaunts itself as if in scorn of the more valuable blade in the neighbouring furrow, and gains more notice from the uninstructed eye, yet it is always a worthless plant, and, as soon as the torrent is dried up by the heat of summer, it withers in a day. So the rich fools' hopes of long life, Luk xii., 16—20. So Goliah's head was cut off with the very sword he hoped to kill David with, 1 Sam. xvii., 44—51.

(166) THE SOUL'S TREASURES IN EARTHEN VESSELS.
2 *Cor.* iv., 7.

The body is compared to an earthen vessel, as being brittle, leaky, mean, of little value, yet it has the souls treasure in it, as the *Bengalis* say—like fine rice in a torn bag.

The Gospel is a treasure, for the reception of it into our hearts makes us "rich in faith;" presents to us "the unsearchable riches of Christ;" and teaches us to lay up for ourselves "durable riches and righteousness." The dying Christian, though ever so rich in this world, loses everything at last which he has in it; but, if he has Christ for his portion, he is richer than all the world he leaves behind him; for every thing belonging to the world must perish, but nothing can deprive us of this treasure, "for who shall separate us from the love of Christ?" Some suppose that the treasure in earthen vessels refers to the lamps which were concealed in Gideon's pitchers till they were broken, when he alarmed the army of the Midianites while asleep in their camp, Judg. vii., 16. So the Gospel is put into earthen vessels, and proves a glorious light to some, while it is hidden to others. Christ says lay not up treasures on earth, or in an earthen house easily dug through by robbers. The *Bengalis* say even in sweet mangoes worms breed, families and water descend, *i.e.*, decay.

(167) THE EARNEST OF THE SPIRIT.
2 Cor. i., 22.

In Guzerat at the ceremony of betrothal the bride's father offers to the bridegroom's father, as an earnest betel-nut, turmeric, and flowers, so in Bengal *pan*, (betel-nut) clothes, and flowers are offerred on a similar occasion.

It is something which one person gives to another to bind a bargain. If one has a house to sell, and any one is disposed to buy it, it might not be quite the proper time for you to give him immediate possession, or for him to settle all the terms; but to make sure of the house, he would give a part of the payment, and this would show that he was in earnest, and engaged to have it, and that you were quite in earnest, and engaged to sell it. Then to have the Spirit of God in us, is to have God's earnest that he will give us heaven. And how shall we know that God's Spirit is acting *in* us? Why, when he is acting *by* us? If we are "led by the Spirit," we shall "walk in the Spirit." We cannot have the Holy Spirit if we lead unholy lives.

(168) CHRIST COMING AS THE LIGHTNING.
Mat. xxiv., 27.

THE sudden flash, which brings so near to us the thought of an awful power that might consume us in a moment, should remind us of Christ's coming. He came at first in great humility, and many years passed by before He manifested forth his glory, that his disciples should believe on Him. But when He shall come again, He will be seen "in the clouds of heaven." "Every eye shall see Him, and they also who pierced Him." From one end of heaven to the other, His presence like lightning will be made manifest; and His coming will be as sudden as it will be terrible to the wicked.

At Christ's first coming.	*At His second coming:*
He was a Babe; Servant, his Forerunner, John in the desert; Fishermen his Attendants; a Mediator; spat on, derided.	King of Kings; the Trump of the Archangel shall sound; Angels, Archangels, his Attendants; Judge and Lord of all.

(169) THE RICH ARE ONLY STEWARTS.
1 *Cor.* iv., 2.

In this place, as in many others, God compares Himself to a master, in order to remind us that we are placed on earth not to do our own will, but the will of Him who placed us here; and that we have nothing which is properly our own, but that whatever we seem to have, is entrusted to us by another, who has left us in charge for a season, and will call us to account when He shall return. There is nothing against which our hearts naturally rise more stubbornly than the idea of being subject to another's will, and of having nothing that is our own; but it is said of true Christians, that they bring into captivity every thought to the obedience of Christ. They know that they are not their own, but are bought with a price; and it is therefore their great purpose to glorify God in their body and in their spirit, which are His.

The various faculties of our soul and body; the opportunities afforded by having our days lengthened; the gifts of station, education, friends, and worldly substance; the knowledge of religious truth and all the means of grace; the various occasions for doing or receiving good; these and numberless advantages and blessings, which are daily and hourly extended to us, must all be accounted for.

All Christians are stewarts, having a great master, the King of Heaven, a great charge their souls, much entrusted to them, and must improve their property, (see parable of the talents, of the barren fig tree, and of the rich who thought they were absolute proprietors.) Christ said it was easier for a camel to go through a needle's eye than for those trusting in riches to enter heaven, *i.e.*, an impossibility in human sight—as the Bengalis say a horse's eggs, or putting an elephant into a narrow dish.

(170) THE TONGUE A HELM.
Jas. iii., 2—5.

A *Bengali* proverb says—his tongue is a sweeper's shovel; and *Solomon*—a soft tongue breaketh the bone; a wholesome tongue is a tree of life. The *Telegus*—if your foot slip, you may recover your balance, but if your mouth slips, you cannot recall your words.

We are told to keep the door of our lips; the tongue is little like a helm, or a bit in a horse's mouth, yet it guides. Senacherib's tongue brought death on 185,000 soldiers, 2 Kings xviii., 28, so Anania's and Sapphira's brought death, Acts v., 8—10.

(171) CHRISTIANS ARE MEMBERS OF CHRIST WHO IS THE HEAD.
Rom. xii., 4, 5.

The Bengalis say are the five fingers equal in length? (See the fable of the belly and members) so the different offices and qualifications of Christians.

The Church is called the body of Christ, and he is the head, Eph. i., 22, which implies superiority and sympathy, 1 Cor., 12, when the head is cut off the body, in one minute life ceases.

Christ, the Head who is in heaven, is also dwelling by His Spirit in all His members, so as to make them one with Him and with each other by an union which is closer than that of parent and child. If we are "the body of Christ," then we have the comfort of knowing that Christ is our life. He is to our souls what the living principle is to our bodies. Being our "Head," He is our counsellor and guide in all difficulties and anxieties. Being our "Life," He is our strength in all assaults of Satan, in all trials and temptations. So that it is not our own strength, nor our own wisdom that we depend upon; but the strength and wisdom of Christ. And if we remember that we are "the members of Christ," we shall regard both our souls and bodies with a more solemn and reverential feeling, and shall fear above all things to defile by any wilful sin what is His and not our own. That is scarcely to be called a member of our body which is of no use to the body, nor can he be called a true member of Christ who is of no use to the Church (which is Christ's body) according to the calling in life which God has appointed for him. The Apostle says, "There are many members in one body, and all have not the same office." All have some office, but all have not the same office. And thus in Christ's body, every member is appointed to some useful office, some work of faith, and labour of love, in the daily duties of his various callings. No two members are appointed to the same office, but all have some service or other assigned to them. The services of some are more honourable than the occupations of the other; but there is no member of Christ that is not called to serve God, in some course of useful and dutiful obedience. The eye cannot say unto the hand, "I have no need of thee," nor again, the head to the feet, "I have no need of you." If any member could sever itself from the rest in a proud independence, it would utterly perish. The members have the same care one of another. The little brook, which waters a few fields, fulfils the office assigned to it by Providence as truly as the mighty river, which bears on its bosom the commerce of a nation.

---

(172) OPPRESSING THE POOR MOCKING GOD.
Pr. xiv., 31, xxxi., 8.

The Bengalis say the love of the zemindar to the ryot is like that of the Mussulman to his fowl which he fattens to kill; or the relation of the carving knife to the pumpkin.

A poor man that oppresseth the poor is like a sweeping rain which leaveth no food. The periodical rains which follow the long-continued drought of summer in Eastern countries, sometimes occasion a devastation unknown in an European climate. The rivers and brooks, in consequence of the periodical rains overflowing their bounds, carry ruin into the most cultivated districts, but especially among the dwellings of the poor, which, being usually built of mud, or of bricks burnt only in the sun, are the first to fall before the torrent, involving the inhabitants in destruction.

The giants before the flood were oppressors, Gen. vi., 4; so were the Egyptians, Ex. i., 13, so Jezebel, 1 Kings xxi., 7—13, not so, Job xxxi., 13—15, or those obeying the law of Moses, Dt. xv., 7—11, xxiv., 10—15. See the parable of the unmerciful servant, Mat. xviii., 30—34.

Oppression of the poor is called a panting after the dust on their head, Amos ii., 7. Thereby the oppressors incline to rob them of everything, and crush them to the dust of death. It is represented as a selling them for a pair of shoes, Amos viii., 6, to mark how lightly the oppressor esteems them, and for how little he is disposed to ruin them. It is called a crushing and treading upon them, Amos v., 11, to signify the grievous, afflictive, and debasing tendency thereof. It is called a slaying of them; a chopping their bones; a frightening and tearing them in the manner of lions, wolves, or bears; to denote the inhuman cruelty contained in it, and the utter ruin effected by it. It is represented as a building of houses and cities by blood, Heb. ii., 12; because oppressors rear these structures with the wealth extorted from others, to the endangering of their life. It is called an eating of God's people as bread to mark the pleasure and greed wherewith wicked men persecute the persons, ruin the character, and consume the substance of the godly.

The widow of Zarephath, 1 Kings xvii., 13, was happier than Queen Jezebel, the oppressor, while the rust of the rich man's gold shall eat his flesh as fire, Jas. v., 2, 3; it shall also like the dust be a testimony against him, Mark vi., 11.

Solomon writes the teeth of the oppressor are knives to devour the poor from off the earth, Pr. xxx., 14.

---

(173) THE ARROWS OF GOD'S VENGEANCE.

"Arrows" mean God's judgments on the wicked, which often fly through the world to punish them. The lightning and tempest, war, pestilence, and famine, all may be his arrows to slay the ungodly, and to cut them off from the earth. So God threatened the inhabitants of Jerusalem by his prophet, Ezekiel, and assured them that for their wickedness he would "send upon them the evil arrows of famine," Ez. v., 16.

Arrows wound quickly and unexpectedly; no noise is made; they stick sharply in the wounds; such are God's arrows of *pestilence*, Ps. xci., 5; *famine* as David had and the *sword*, Job said (vi., 4) God's arrows of disease and the sword were within him; God's arrows for crushing the wicked are compared to treading down the grapes in a wine-press, Rev. xix., 15.

---

(174) CHRIST THE BREAD OF HEAVEN.
John vi., 51.

Man has a soul as well as a body, and as the body cannot live without food, so neither can the soul. The soul can never die like the body, but then there is a sort of death which can happen to the soul, when it has no life to love and serve God. It is then like a dead body which can serve no one. It is then displeasing to God, as a dead body is offensive to us. Our Lord Jesus is called " bread," because all our spiritual life must come from him. We have no inclination or strength to serve God, but as he helps us. Bread, to do us good, must be eaten; and, by faith, we may get all our spiritual life from Jesus Christ, that is to say, all our ability to love and serve God. Faith then is as the mouth of the soul, or the way by which this spiritual nourishment is received into the soul. Jesus is called the " Bread of Life" and " the Living

Bread," to those who believe or trust in him; he gives this spiritual life to serve God here, and this is but the beginning of a life which shall never end, for he who eats of this broad "shall live for ever."

The hungry know the value of bread, Pr. xxvii., 7; gold is no use in a starving city, and all need it, for hunger will eat through a stone-wall—*Khudanám nechi pátra sudhi.*

---

(175) THE BODY A HOUSE.
2 *Cor.* v., 1.

The *Probodh Chandrodaya* compares the soul to a taper confined in a dwelling which has nine openings. The *Shanti Shatak* says it is absurd to lament the loss of youthful joy and a lively countenance which floated off like the sportive and short-lived billows in the Jumna. *Vemana* writes when a bubble stands on water, a rapid rush in passing destroys it. Alas! what affection men feel for the frail earthen vessel of the body."

The word house sometimes means property, as when referred to the Pharisees who devoured widow's houses, Mat. xxiii., 14.

But "house" more generally means a place to dwell in. The body is the earthly house in which the spirit dwells, 2 Cor. v., 1. The grave is called "the house appointed for all living," Job xxx., 23, because every one now living must at last abide there as in a house. The tabernacle and temple were called "the House of God," Judges xviii., 31, 2 Chron. v., 14, because there God dwelt among his people by the signs of his gracious presence, and his glory appeared in the cloud, and shone forth from between the Cherubim over the ark. And thus Jacob, when he set up the stone which had formed his pillow, called the place Bethel, or the house of God, to signify that the Lord had revealed himself in that place, Gen. xxviii., 19.

Solomon says in old age *the keepers of the house*, the knees, chaukidars, or pillars tremble with paralysis; the grinders or teeth are like the women who ground meal; the eyes are the windows, the sight becomes dim, Gen. xxvii., 15, xlviii., 10, 1 Kings xiv., 4; the lattices of the windows afford less light to pass through, Judg. v., 28, 2 Sam. vi, 16; the doors are shut to enable the old to sleep 2 Sam. xxx., 35, the *daughters of music* brought low, are singing or natch-girls; the house tumbles, and its tenant goes to his long home. Who builds stronger than a mason, a ship-wright, or a carpenter? The grave-digger, the house that he makes, lasts till Doomsday. The Christian's sun breaks through the clouds of old age; the golden chain, which binds his heart to heaven, is waxing stronger and stronger, its links are growing more firm; the Christian's house is tumbling, but he has a building made without hands, 2 Cor. v., 1, in a city without foundations.

(176) The Smoke of God's Anger.
Is. lxv., 2—5.

Nothing is more offensive to the nostrils than smoke When it is said in Is. lxv., 2—5, that Israel was to God as a smoke in his nose; such language signifies that he was greatly offended with their idolatries. When it is said, "There went up a smoke out of his nostrils," it is to express God's wrath against those who did what was offensive to Him.

When Sodom and Gommorah were destroyed by brimstone and lightning, a dense smoke arose from the ruins indicating the terrible fire that was there, Gen. xix., 28; so God is said to be to the wicked a consuming fire, Heb. xii., 29; as fire he appeared in the burning bush, Ex. iii., 2; on Sinai, Ex. ixi., 18, to Isaiah vi., 4, Ezekiel i., 4, John, Rev. i., 14, and as a flaming fire will he appear at the Judgment Day, 2 Tim i., 8, then all will be *confusion*, as when a fire breaks out, Rev. vi., 10; it will be sudden like as at Belshazzar's feast, Dan. v., 5; it will destroy everything; while the wicked will be only stubble, Nah. i., 10, the righteous will be as the burning bush on which fire had no effect. God's anger is described in Job, 37th chapter.

Smoke quickly disappears, not so the smoke of God's anger, Rev. xiv., 11. In Rev. ix., 2, the smoke which rose from the bottomless pit is supposed by many to refer to the gross errors of Muhammadanism which darken the understanding.

(177) THE GREAT FAMILY OF CHRISTIANS.
Eph. iii., 14.

God is our father, the Church our mother; all Christian people our brethren in Jesus Christ, who is the eternal Son of God. We all make one family under the same head, and the same Saviour; and the many millions of Angels in heaven are comprehended within this family as well as the saints upon earth. If God is our father, we may depend upon his goodness and affection to us, but we must pray to him, as we make our wants known to our earthly parents. We must also expect that God will chastise and correct us for our faults, even as every wise father punishes the child in whom he delights. Christian people are our brethren; it must be our duty to love them, and to bear in mind that wise advice of *Joseph* to his brethren, *see that ye fall not out by the way*, Gen. xlv., 24. In our journey through life, we are under so many trials and afflictions, that it is both foolish and wicked for Christian brethren to add to one another's troubles by strife and envying by quarrellings and disputings. Proud people are ashamed of their poor relations; but we must not be ashamed to own the poorest child in the family of God, who, perhaps after a laborious life of faith and patience, will be our superior in the kingdom of heaven.

A family is a resting place for worldly cares, so is the Christian family whose father is God; Christ the elder brother or head, Col. i., 17; the Holy Spirit the guide; and all true Christians members.

(178) LIFE A WARFARE.
2 *Cor.* x., 3.

The *Niti Shatak* states time no more conquers the wise than a straw the elephant; he, whose cheeks are streaked with the marks of passion, is not fastened by the filaments of the *lotus*. Life is compared in the Bible to a dream, an eagle hastening to its prey, a hand-breath, a swift ship, a tale told; in the text to a war.

What a strange thing is war, yet we see it everywhere, and vile as is war and very destructive to life and comfort, we ourselves are engaged in it, whether we will or not, there is war in the natural creation: the hawk is always in arms for the seizing of his prey; the tiger and the wolf are at war with cattle; birds and beasts are persecuting one another; and the innocent birds are destroyed by the cruel and rapacious. Even in seas and rivers, there are *bol* fish, sharks, and alligators which devour other kinds. If we turn our eyes to mankind, we see nation rising in arms against nation, and kingdoms divided against themselves. The invisible world is also at war; *there was war in heaven*, Rev. xii., 7, when Satan and millions of Angels rose in rebellion against God prompted by pride and jealousy, God himself has his enemies among Angels that excel in strength; principalities and powers are confederate against all the great and merciful designs of heaven; and the war, which they began there, is carried on upon earth against us (men) and our salvation. We are, therefore, born to a state of war, and are accordingly enlisted as soldiers at our baptism; and Jesus Christ is the *captain of our salvation*, under whose banner we are to fight against his and our enemies. Our Christian profession is called *a fight of faith*, because it is subject to all the dangers, losses, fears, and miscarriages of war; and the same rules are to be observed, the same measures followed in the one case as in the other; with this difference, that spiritual dangers are a thousand times worse than bodily, and call for more valour and more vigilance. Being, therefore, soldiers, we are to do as soldiers do. We are to put on the whole armour of God. There is the helmet to save the head in natural war; and there is the protection of God, the *helmet of salvation* in spiritual war. There is the *shield of faith*, which we are to hold up against the fiery darts of the enemy. There is the *sword of the spirit*, the word of God, *sharper than any two-edged sword*, which, when skilfully used, will give mortal wounds to the adversaries of our faith. We must practise the prudence which is necessary in earthly war, considering that we are here in an enemy's country, in continual danger of being surprised by evil spirits, who are always upon the watch, and, therefore, we must be sober and vigilant. A drunken soldier, in a time of war, is in danger of death— a drunken Christian is in danger of damnation. All levity, dissipation, and foolish jesting are to be avoided, as tending to make the mind effeminate and careless, and insensible of its dangerous situation in this life; in consideration of which we are to *pass the time of our sojourning here in fear*, as they do who are encompassed with enemies. We are to study the interests of the two parties at war. We are to know that the grand enemy of man which is the devil has his allies who assist him in his warfare against us; these are the world and the flesh. The world receives his principles, and works with him by the great force of custom, fashion, and example; the flesh wars against the spirit, and is to be denied and mortified as we stop and seize the supplies of provision when they are upon the road to the camp of an enemy. As the mind of a soldier is intent upon victory, and he runs at all hazards to obtain it, so has the Christian the same object in view; sin and death are to fall before him, and the kingdom of heaven is to be the prize.

In war soldiers must submit to hardships in clothes, houses, food, sleep; they look forward with joy to the expiry of their time of enlistment, Job vii., 2. So Christians wish like the dove to flee away and be at peace, Ps. xi., 1.

(179) THE DEVIL THE FATHER OF LIES.
John viii., 44.

The *Shanti Shatak*, treating of the marks of the friends of truth, states they have as a father patience, as a mother forgiveness, as a wife peace of mind, their heir truth, their sister pity, their brother temperance, the earth their bed, their garment the air, and wisdom their nectar. The *Markanda Purana* writes of truth :—

Satyena arkah pratapati satye tishtati medini,
Satyam ea uktam paradharmah, svargah satye pratishtati ;
Asvamedh sahasram ea satyam satulat dhritum,
Asvamedh sahasrad hi eva vashishyati.

Through truth only the sun shines, on truth the earth stands,
  To speak the truth is the highest duty, on truth the heaven rests ;
Though we weigh a thousand Asvamedhs against truth,
  Yet will truth outweigh a thousand Asvamedhs.

Jesus Christ is the true light; but the devil is the prince of darkness, the god of this world, who blinds men's eyes that they may not see the truth. The Saviour is a shepherd who gives his life for the sheep; but the devil is a lion who goes about seeking what he may devour. The one is a lamb, meek and harmless, the other a serpent, full of devices and more subtle than any beast of the field. The one raises men to life; the other was a murderer from the beginning. The one is our advocate with the Father, suffering and pleading for the pardon of our sins; the other is the accuser of the brethren; first tempting them to fall into sin, and then accusing them that they may fall under the judgment of God. Jesus Christ is the truth, and the devil is the father of lies. And lastly, Jesus Christ is the true God worshipped by all believers, and the devil is the false god worshipped under a variety of names by the heathen world. The children of the devil are like the devil, as the young viper is like the old one. There have always been two sorts of people in the world—the sons of God and the seed of the serpent; and God has put such enmity between them, as shall last as long as the world does. Why did the Jews crucify Jesus Christ, and why did the heathens persecute the Christians, and put them cruelly to death?—but because they were of their father, the devil, and filled with the same spirit of envy and hatred as he is? His name is called *Satan*, which means an *adversary*, because he is the adversary of God and man. Peace and quietness are never promoted by him, but opposition and confusion; he sows the seeds of discord, and stirs up men to tumult and rage, as the stormy wind stirs up the waves of the sea. He is pleased when men kill one another with the sword in carnal war, but more so when they are set at variance by perverse disputings which are the wars of the mind, and such as spirits are most fit for.

Judas, the traitor, was also called a devil, John vi., 10, as God is called the father of mercies, so is the devil of lies; he was first an angel of light, and then by his lies induced one-third of the angels to rebel against God; he told lies to Eve in the garden, Gen. iii., 6, and to Christ in the the desert. The devils are also compared to *birds of prey* for their piercing eye, sudden pouncing, residence in the air, Eph. ii., 2, yet Satan was once called the son of the morning, Is. xiv., 12.

(180) TREASURES LAID UP IN HEAVEN.
Mat. vi., 20.

Vemana states if you consider your possessions as your own fools alone will agree with you; that alone is yours which you have bestowed on others. The *Telegus* say worldly possessions are like a drop of water on a *lotus* leaf.

Earthly treasures can be destroyed by fire, floods, thieves, white ants, rust, Job xx., 15. No treasures of the Hindus could be secured against Mahrattas and Moguls. The earth itself is kept in store reserved unto fire; Solomon calls ill-got riches treasures of wickedness, as Rehoboam found, 2 Chr. cxxi., 4—9, so did Nebuchadnezzar, Dan. iv., 31.

See the parable of the hid treasure, Mat., xiii., 44.

---

(181) THE LORD OUR SHEPHERD—BELIEVERS SHEEP.

Ps. xxiii., 6.

The shepherd knows his sheep, so as to be able to distinguish them individually, John x., 14, and "when he leadeth them out to call them by their names," John x., 14. Christ knows his, their number, names, place, character, and condition. "I am the good shepherd, and know my sheep." He provides for them; his name is Jehovah-jireh, "the Lord will provide." The sheperd protects them, and for this purpose, he is usually provided with a staff or rod, a sling, and if need be, with a sword or spear. So "David took his staff in his hand, and his sling was in his hand, and he drew near to the Philistines," 1 Sam. xvii., 40. Christ is the protector of his. Having purchased them by his blood, he protects them by his power. He leads and guides them often in a barren wilderness with no paths or water surrounded by wild beasts; so Christ guides his people by his Providence, Word, and Spirit. "I will go before thee, and make the crooked places straight," Is. xlv., 2. "He leadeth me," says the Psalmist, "in the paths of righteousness in an even and quiet path, in opposition to a path among thorns and stones and cliffs. When exposed to the scorching heat of the sun, or when weary and exhausted, he conducts them to some shady place where he "causes them to rest at noon." By "noon is meant" "fiery trial," whether arising from temptation, affliction, or persecution, or all together. The lambs are the objects of his special care and affection. When the lambs become tired, or come to some difficult part in the track, which they cannot get over, the shepherd may be seen "gathering them in his arms," and even "carrying them in his bosom."

Christ said, "Suffer the little children to come unto me, and forbid them not, for of such is the kingdom of heaven. And he *took them up in his arms*, put his hands on them, and blessed them," Mark x., 14—16. Hence also his charge to Peter, "Feed my lambs," John xxi., 15. He *numbers* them when they return to the fold to see that none be missing, and if there be an under-shepherd, that he may account to the owner for the sheep committed to his trust and care. When the flocks are large and numerous, and several shepherds are required, *one* is appointed over the rest as the *chief* shepherd. He restores the sheep that has strayed, and goes after that which is lost until he finds it. This Christ does for his. God, as a shepherd, has an immense flock all over the world; gives them peculiar food; always abides. Believers are sheep, easily scattered when away from the shepherd as were the Jews by the Babylonians.

(182) Sinners are Blind.

Rev. iii., 17.

The *Atmabodh* states, "The eye of ignorance does not behold God, as a blind man does not see the light." Sinners are like the blind, in not being able to see the sun, to know what colors and light are; they see not the dangers in the road. Those naturally blind regret not seeing the light of the sun, and wish for a guide; not so those spiritually blind; the eyes of the rich man's understanding were not opened till he reached hell, where he lifted up his eyes being in torment.

Chanakya writes he who has no sense what does the Shastra do for him? What does a mirror do for a man without eyes? What does an eloquent man where there are no hearers? What do washermen in a country of naked *fakirs*?

(183) THE WORM OF CONSCIENCE.
Mark x., 44.

The *Bengalis* say no sin is hidden to the soul, only strike the ground, and the guilty start up in terror.

The reproaches of conscience are compared to a worm—(1) sprung from filth; earth is a dunghill; (2) *produce death* by gnawing the internals, so Herod was eaten up of worms; (3) scourge of great *pain*; (4) *medicine* required, otherwise no internal cure.

Conscience is compared to a candle, such as Joseph's brethren found it, Gen. xlii., 21, xliv., 16, Pharoah, Ex. ix., 27, x., 17, Saul, 1 Sam. 24, Herod, Mark xii., 16, Judas, Mat. xxvii., 4. It is called a witness, Rom. ix., as Cain's wounded spirit led him to wander as a vagabond.

(184) THE SOUL SHIPWRECKED.
1 *Tim.* i., 19.

The body is compared to a casket, the soul to a jewel; in the text the soul is like a ship, launched at birth on the river of life, constructed with great skill; fitted up for a long and dangerous voyage over the ocean of life, exposed to the storms of temptation, the rocks of sin, the waves of passion, a good bottom is necessary to prevent a leak, and the wind of God's Spirit to fill the sails of the affections, the compass of God's word is required, 2 Pt. ii., 19; Christ is the pilot.

(185) THE NECK HARDENED.
Prov. xxix., 1.

The Jews were called a stiff-necked people, Acts vii., 51.

The old world had its neck hardened by resisting the preaching of Noah for one hundred and twenty years, 1 Pet. iii., 20, 2 Pet. ii., 5; its people were swept away by the flood altogether unexpectedly to themselves.

Pharaoh's hard neck was reproved by the ten plagues:—The waters of Egypt turned into blood, Ex. vii., 19-25, the plague of frogs, viii., 1-15, of lice, Ex. viii., 16—19, of flies, Ex. viii., 20—32, the murrain of the cattle, Ex. ix., 1-7, the plague of boils, Ex. ix., 8-12, of rain with hail and fire, Ex. ix., 13—35, of locusts, Ex. x., 1—20, of darkness, x., 21—27, the death of the first-born, Ex. xii., 29. But continuing obstinate in his rebellion against God, Pharaoh was overtaken with sudden destruction, Ex. xiv., 28, at the moment he thought himself sure of his prey, Prov. xvi., 5. So Ahab, 1 Kings xvii., 1, xviii. 18, xx., 42, xxi., 20, xxii.

(186) THE WORDS OF THE WISE GOADS AND NAILS.
Ecc. xii., 10, 11.

As the elephant, when sluggish and disobedient, must be quickened and corrected by the goad, so does our sleeping conscience need the continual pricks and admonitions of a faithful expounder of Scripture, both for correction, and instruction in righteousness, 2 Tim. iii., 16. And as it is the use of "nails" to fasten what is loose, or what would otherwise drop to pieces, so the exhortation of a wise preacher should fix in our treacherous memory what we might otherwise soon "let slip."

God's word is compared to a *hammer* breaking the rock in pieces, but the hand of God is required; according to the strength and skill of the holder is the blow; this hammer fastens the nails of conscience and of promise; it pierces even a stone.

(187) SINNERS HAVE A BROW OF BRASS.
Is. xlviii., 4.

Brass is a strong metal, hence the brazen serpent in the wilderness was made of it, Num. xxi., 9, so were the gates of Babylon. Sinners' obstinacy is compared to a brow of brass, while the righteous set their faces like a flint against sin; of the former were

Pharaoh, Ex. v., 1, Saul, 1 Sam. xv., 9—23, Jeroboam, 1 Kings xii., 28—33; of the latter, Jacob, Gen. xxxii., 24—28, David, 1 Sam. xvii., 45, Stephen, Acts vii., 57.

Sinners are also said to have a hard or stony heart, a seared conscience, to be past feeling; they are likened to the deaf adder which will not hear the voice of the serpent-charmer. Such were Samuel's sons, 1 Sam. ii., 25, vi., 11, Jerusalem, Ez. ix., 9, 10.

---

(188) HEARING AND NOT DOING.
Mat. vii., 24,—27.

There are four different kinds of hearers, those like a *sponge* that suck up good and bad together, and let both run out immediately—having ears, and hearing not; those like a *sand-glass* that let what enters in at one ear pass out at the other—hearing without thinking; those like a *strainer*, letting go the good and retaining the bad; and those like a *sieve*, letting go the chaff, and retaining the good grain.

The *Bengalis* say in name he is *Dharmadas* (a servant of righteousness), but he has no virtue. *Chanakya* writes knowledge only in books (without practice), and wealth in the hands of others, are of no use, as in the time of action they are not available.

Profession without practice is compared to failing fountains, shells empty of kernels, tares among wheat, Mat. 13, foolish virgins without oil, Mat. xxv., 1—13, the mirage; lilies fair in show, foul in scent. Dead fish float down the stream; living fish struggle against it.

---

(189) A CRUEL MAN TROUBLES HIS OWN FLESH.
Pr. xi., 17, xxii., 10.

The tender mercies of the wicked are cruel. Joseph's brethren illustrated it in their treatment of their brother whom they put into a pit, Gen. xxxvii., 42. Adonizebek had his barbarity in cutting off men's toes visited on himself, Judg. i., 6, 7. Haman's cruelty involved his own sons, Esth. ix., 25; on the other hand, David shewed his kindness by rescuing a lamb, even endangering his own life for it, 1 Sam. xvii., 34.

(190) EARS THE WICKED HAVE, BUT THEY HEAR NOT.

Mark viii., 18.

The wicked are said to have uncircumcised ears, Acts vii., 51, heaping up teachers they have itching ears, 2 Tim. iv., 3, stopped at the cry of the poor, Pr. xxi., 31.

God is represented as having ears, because he knows better what all men say than we should know if we heard their words. He hears the words of rage and anger, and he hears the profane wretch that takes his name in vain, and will not hold him guiltless. He also hears the cry of the humble that look to him for help and mercy. He hears the prayers of the most humble child, and he marks his lisping praises. See how delighted Christ was with the children in the temple, and observe what he said about them! The blind and the lame came to him in the temple, and he healed them. And when the chief priests and scribes saw the wonderful things that he did, and the children crying in the temple, and saying, Hosanna to the son of David, they were sore displeased, and said unto him, "Hearest thou what these say?" And Jesus saith unto them, "Yea; have ye never read, out of the mouth of babes and sucklings thou hast perfected praise?"— Mat. xxi., 14—16. God really waits for us to pray, and prepares his blessings for us, for that is clearly the meaning of those words, "And it shall come to pass that before they call, I will answer, and while they are yet speaking, I will hear." The worshippers of Baal cut themselves with knives, and cried to their god as the Hindus do to Ram from morning till night, "O Baal, hear us!"—but Baal never heard, and as soon as Elijah called to his God, he heard, and, in proof that he heard him, sent fire from heaven to consume his sacrifice.

(191) The Inner and Outer Man.
2 *Cor.* iv., 16.

The *Telegus* say the tamarind may be dried, but it loses not its acidity, so Paul's outer man the body decayed, though the inner man was renewed; his setting sun was as fine as the rising one; he was like the bird who sang as sweetly in winter as in summer. The *Atmabodh* states the wise man, during his residence in the body, is not affected by its properties, as the firmament is not affected by what floats in it. The *Bengalis* say of a clever woman that though old, she is not aged, but has the sweet sap of wit in her. The Hindus write of various *kosh* or sheaths enveloping the body, as also of the different kinds of spirit, the breathy, the breaden, the mental, the intelligent, the inmost (joyful).

Paul means by the outer man the body, and senses by the inner, the heart, and spirit; the bodily eye might grow dim, while the eye of faith grew brighter.

---

(192) Born again of Water and the Spirit.
John iii., 3.

A Brahmin is called *dija*—twice-born, *i.e.*, first by nature, and second by dedication to his religion. A Christian is twice-born in regeneration which is compared to an old tree grafted, through which its nature is changed and improved, and the old stock is made to bear good fruit. A child when new born is a perfect man as to limbs, though not yet at their full growth and size; similar is God's grace in the new birth. Christ, in his conversation with Nicodemus, shewed the need of the new birth.

The new birth of a Christian is called a resurrection Col. iii., 1; a transformation, Rom. xii., 2, having a heart of flesh, Ez. xxxvi., 26; a new creation, 2 Cor. v., 17; putting off the old man, Eph. iv., 22; metal figures cast in a mould, Rom. vi., 17.

Believers are called by the world its offscouring, yet though by nature children of wrath by the new birth, they become sons of God; like the angels they have access to their father, Rom. viii., 14; their petitions are heard, Mat. vii., 7—11, and they become heirs of God, Gal. iv., 7.

(193) THE RIVER OF GOD'S GRACE.
Rev. xxii., 1.

A flowing river is often spoken of in Scripture, when it is intended to describe the abundance of anything, Job xxix., 6. "The rock poured me out rivers of oil;" that is, great plenty and abundance of oil, Psalms xxxvi., 8; "Thou shalt make them drink of the river of thy pleasures;" that is, thou shalt make them partake of that abundant pleasure, delight, and satisfaction, which thou didst not only enjoy thyself, but bestowest upon thy people; and "river" may denote the constancy and perpetuity of these pleasures as well as their plenty, John. vii., 38. "He that believeth on me, out of his belly shall flow rivers of living water;" that is, he shall be indued with the gifts and graces of the Spirit in a plentiful measure which shall not only refresh himself, but shall break forth, and be communicated to others also for their refreshing. In Job xl., 23, it is said of the hippopotamus, "He drinketh up a river;" that is, a great quantity of water, Psalms lxv., 9. "Thou waterest the earth with the river of God;" that is, with plentiful showers of rain from the clouds. In Psalms xlvi., 4, the words mean the gracious presence of God, and the blessings following thence which shall make Zion, or the Church of God glad. In this text, as in various others in the Bible, there is an allusion to the flowing rivers, on the banks of or near which the eastern gardens were planted and cities were erected, and the church of God is called a city, because like a city it is composed of many individuals living together having the same common privileges; it is refreshed and delighted by this river common to all, *i.e.*, by the spiritual blessings which God bestows upon it, regaling all its spiritual senses, and supplying all its spiritual need.

God is compared to a place of broad rivers, Is. xxiii., 21; by him saints, in their situation and blessings, are adorned and beautified; by him the air, *i.e.*, the soul's breathing is rendered pure and wholesome; by him they are completely defended from every foe; by him they have full access to the profitable commerce of the celestial country; in him how wide their prospect into eternity into things in heaven and on earth! How inexhaustible his fulness to quench their thirst; to satisfy their desires, refresh their souls, and purge away their filth.

A river, however large, like the Amazon which is 180 miles wide, springs from a small *fountain*, scarcely seen like the founts of the Ganges at Gangautri; the river of grace rises in heaven from the throne of God; a river, not like a tank, has much water constantly flowing; all may come to it, Is. lv., 1. It sometimes overflows so at Pentecost, and in the time when God's knowledge shall cover the earth. In its course it is impetuous, carries away impediments, so Paul went out a lion, came in a lamb, Acts ix., 6; it fertilises; the righteous are compared to willows by the watercourses, Is. xliv., 4; the banks of Indian rivers are very fertile; its waters are carried to the ocean, so all grace ends in God; the water is always new and fresh hence grace compared to a tree of life bearing twelve manner of fruits every month. The river of God's grace differs from earthly rivers in these points; it never dries up; is never frozen up; breeds no noxious animals; its channel is not shifted; never muddy; cleanses the soul; its fountain—the Holy Spirit—is eternal; its waters as clear as crystal; no trail of the serpent; no tigers near this river; no gold alloyed; no blighted flowers.

---

(194) Christians are Servants of Christ.
2 *Tim.* ii., 24.

The Jews had a class of house servants, as the Hindus had who were slaves sold for debt or by their parents; but among the Jews they were set free on the seventh year, unless they had with their own consent their ears bored with an awl, and fastened to the door-posts; the devil's children are like them—bond slaves of sin; but Christians, as the sons of a king by regeneration, have a higher dignity in the court of heaven; such was Joshua to Moses, Elisha to Elijah. Moses was the servant of the Lord, Jos. i., 2. Believers were slaves to the world, the flesh, and the devil, but were redeemed by Christ who freed them from hereditary bondage.

Christians are servants of Christ as *appointed* thereto, Is. xl., 10; *obedient*, Luk. xxii., 27; *entrusted*, Gen. xli., 14; *delight* in work, Gen. xxxiv., 33; act according to *orders*, Ex. xxv., 40; expect *wages*, so Jacob labored seven years for his wife; render an *account*.

Angels, though far higher in rank, power, and intellect than any kings of earth, yet took charge of a beggar's soul, when only the dogs attended to his body; these angels are called servants, Heb. i., 14; they proclaimed their master's will to Lot, Gen. 18; to Elisha, 2 Kings i., 3; to Daniel, ix., 22; opposed God's enemies, so Michel fought with the dragon, Rev. xii., 9; executed God's judgments in Egypt, Ex. xii., 23; blinded the Sodomites, Gen. xix., 11, and others, so Act xii., 23; defended the godly; they hold the four winds, Rev. vii., 1—3; protected Elisha, 2 Kings vi., 14; were guides, and carried Lazarus into Abraham's bosom; are the reapers in the day of judgment, Mat. xxiv., 31.

(195) Christ a Propitiation through Faith in his Blood.

Rom. iii., 25.

Christ's death as an atonement was typified by the paschal lamb, Ex. 12; the smiting the rock, Ex. xvii., 6; our sins are imputed to Christ, as Adam's were to us, Rom. v., 12—21; in England when a woman is married, her husband is responsible for her debts; the Church is Christ's bride, and he pays her debts, so David was kind to the house of Saul for Jonathan's sake, 1 Sam. xi., 1.

The atonement was also typified by sacrificing the firstlings of the flock, Gen. iv., 4, by Isaac about to be offered, Gen. xxii., 2 ; the mercy seat was not approached without blood, Lev. xvi., 24, the scapegoat was a type, Lev. xvi., 21. The atonement is a washing out stains, Ps. li., 2, a passing by, Mic. vii., 18 ; scattering a cloud that hides the sun, Is. lxiv., 22 ; removing sin far away, Ps. ciii., 12 ; healing, Ps. vi., 2. The brazen serpent which cured the Jews bitten by the snakes on their looking at ; it typified the eye of faith looking on Christ, curing the soul bitten by the serpent—sin.

If the mercies of God be not loadstones to draw us to heaven, they will be millstones to sink us to perdition ; the wicked are no better for mercies, as the Dead Sea or ocean is no sweeter from the rivers of fresh water that flow in.

(196) THE WAGES OF SIN IS DEATH.

The wicked are said to be holden with the cord of their own sins, Pr. v., 22 ; such was Saul. Death to the wicked is called the king of terrors, Job xviii., 4 ; is likened to a wolf, Ps. xlix., 14 ; a flood, Ps. xc., 5 ; darkness, Job. xii., 21.

The devil is a bad master ; his servants work hard ; they are fed with husks in this life and with everlasting fire in the next. God's punishment of sin is compared to dashing in pieces like a potter's vessel ; treading down as the mire of the street or ashes ; grinding to powder ; melting as a snail ; gnashing of teeth. Even in this life the wages are—sickness, Lev. xxvi., 16 ; famine, Lev. xxvi., 19 ; war, Lev. xxvi., 25—33 ; fear, Job, xviii., 11 ; in the next, it will be the blackness of darkness, 2 Pet. ii., 17 ; the wine of God's wrath, Rev. xiv., 10 ; everlasting contempt, Dan. xii., 2.

(197) FIT WORDS APPLES OF GOLD IN PICTURES OF SILVER.

Pr. xxv., 11.

This is a definition of a parable or a proverb which sets off grave sentiments by elegant language, as the appearance or imitation of finely colored fruit is improved by its shining as through a veil, through the net-work of a silver vessel finely carved, or like oranges in baskets of silver. The beauty of truth is heightened by the veil of imagery. Christ, without a parable, spoke not unto the people.

(198) The City of God in Heaven.
Heb. xii., 22.

A city from its numerous inhabitants is called a mother, Is. ii., 23, while Babylon was called a widow when desolate, Is. xlvii., 3—4; Abraham looked for a city without foundations, Heb. x., 10. The city in heaven is—(1) well situated far above earth, Ps. xlviii., 2; (2) surrounded by walls of salvation, Is. xxvi., 1; guarded by holy angels, Ps. xxxiv., 7; (3) various nations in it, Eph. ii., 19—21; a great multitude which no man can number, Rev. vii., 7; (4) enriched by the beast of earth and creation.

Its citizens are all first-born, i.e., the choicest first-born had a double portion, and were superior in rank, Gen. xlix., 3, applied also to inferior things. Job calls worms the first-born of death, xiii., 13, and death is called by the Arabs the mother of vultures.

Earthly cities were often founded by blood and rapine, Mic. iii., 10, or like Babel to perpetuate a name, Gen. xi., 4; built of stone or wood surrounded with walls, infested by dogs, often burnt or sown with salt, Judg. ix., 45; the city of the heavenly Jerusalem has God as its architect; nothing evil in it; its walls of gold and streets of pearl; no enemy can approach it; the palace and court of the king.

(199) The Hoary Head of the Righteous a Crown of Glory.
Pr. xvi., 31.

The Jews required persons to rise up when at a distance of four cubits from an old man. The Romans punished with death those not rising up before the hoary; and God sent two bears to devour the men who called Elisha bald-headed, 2 Kings ii., 23.

The Germans call grey hairs death's blossoms. The Bible says, *if,* found in the way of righteousness, they are a *crown* of life, *i.e.,* unfading, and an ornament, a sign of dominion and victory. Men are like wine; age renders the good mellow, but makes the bad sour, or like chimneys long foul, which, if not swept, are at length fired. Old sinners are like vessels long abroach in which nothing is left, but the lees and dregs of ignorance and sin.

Examples of good old Christians, in Samuel, 1 Sam. xxv., 1, 1xix., 12, Elisha, 2 Kings, xiii., 14, Jacob, Gen. xlvii., 10, Annah, Luk. ii., 36. Polycarp.

---

(200) TO THOSE NOT WATCHING CHRIST COMES AS A THIEF.

Rev. iii., 3.

The day of Christ's coming is described in Mat. 24, and the suddenness of it is compared to the midnight cry of the virgins, "Behold the bridegroom cometh," Mat. 25; the heavens shall pass away with a great noise, and the elements shall melt, 2 Pet. iii., 9, 10. The thief comes to *destroy,* so in the day of the Lord, the wicked shall be cut asunder, Mat. xxiv., 37. The thief comes with *weapons,* so Christ comes in flames of fire, 2 Thes. v., 7—8; and he comes *unexpectedly* like as in the days of Noah, Mat. xxiv., 37; all will be confusion; they will call on the rocks to cover them, Rev. vi., 16, 17. The thief comes with *wicked intent,* Christ, on the other hand, to punish injustice, and deliver his people; the thief's coming may be prevented, but the day of the Lord *will* come, 2 Pet. iii., 10. The thief injures a few; Christ executes judgment on all.

(201) THE TONGUE SETS ON FIRE THE WHEEL OF NATURE.
Jas. iii., 6.

"This course of nature," means the *wheel* of nature; and refers to a wheel catching fire from its rapid motion, spreading its flames around, and so destroying the whole machine. The tongue sets on fire the wheel of human life, and thus destroys the whole life. So Korah's party, speaking evil of dignities, were punished, Num. xvi., 1, iii., 31—34.

This figure shows us that as the rapid movement of the wheel will set it on fire, if not carefully greased or oiled to prevent friction or hard rubbing, so will the words of the tongue inflame the mind, and burn up the whole body with fever, and the whole heart with anger, if the oil of love and humility be not applied. The wild birds, the fierce beasts, the angry serpents have been tamed; but the tongue has always been an evil to the world, and full of deadly poison. With the tongue, people bless and curse, and some do both with the same tongue. And those that quarrel and rage, and rave, are in very great danger of being "set on fire of hell;" for there have been many instances where quarrelling has ended in fighting, and fighting in killing, as with Cain, and so, "Behold how great a matter a little fire kindleth!" Jesus Christ was never angry but at sin. He was "meek and lowly of heart;" and even when he was treated in the most cruel manner, for no cause whatever, and mocked, and scourged, and spit upon and crucified, he prayed for his enemies, "Father, forgive them;" like a sheep before her shearers he was dumb.

---

(202) CHRIST'S KINGDOM IMMOVABLE.
Heb. xii., 28.

Christ's friends are heirs of a kingdom, but not of this *world*, where every thing is so uncertain. Christ said his kingdom was not of this world. This kingdom differs from earthly kingdoms in—

1. Its *throne is stable* : a throne is a great object of human ambition, yet like a *high tree* yields soonest to the storm, Job xii., 21, as we see in the Mogul, Mahratta, Portuguese, Sikh kingdoms in India, but in heaven " the Lord reigneth." Christ once took the form of a servant, " but he is now highly exalted," with the *ancient days of* God the Father; he has an everlasting dominion, Dan. iv., 34.

2. Its *constitution unalterable, i.e.*, these fundamental ordinances which determine the form of government. Christ's is an absolute monarchy, but it is the rule of absolute wisdom, goodness, and truth ; a change of earthly government upsets men's minds, but Christ's kingdom is stable.

3. Its *laws immutable*: *Persian laws* were so, but many were bad ; *interpretations* vary, but the Bible laws are in their essence in ten *precepts* and two *golden* rules ; human laws are repealed, and others are substituted, but God's law the same ; it is not " the glorious uncertainty of the law" as with human laws.

4. Its *privileges inviolable* " life that never ends," secured *property*, " an inheritance incorruptible," *liberty* " from the bondage of corruption," " the son makes free." Every Englishman's *house is his castle*, but the believer's abode is more so ; he dwells under the shadow of the blood of sprinkling. Every Englishman has the right to be tried by his peers ; Christians have a divine advocate ; every Englishman has the privilege of *habeas corpus*, but " who shall lay anything to the charge of God's elect," Rom. viii., 33. All in this kingdom are *brethren* ; all *things* are yours—the true *equality*—all raised to be *kings* and *priests*.

5. Its *prosperity imperishable* ; *wealth* takes wings ; all the old empires have perished ; weather and disease blast the best expectations ; to the believer *all things* shall work together for good ; the *poor* of this world are rich in faith.

6. Its *duration eternal* : *Egypt, Babylon, Greece, Rome* all decayed. *David's stem* buried in the rubbish of a carpenter's shop, but *Christ's kingdom* is eternal, not supported by human ambition or an arm of flesh. "The kingdom of this world will become the kingdom of our God." Christ will be "king of kings."

---

(203) CHRIST A FRIEND.
John xv., 15.

Friendship implies *sympathy*: such Job's friends showed not, but Christ is touched with a feeling of our infirmities. *Union*: can two walk together unless they be agreed? Saul and Jonathan had their hearts knit, 1 Sam. xxviii., 4, so Christ to his people, Eph. ii., 14—16. *Love:* the offspring of desire; Christ loves to the end, and has peculiar knowledge the fuel for this love, Jon. x., 27; but the love of Christ passes knowledge. *Intercourse:* Christ is said to sup with the believer, Rev. iii., 20. John lay on Christ's bosom, Jon. xiii., 23. *Secrets* are made known, so Abraham, the friend of God, found, Gen. xviii., 17; Christ was a great friend to Lazarus and the Bethany family, Jon. xiii., 23, xx., 2, xxi., 7—2.

Christ's friendship thus differs from earthly friendship —it is never broken up—formed with useless persons —Christ forsakes not in adversity, and lays down his life—no king a friend to a beggar; Christ the companion of publicans and sinners—no time or circumstances change it—always able as well as willing; as shewn in Dorcas and Lazarus's case.

---

(204) REDEEMING THE TIME.
Eph. v., 16.

The English say time and tide wait for no man, and the Bengalis say, there is no hand to catch time. When the rice rises in the pot quick, quick, quick; in hell they know the worth of time; the sinner's to-morrow will never come; Jerusalem had its time, but it knew it not, Luk. xix., 42; a Jewish rabbi, asked when a man should repent, said one day before his death. Christ came in the fullness of time, Gal. iv., 4; and our times are in God's hands, Ps. xxxi., 15. The text treats of laying up time as a thing of value, such as the dying who know the preciousness of time. Solomon says, Ecc. iii., 3—7; there is a time to break down such as happened to the walls of Jerusalem, 2 Kings, xxv., 4—15; there is only one building eternal, 2 Cor. v., 1; there is a time to cast away stones as memorials, Gen. 30, Jos. iv., 1—9; so Paul threw things over board in the shipwreck, Acts xxvii., 38.

Time brings changes, thus one man who in the morning was worshipped, in the evening was hung up as food for crows, Esth. iv., 12, vii., 1—10; one great king became mad, Dan. iv., 30; see the fate of a king in the midst of a feast, Dan. v., 30.

(205) God a Builder.

Heb. xi., 10.

A good builder must be clever to *plan*, so known to God are all his works; there was the pattern on the mount; he lays a *good foundation*, so God laid the pillars of the earth; man's foundation, as is frequently seen in India, has often bad materials in it; employ, a variety of *workmen*, so God has seven orders of angels; men, nature, the firmament are in his hands, Ps. xix., A *variety* of work—God made the fountains of the great deep, the windows of heaven, hell the prison, and paradise the garden; he tells the number of the stars.

Earthly builders are mortal; limited in knowledge; build for others; improve in their plans; require materials for a building. The *Telegus* compare one who uses bad agents to one scratching his head with a fire brand, but God can make the wrath of men to praise him.

(206) Hell is outer Darkness.
Mat. viii., 12.

Heaven is compared to a banquet in which amid blazing lights chosen guests sit down, but hell is the cellar outside all in darkness; this implies *terror* as in Egypt, Ex. x., 21; *separation* from good people, they stumble and wander, Is. iix., 9., 10; evil deeds in secret are called chambers of imagery, Ez. viii., 12.

Hell is the blackness of darkness; in earth there may be some light; in hell none natural, artificial, or spiritual; in earth some comfort; in hell none.

---

(207) A false Witness a Mall, a Sword, and a sharp Arrow.
Prov. xxv., 18.

The slanderer wounds three at once—himself, him he speaks of, and him that hears. If we cannot stop other's mouths, let us stop our own ears. As soon as a person takes pleasure in hearing slander, he is to be ranked in the number of slanderers. By the approbation of evil we become guilty of it. The witnesses against Naboth showed that a false witness is, in some respects, as bad as a murderer, 1 Kings xxi., 13.

In the case of the two false witnesses against our Lord the words were true, the evidence false, while they reported the words, they misreported the sense, and thus swore a true falsehood, and were truly forsworn, Mat. xxvi., 60, 61. So the witnesses against Stephen, Acts vi., 13, 14, Pro. xii., 17. In these two last instances it was not by direct falsehood, but by a partial statement of truth, that they involved themselves in the murder of the innocent; such were the masters of the damsel possessed with a spirit of divination, Acts xvi., 21.

(208) The Eye that Mocks Parents Eaten by the Crows.

Prov. xxx., 17.

It was a common and much dreaded punishment to expose in the open fields the corpses of malefactors to be devoured by wild animals; the eye is the first part eaten by birds of prey. Moses commanded that a rebellious son should be stoned to death, Dt. xxi., 18.

---

(209) The Straight Gate and Narrow Way to Eternal Life.

Mat. vii., 12.

The *Katha Upanishad* of the *Yajur Veda* states, the way to the knowledge of God is considered by wise men difficult, as the passage over the sharp edge of a razor. Though the way to heaven does not allow the unclean or lions to pass on it, the way-faring man though a fool may find it; it is not like the broad way crowded or on an inclined plane, or easy like a boat going with the tide or ending abruptly as Sodom did in brimstone; the way of transgressors is hard, as Samson found, Judg. xvi., 16, and Saul, 1 Sam. xvi.; 14, so the licentious experience, Pr. ii., 18, v., 11; Josiah found the way that seemed right to him ended in death; the way of life goes to the eternal city; the broad way has many on it, and is easy.

Paul uses a *door opened* to devote the free exercise of the Gospel, 1 Cor. xvi., 9. Christ calls himself the *door of the* fold, John x., 9. In Joshua ii., 15, the valley of Achor is called a *door of hope,* for immediately after the execution of Achen there God said to Joshua fear not. A gate or door is a passage to a city or house. Hezekiah spoke of his going to the gates of the grave, Is. xxxviii., 10. Mordecai sat at the king's gate as a Magistrate sat at the gates of the city. Cities had high walls, so the gate was the only entrance.

(210) Heaven our Father's House.
John xiv., 2.

Allusion to the *temple of Jerusalem* where God dwelt, 1 Kings viii., 10, 11, with many chambers for priests and Levites. King's palace have many rooms. The *Vatican*, the Pope's residence, has 4,000 chambers.

In this world we are only *pilgrims*; heaven is our home. Heaven is represented under the emblems of "a better *country*," "*a paradise*" without any serpent, "*a city*" paved with gold, "a *palace*;" but "home" is an emblem familiar to all—all can understand the "*father's house.*"

1. *Place of birth—earliest recollections*: early recollections, like the *tamarind* roots not easily pulled up, cling to the memory, so *heaven* to the believer; he is "*born* from above." *Jerusalem*, the mother of us all, "light from heaven first illumined him," hence he seeks the things above; his religious affections fixed on an unseen world.

2. *Residence of our best friends*, our family, and the old servants attract us to it, so heaven the residence of the father of mercies, of "Christ, our eldest brother," the spirits of just men made perfect "our younger brethren" besides ministering spirits. No family contentions there; the father of lights there without variableness.

3. *Source of sweetest comforts*: the child found in clothes and education, the prodigal son thought of his father's house, so the Christian has *bread* from heaven and the *water* of life they shall go no more out; "the lamb shall feed them."

4. *Security*: a father's house a sure refuge; "no plague comes nigh our dwelling," Ps. 91; "no lion shall be there." "Under the shadow of the wings of Almighty."

5. Habitation to which a *right is claimed*: the child considers the father's things "ours," my father, your father. Though here we may not have where to lay our head "in heaven, a building of God."

6. *Free of care*: children have no anxiety to provide for the family; "they shall enter into peace." They shall sit down with Abraham, Isaac, and Jacob.

7. Enjoyments regarded as *permanent*: in after year's neither time nor distance destroys the link. "Oh! Absalom my son, my son," said David, and the father made merry for the prodigal son's return.

The earthly father's house often *desolate* after years, but Christ the "same yesterday and for ever." Jacob vowed obedience to God, if he would restore him to his father's *house*; earthly abode a shifting one, small in tents; the heaven has *many* mansions, the "palace of the great king," "if children the heirs." David said, "Though father or mother forsake me," believers, though here wandering in dens and caves, Heb. 11, "shall sit with Christ on his throne," "as one whom his mother comforted, so will God." "Forget thy father's house," *i.e.*, the earthly.

---

(211) Rend your Hearts and not your Garments by Repentance.

Joel. ii., 13.

The Russians have a proverb people sometimes sin like David, but do not sorrow like him, 2 Sam. xii., 13. The tear of repentance is dropped from the eye of faith; repentance consists in attrition, as when a rock is broken in pieces and in contrition, as when ice is melted in water; the former is the work of the law, the latter of the Gospel—the one is like a hammer, the other like dew. Ice must not only be broken, but melted, so the coldness must be taken out of the heart. False repentance is the sudden torrent after rain in the mountains; the true is the streams flowing from a living fountain; false repentance is like people who throw their goods over in a storm, and wish for them again in a calm.

Rending the garment a sign of grief, as in Reuben's case, Gen. xxxvii., 29, David's, 2 Job. i., 20.

Examples of true repentance in rending the heart in Manasseh, 2 Chr. xxxiii., 12, 13, Nineveh, Jonah iii., 5—8, Peter, Mat. xxvi., 75, the thief on the cross, Luk. xxiii., 40, 41. Examples of false repentance in Saul, 1 Sam. xv., 24—30, Ahab, 1 Kings xxi., 27—29, Judas, Mat. xxvii., 3—5.

---

(212) CHRIST AN ALTAR FOR BELIEVERS.
Heb. xiii., 10.

Christ's sacrifice for his people was like an altar—(1) All even the most polluted might *approach* it. Christ was also the brazen serpent on high, John iii., 4; (2) Its horns or four corners a place of *refuge* for the guilty, Ez. xliii., 16, 1 Kings, i., 50, Ex. xxvii., 2; (3) The altar the only place for sacrifice, so prayer can be offered only through Christ's mediation, Heb. ix., 27; (4) The *incense* for it beaten and prepared, so prayers must be from an humble spirit, Ps. xli., 2; no strange incense allowed to be offered; incense to be offered morning and evening, so special prayer then; (5) The altar was sprinkled with *blood* once a year, so Christ was once offered; (6) *Fire* was necessary to kindle the incense, so the Holy Spirit's influence is requisite.

---

(213) THE RIGHTEOUS GROAN IN THE TABERNACLE OF THE BODY.

2 *Cor.* v., 4.

The soul dwells in the body as in a tent which is easily taken down, and made of frail materials that flood or fire soon destroys; the body soon returns to dust.

> The soul's dark cottage battered and decayed
> Lets in new light through chinks which time has made.

Few care to ornament a tent as they are but a short time in it; it is crazy and leaky in bad weather, so disease makes the body.

It is better to groan for a while in this tabernacle than for ever under God's vengeance; the tears from groaning God puts in his bottle. This groaning arises from the burthen of the *body*, which hinders the soul rising on eagle's wings from *Satan's* temptations, 1 Pet. i., 6; bad *company*, Gen. xlix 16; *afflictions*, Ps. xlii., 7; *in dwelling* sin, Rom. vii., 24; *creation* itself groans, being under a curse for sin, Rom. viii., 22.

(214) THE WORD OF GOD THE SWORD OF THE SPIRIT.

Eph. vi., 17.

There are two words of God, one written on paper—the Bible, the other written by the Spirit on the heart. Christ is called the word of God as being the eternal son.

The Bible is compared to—a *letter* from the father of mercies to his children at school—a *banquet* where all are invited—a *prism* which only glistens when in the light—a *portrait* of an absent friend—a *storehouse* of spiritual weapons—a *telescope* revealing the glories of the upper world. David compares it to silver tried in a furnace of earth seven times refined, Ps. xii., 6.

(215) THE CHRISTIANS OLD AGE AN UNSETTING SUN.

Is. xx. 19, 20.

The righteous dying sets like the sun to our part of creation, but it is only to rise amid glowing clouds and a clear blue sky in another region; but even when setting his light lingers and the western clouds are bright with his beams. Even the twilight is beautiful, so that though dead he yet speaks—at even tide it shall be light. The Hindu writings state, on the other hand, that old age is like a dried up stream, fallen as a tree levelled by thunder, dreaded as a house in ruin; it takes away vigor as if a man were placed in a marsh. Very different is the Bible view, for Solomon compares the path of the just to the light shining more and more to the perfect day, though the morning might be cloudy and stormy; such were Simeon, Luk. ii., 28—32, Peter, 2 Pet. i., 3, 11—16; they were not like the wicked *driven away* in his wickedness.

As the *Aloe* is green and well liking, till the last best summer of its age,
And then hangeth out its golden bells to mingle glory with corruption,
As the *Meteor* travelleth in splendor, but bursteth in dazzling light;
Such is the end of the righteous; their death is the sun at its setting.

(216) Believers are Kings.

Believers are like kings occupied with *high* things, Ph. iii., 20; shall *rule* the kingdoms of this world, when they become the kingdom of God, Rev. xi., 15; the saints shall rule, Dan. ix., 27, highly *honored*; high *born* Christians born from above, 1 John iii., 1; well *attended*; angels their servants; crowned, 2 Tim. iii., 8.

Chanakya says a learned man and a king are not on an equality; the king is honored only in his own country, the learned everywhere. Death is called in the Bible the king of terrors, Job xviii., 14, as the alligator is called a king, Job xli., 34. The Turks are considered by some the kings of the East, Rev. xvi., 12.

Christ is called king of kings, while the church is styled his daughter all glorious within, Ps. lxv., 13. Christ is the only begotten son; the treasures of wisdom are hid in him, 1 Cor. i., 24; he was proclaimed by a star, and by the angels singing to the shepherds; his palace was the heaven of heavens; angels his attendants and ambassadors; all are his subjects, even the winds obey him, while heathens like Cyrus and Nabuchadnezzar work out his will.

(217) The Sacrifices of the Body and of Praise.

Rom. xii., 1.

Paul wished to be delivered from his body as from a putrefied corpse fastened to him, and yet this vile body is to be used in God's service, but the sacrifices to God are a broken spirit. Sacrifice was the immediate commerce of a creature with its God in which the Lord of all condescended to receive offerings at our hands. Paul in this view offered his body as a sacrifice, and he was beheaded, 2 Tim. iv., 6. We are to offer the meat-offering of charitable distributions, the drink-offering of penitent tears, the hen-offering of prayer, the peace-offering of praise, and the whole burnt-offering of concupiscence. The priests before offering sacrifices must be washed, anointed, and put on white garments; they must have clean hands, Job. ix., 17, so must we spiritually. The sacrifice was not to be offered with strange fire; Nadab and Abihu were killed for doing so; neither were the blind to be offered, Mal. li., 8.

(218) CHRIST RISING AS THE SUN WITH HEALING ON HIS WINGS.

Mat. iv., 2.

In the *Vedas* the sun is called ray-diffuser, deep quivering, life-bestowing, golden-handed, the eye of the universe, the soul of all that moves.

In Judea every morning about sunrise a fresh breeze of air blows from the sea across the land, from its utility in clearing the infected air, it is called the doctor; this salubrious breeze, which attends the rising of the sun, may be considered the wings of the sun. Christ is the one mediator, the sun of our system; he is the eye of the world, gives light to all, drives away gloom; like the sun he operates differently, hardens clay, and softens wax, eclipses the light of the stars by his own. Flowers as the tulip and marigold open to the solar, so do believers' hearts to Christ's beams.

Sick or delicate people generally feel worse during night when the sun ceases to shine; the morning dawn often revives them after a bad night. All the candles in the world put together could not give the light of day; it can come only from the sun; so with human intelligence compared to Christ.

(219) The Devils in ever-lasting Chains of Darkness.

Jude. 3.

Chains signify the degradation of the devils; they are—(1) marks of *bondage*, as Paul wore them before Felix, Acts xxvi., 24; pride compassed the wicked as a chain, Ps. lxxiii., 6, while love is to the good, the bond of perfectness, Col. iii., 14; (2) *heavy*, 1 Kings xii., 10; Peter was fastened with two chains to prevent his escape, Acts xii., 6; (3) subject of *reproach*, 2 Tim. i., 6, Acts xxvi., 29. The devils are banished from the presence of God, the light of heaven, and now in their dungeon, lead a more cruel captivity than the Jews did in Egypt.

(220) The safe Guide.

Ps. xlviii., 14.

A guide is necessary in a strange place; the world is a wilderness where there are no roads, few wells, storms of sand arise, and the dread of robbers. We have to die alone, but Christ has gone before; Christ and his angels, are safe guides, and relieve the dreariness of the road; the disciple's hearts burned within them going to Emmaus; Stephen and Jacob dying had the eye of faith opened; Christ's death threw a light on the tomb's darkness, shewing the king in his beauty and the land very far off. Christ has the keys of death and hell; hence the believer will not be afraid at the swellings of Jordan. Christ like Joseph will introduce his brethren to the new country; he, who bore the sheep through the wilderness, will not desert them in the fold.

(221) The Holy Spirit's Influence like Oil.
Ps. xxiii., 5.

The Holy Spirit's influence is like oil in its effects; in —*softening*, hard tumors are mollified, so the swellings of pride; *healing*, draws the bad humors out, so the wounded traveller had oil poured into his wounds, Luk. x., 14; the sick were anointed with oil, Jas. v., 14; *refreshing*, used in banquets, and called the oil of joy, made a person *active*; hence wrestlers and warriors used it for their limbs, makes the face to *shine*. Stephen's face shone like that of an *angel*, Acts vi.

Men were appointed to office by anointing with oil; in this way Saul was made king, 1 Sam. x., 1. Christ was anointed to heal the broken-hearted, Luk. iv., 18, hence his name. Cyrus, though a heathen, was called God's anointed, Is. xlv., 1.

Christ's name is compared to ointment poured forth in its *preciousness*, Mat. xxvi., 7, *fragrance*. *Brotherly love is* compared, Ps. cxxiii., 2, to oil in its qualities of softening, making supple, fragrant, healing, precious, poured forth.

---

(222) Christ a Root out of a Dry Ground.
Is. liii., 2.

Christ was called the root, and yet the offspring of David, Rev. xxii., 19; David's lord, and yet his son, the branch as well as the root. Christ in relation to believers is a root—(*a*) the origin of the trunk and branches; he diffuses life which is often in the root when the branches are dead; (*b*) *hidden* under the earth, so Christ's divinity veiled in flesh; (*c*) keeps the tree *firm* in storms; in New Zealand there are trees 300 feet high which would be blown down, were it not for the roots; (*d*) draws *nourishment*, for the tree by sending suckers into the soil which spread laterally to get food.

Christ's root was in a dry ground, *i.e.*, his person was ugly, Is. lii., 14, liii., 2. God thus rebukes the pride of beauty. Christ took the form of a servant, so Paul's appearance was mean, 2 Cor. x., i.

(223) The Sting of Death Sin.
1 *Cor.* xv., 56.

There are various stings those of a nettle, a wasp, an asp, a bee—all infuse poison quickly and sharply, give pain, and are dreaded beforehand, so the devil is the old serpent who infuses the poison of his sting into afflictions and death; while Christ is the brazen serpent looking to whom the wounds are healed; the death of the righteous is called a sleep, or rest; no sting in death was felt by Jacob, Gen. xlix. 18, Joseph, l., 24, David, 2 Sam. xxiii., 5.

(224) Love as Coals of Fire on an Enemy's Head.
Pr. xxv., 21, 22.

Metal is difficult to melt even placed on the top of a fire of burning coals; it may be placed at the sides, still no melting, but put the coals on the top or head of the vessel, and the metal soon flows down in a stream; so your enemy's hostility to you may be softened by kindness in every way, as fire to the metal, so kindness to an enemy. Christ prayed for his murderers.

(225) Crucifying the Flesh.
Gal. v., 24.

The mark of a living Christianity is not mere baptism, but crucifying the flesh; they, who take Christ as their prophet, priest, and king, mortify the flesh—the flesh is the fuel, and lust the flame thereof. God made the soul pure, but coming into the body like water into a dirty sewer, it becomes filthy or fleshy; the body like a snail's shell always accompanies the spirit, and death alone releases the soul from its cage.

Crucifixion caused *death*, so believers die to sin. Paul said, however, he was crucified, yet he lived, Gal. ii., 20, Ph. iii., 10; the old man is crucified, Rev. vi., 6; sin must be killed, not wounded like a serpent; crucifixion was a *violent death*, sin must be fought against fully, a *painful* bitter *death*; the body in crucifixion hung on a post, the nails piercing through the hands and feet, hence a stupifying draught was given to stop the pain arising from all the joints being stretched; *a shameful death* inflicted on slaves and malefactors.

Our bodies are called temples of the Holy Ghost, 1 Cor. vi., 19, and as a temple are to be kept clean.

---

(226) THE PURE IN HEART SHALL SEE GOD.
Mat. v., 2.

The Hindus express by *darshan* the privilege after a long pilgrimage of seeing the idol. Our knowledge of God in heaven is expressed by seeing, because sight is *(a)* the *clearest* of the other senses, as light is given, so our knowledge comes from God; *(b)* the sense most *universally* exercised; *(c) pleasant*, Ecc. xi., 7, seeing a friend is very different from hearing about him, the eye is the window of the soul; *(d)* the most *comprehensive*; the eye is never satisfied with seeing.

Dirt loves not a sunbeam, nor the impure to see God, Gen. iii. 8, iv., 14. Moses saw God through Christ, Num. xxii., 8, so Jacob, Gen. xxxii., 30. Believers while pure walk in the light of God's countenance; like the moon dark when away from the sun; bright when facing it.

---

(227) THE LORD THE STAY OF THE RIGHTEOUS.
2 Sam. xxii., 19.

A house or wall is tottering, a beam of wind stays it up, so are the ropes to a ship, so creeping plants, like the betle-palm, unable to stand upright, cling by their tendrils to some stick which becomes their stay; similarly the soul clings to Christ by the tendrils of faith.

---

(228) God has his People graven on the Palms of his Hands.

Is. xl., 15, 16.

God says a mother may forget her sucking child, but He will not forget his people, Is. ixl. 15; as they are not impressed on the surface as writing, but cut in or graven as with a pen of stone or iron; the writing on which is not rubbed out like ink or palm leaves, but remains like the impression of the style on *ola* leaves, God's having his people on the palms of the hands, means their being in a secure place, and one easily observed by the individual.

---

(229) Christ's Yoke easy and his Burthen light.

Mat. xi., 28—30.

Asses or oxen are yoked or harnessed to a cart; sometimes this yoke is heavy, and the burthen of the cart falls on the neck which becomes chafed; the animal is, however, the property of the owner who does what he likes. Men are under the yoke of Satan; they are slaves, and Christ comes with the ransom money. Bullocks often, though well-fed, do not like to submit to the yoke, and kick against it, but must at last submit, so the sinner must bridle his tongue and passions; he must not be stiff-necked.

---

(230) The Believer rescued from a horrible Pit.

Ps. xl., 2.

This text alludes to the custom of digging pits to catch wild beasts, and covering them with straw or dust, or such like things that they might not be discerned.

The Psalmist in this, as in some other passages of his writings, means by digging a pit to express the mischievous designs of the wicked, who, in trying to do him harm by their subtlety, treated him as men did wild beasts which they endeavoured to catch.

"Pit" also signifies the *grave*, and the Psalmist expresses the despair he should be in, if God slighted him. He should become as a dead man, lost and undone. Nothing is so painful to a gracious soul as the want of God's favour and the sense of his displeasure. His frowns are worse than death and the grave. "Pit" also means *trouble*. Despondency of spirit under the sense of God's withdrawings, and prevailing doubts and fears about our eternal state, are like unto a horrible pit and miry clay. David found himself sinking more and more into inward disquiet and perplexity of spirit, out of which he could not work himself. *Hell* is also called "the bottomless pit," because there is no possibility of ever escaping from it, a pit too deep for any one ever to get the sufferer out. Joseph was cast into a pit by his envious brethren, where they would have left him to perish, if Juda had not interposed on his behalf, Gen. xxxvii.

(231) GOD OUR REFUGE.
Ps. xvii., 1.

God is a hiding place and a strong tower. But the name "refuge" has a very particular meaning. If any Israelite killed a man by accident, God told Moses that he must not be treated as a murderer, because he did not design to murder. But, lest the kinsman or relation of the person killed should take away the life of the manslayer, which was allowed to be done in the case of murder, he was to hurry off with all speed out of his way, and to take refuge in one of the six cities appointed for the protection of such persons. These cities were well supplied with water, and they had plenty of provisions, so that there was no occasion to go out of them to buy which would endanger the manslayer. The roads to these places were all plain and easy of access, kept in good order, and provided, wherever it was necessary, with bridges to cross streams of water, and wherever two roads met, there were hand-posts pointing to the proper direction, on which was written in large characters, so that it might easily be read, " Refuge, Refuge." So God is our refuge, to whom we may flee in distress, as the manslayer did to the city of refuge.

(232) All Flesh is Grass.
Is. xl., 6.

What is more frail than grass? It comes up in the spring, flourishes for a short period, and is then cut down; or, if not severed from its root by the scythe, it soon withers away. In India especially the great heat of the sun quickly withers away the grass; in the North-West Provinces, the grass becomes quite brown, or disappears in the hot weather. So weak are we, and so unable to resist the stroke of death. We come up, and are cut down! The spring-time of life is soon gone, the season of harvest comes, and death strikes the fatal blow. Nothing can make man a solid substantial being, but the being born again of the incorruptible seed, the word of God, which will transform him into an excellent creature, whose glory will not fade like the flower, but shine like an angel's face.

(233) Christ a Well of Water.
John iv., 14.

These words were uttered by Christ when wearied and thirsty in the heat of the day; he drank well-water received from a Samaritan woman—a pariah. Wells were greatly valued in deserts, and the march of caravans was regulated by the wells; we see Lot's and Abraham's herdsmen strove about the possession of a well, Gen. xxvi., 15. But wells often dry up, or are filled up with sand. Christ is the same yesterday, to-day, and for ever; his grace ever flowing comes like the rain from heaven on the mown grass.

---

(234) BELIEVERS AS BRANDS PLUCKED FROM THE FIRE.

Zech. iii., 9.

The fire is already blackening and scorching the brand; but there is yet time to snatch it from the flame, and to save it for some nobler use. Linger not, but seize it, ere too late. Another minute, and you could not have plucked it from the fire. It bears the marks of the peril from which it has been scarcely saved; but having thus far concerned yourself to preserve it, you will not lightly throw it back again into the flame. When the Jews were brought back from Babylon, the prophet Zechariah in a vision saw Joshua, the high priest, standing, as a representative of the Jewish Church, before the angel of the Lord, and Satan standing at his right hand to resist' him. "And the Lord said unto Satan, the Lord rebuke thee, O! Satan; even the Lord that hath chosen Jerusalem rebuke thee; is not this a brand plucked out of the fire?" The Jewish Church, at that time of recent deliverance, had many marks of sin as well as of suffering; and Satan was ready to take advantage of whatever spots and blemishes he could find in her. But God had not released his Church from her long captivity, in order to deliver her to the malice of a more cruel enemy than the king of Babylon. She was a brand plucked out of this fire, and bore indeed the marks of that scorching flame; but God had not plucked out the brand only to cast it into a yet fiercer furnace. The Apostle Judas bid us, "save others with fear, pulling them out of the fire." Each of us is as a brand plucked out of the fire; and it is owing to the distinguishing mercy of God that we were not left in the guilt of original sin, or were not left to perish in our sin's fuel for hell-fire. How many who seemed perhaps less guilty than ourselves have been cut off, while we have hitherto been spared! And which of us does not bear the scars of those wounds which we have received, while doing the deeds of Satan?

(235) THE SWALLOW KNOWS HER TIME, NOT SO THE IGNORANT.
Jer. viii., 7.

The swallow is a bird of passage. What was it that skimmed over the stream, where the ripples are so bright in the morning sunshine? It was the first swallow of the returning spring. It has come back in its season—the spring and summer—nor will it leave again till the leaves, which in spring burst from their buds, are withered and falling. When cold and winter are coming in the winter, the swallows often remain in a torpid state in the holes of walls or the banks of rivers. The swallow, like the Indian adjutant, is true to the divine law which concerns its return and its departure. It knows the time to come and the time to go, and neither loses the summer pleasantness by delaying its return, nor runs the risk of suffering from the winter frost by prolonging its stay too late. How many do not begin the work of salvation till summer is over, and the winter of life is well-nigh at hand; when, if they work at all, they work with every disadvantage!

(236) THE GOSPEL IS A NET AND A PLOUGH.
Luk. ix., 62, Mat. iv., 18—20.

As the sea is a frequent type or emblem of the world, so "the fishes of the sea," which take their course at will, and so often prey upon one another throughout that waste of waters, represent the vast numbers who know not God, and walk in the way of their own hearts, without any sure guide or rule of conduct, and too often, only envying and provoking, hating and devouring, one another. Into this broad sea of the whole world a net was to be cast; and instead of their lowly labours on the little sea of Galilee, the Apostles were to be employed in gathering men out of every clime and country into the Church of God, and in drawing them under the blessed restraints and holy discipline of "the obedience of faith." A net will indeed gather of every kind, and when it is drawn to the shore, a separation is made of the fishes which are worth the pains of taking out of the sea, and of such as are nothing worth, and may be cast away. Thus we are reminded, that among those who are gathered into the visible Church of Christ, there "are good and bad," many false professors as well as sincere servants of God; nor will the good be separated from the bad until the net is drawn completely to the shore, which will not be till the end of the world. The fish whether big or little are taken out of the sea of this world, a stormy place full of rocks, subject to tempests.

Divinely applied to our heart, the Gospel not only a net but a plough, breaks up the fallow ground, tears up the roots of corruption, and prepares us for receiving the good seed of grace. How proper for its operation, the winter of adversity, and spring-tide of youth! How necessary that every application be attended with the dewy influence of the Holy Spirit!

---

(237) CHRIST THE LILY OF THE VALLEY.
Cant. ii., 1.

Christ is compared to a lily among thorns, like a lily he is *fragrant*, Gen. viii., 20, *white* and *pure*, Rev. xix., 8, *fruitful*, not destroyed by the snow of persecution, *beautiful*, like a lily among thorns. Sadi compares an amiable youth to a white lily in a bed of nercissuses.

The simple beauty of the lilies drew on them their Creator's approving notice, when, in the days of his flesh, he went in and out among men, and was himself capable of being soothed by the works which he made so fair and pleasant for the children of men. Those sweet and lovely flowers were then as unreprovable in his sight as in the day when he first " saw that they were good." Man, for whose delight and solace they were made, was now sinful and fallen ; but the handiwork of God in these his humbler creatures, was still such as he could behold with complacency. "They toil not, neither do they spin ;" the bright clothing, which it is so pleasant to behold, is furnished for them without any task imposed on them of painful labour ; and they close their flowers at night without any anxious care, lest the kindly shower or the genial sun should fail them on the morrow.

Our Saviour does not mean to discourage the toils of honest industry and wise foresight, or obedience to the law which is laid on all of us, "Six days shalt thou labour ;" but he means, that in these innocent "flowers of the field," we should see an emblem of those who are "without carefulness ;" and who, having diligently done "whatever their hands find to do," are enabled to trust God for the result.

(238) CHRIST THE SURE FOUNDATION.
Is. xxviii., 16.

A *mansion* is required with an estate to enjoy it and superintend, so "God's *tabernacle*" with his people. *God's Church* is compared to a building, as the temple was the visible residence of God. "Ye are the temple of God."

A building must—

1. Have a regular and *orderly erection*, the rule of *architecture* applied to its building, so Israel's Church was " according to the *pattern* shown in the mount." Sin breaks up the harmony of society, grace *unites* in a Church, " God is not the author of confusion." "That he *might gather together* in one all things." On the *regularity* of a building depends much of its strength, so "the unity of the spirit in the bond of peace,"

how symmetrical was *Solomon's temple*, so the spiritual one, "the *whole building* fully framed."

2. Be erected on a *solid foundation*. Christ is the "*rock* of ages," "the foundation of *Apostles and prophets*, Christ being the chief *corner-stone*" as well as the foundation. Some build on the *sand* of self-righteousness, "God lays in Sion a tried stone, a precious corner-stone," Heb ii., 16.

3. Be composed of many *stones*. Every stone has *its place*, though there be many; some are polished as James, Cephas, John "pillars," some hidden, some form the *coping*, yet all on the foundation. Some houses are of turf or layers of brick or sandstone or marble, but God's houses are of *living stone*, 1 Pet. ii., 4; *pictures, statues* sometimes seem *alive*, but here the stones are *living, i.e.,* active.

4. Undergo *a great transformation*. Polished statuary and fine buildings are originally from the *quarry*, so believers were *encrusted* with fleshly lusts, sunk in the *mire* of spiritual corruption; so *Paul* the blasphemer preached the faith he once destroyed, "Look unto *the rock* whence ye were hewn."

5. Have *appropriate agency* in their transformation. Stones are *inactive* to raise themselves from the quarry; *scaffolding* and *masons* are required; so in *Solomon's* temple. Jews, Canaanites, Tyrians were employed; *Cyrus* was subsequently God's servant for its rebuilding; in the scaffolding of Solomon's temple no noise of axe or hammer hard.

6. Be *cemented in the strictest* way. Their *position* unites stones, but the best union is *cement*, the whole body composed of that which every joint supplieth, Eph. iv., 6; love is the *bond* of perfectness. Earthquakes may split the building without breaking the cement "who shall separate," Rom. viii., 35.

7. Be *formed into a complete habitation*, *vast* in extent and *ornamental*, "*a fount* for cleansing, *illuminated* by the seven spirits of God;" it has a *throne of*

grace. In Solomon's temple the vessels were of pure *gold*; this has holiness, "the beauty of believers," not yet *completed*, soon however the *copestone* will be brought out with the shouts of grace, grace. The Disciples said of the *old temple*, "Behold what manner of stones," but that was soon destroyed, not so this, its "foundations of sapphires." God is its *architect*; a *plan* is laid before the building was begun, so "chosen in Christ *before the foundation* of the world;" *taste* and *science* required for an *architect*; the Lord knows every stone in his temple; no *change* in place for 6,000 years it is going on. God the *builder* also, as he gave the *pattern* in the mount," so here. "Except the Lord build the house," "the stone the builders rejected," God the *owner* has given the site; believers are lively stones *purchased* with his own blood. "Then *much* people in this city believed." How *costly* Solomon's temple; it had never been built had not "gold been as stones in Jerusalem." *God the inhabitant*, the earth is his *footstool*, yet he dwells in this; it is his *jewel* house, his council house, his banqueting house, his place of rest. *Babylon* built as a monument of pride turned its builder mad.

David preferred being a *door-keeper* in God's house to dwelling in the tents of the wicked. The Christian conqueror promised to be a *pillar* in the heavenly temple.

---

(239) THE WICKED ARE WOLVES AND LOCUSTS.
Mat. x., 16.

Stephen, surrounded by the fierce Council, when they gnashed upon him with their teeth, stopped their ears, and ran upon him with one accord, although they had just before seen his face, as though it had been the face of an angel, was like Him who is brought as a lamb to the slaughter, and as a sheep before her shearers is dumb, so he opened not his mouth."

Wolves are fierce and cowardly near Agra; they often carry off children and devour them; they love to hunt in packs, are particularly fierce against sheep, fond of darkness, hence bad Judges were compared to evening wolves, Zeph. iii., 3.

The wicked are also called slaves of sin, Jon. viii., 34, dry bones, Ez. xxxvii., and are compared to locusts as being cunning, Pr. xxx., 24—27, voracious, rapid in movement, carried about by every wind, very numerous.

(240) Satan a Fowler.
Ps. xci., 3.

You sometimes see a fluttering of wings among the grass on a bank, which shows that some poor bird is taken in the snare, and is vainly struggling to be free. The snare was so skilfully set that the bird could see nothing of its danger, but flew into it unawares.

There is an enemy who is ever setting snares in our path—Satan; and the snares are those many false reasonings and vain seductions by which he misleads to their ruin, such as are unwary and unstable. To one he says, "Stolen waters are sweet, and bread eaten in secret is pleasant." Satan tried to sift Peter like wheat, Luk. xxii., 32, against some he sends fiery darts, Eph. vi., 16, with others he wrestles, Eph. vi., 11; Satan as a fowler is crafty, cruel, hunts and persecutes God's people, while the righteous are like the dove before the hawk. Satan in this respect is also called a goat from his mischievous propensities, while like the fowler he appears in disguise as an angel of light, 2 Cor. xi., 14; he is also for his destructiveness called the great Dragon, Rev. xx., 24.

(241) The Righteous a Tree planted by the Water Side.
Ps. i., 3.

The righteous are in another place compared to willows, which love the water, not like the cactus flowering in a desert; true Christians like a tree must have roots firmly fixed in Christ, the rock of ages draw sap from earth by the spongioles of faith and love, grow upwards and heavenwards, some are weak, some strong, so the centurion, Mat. viii., 10, the woman of Canaan, Mat. xv., 28, some are fruitful, so Dorcas, Acts ix., 36, and flourish like a tree exposed to all weathers.

How many do not begin the work of salvation till summer is well-nigh over, and the winter of life is nigh at hand, when, if they work at all, they work with every disadvantage!

---

(242) THE WILD GOAT ON THE MOUNTAINS PROTECTED, SO THE CHRISTIAN.

Ps. civ., 18.

How safely does the wild goat rest on the side of the precipitous mountain, or climb the dizzy height, where man's brain would turn, and his feet would inevitab'y slip! How freely and fearlessly does she leap from rock to rock! Her eye is as true, and her foot as sure upon the steep and slippery crag, as on some beaten road! God has fitted her for "the high hills," on which he has appointed her to live, and has endued her with those faculties of the foot and of the eye, which enable her, even in the darkest night, to walk on rocks and precipices where man could not tread securely under the noonday light.

The lesson taught is God's protecting Providence which tempers the wind to the shorn lamb; it is like *Jacob's ladder*, extending from heaven to earth, though God's way to us may be *in the sea, i.e.,* leaving no track; his acts are like *clouds*, which though black have the rain-bow from Christ, the sun of righteousness in them, or like wheels, of quick and easy motion, which, though wheels within wheels, are regulated by the main wheel.

(243) The Believer begotten to an Inheritance that fades not away.

1 *Pet.* i., 4.

Heaven is the inheritance of those who, by the new birth, belong to the Church of the first born, who get the blessing of the spiritual birthright. Esau was entitled only to the temporal one; the heirs are heads of the house, the prop of the family; believers are joint heirs with Christ, who is the heir of all things. The heir must be qualified to manage the estate properly, so believers are made partakers of the Divine nature, 2 Pet. i., 4; the proud God knoweth afar off; the estate is in proportion to the wealth of the donor. God is Lord of all. This inheritance is future, but is as certain as money in a good bank; here the heirs have little, but are like the Jews in the wilderness who had no house, yet called God their dwelling place. God's promises are a heritage, Ps. cxix., 11.

Earthly inheritances are small, limited in duration, unsatisfying, common to the wicked and good, often wasted as the prodigal son did his.

---

(244) Looking to Jesus.

Heb. xii., 2.

The wicked look to a fearful judgment day, believers for Christ's coming in the clouds, Ph. iii., 20. As the weary traveller at night looks for the morning star, so is Christ's advent regarded.

A man's looks often indicate his frame of mind; the eye is a mirror of the passions of the soul; it expresses like the tongue, joy, and grief, thus the look of a *dying husband* on his surviving wife or of a *drowning* man wishing aid.

Looking to Jesus implies—(1) *distinct knowledge*, Hos. iv., 5; (2) *eagerness for relief*, Ps. xxv., 15, Jonah ii., 4; (3) *humble dependance*, 2 Chr. xx., 12, Mic. iiv., 7; (4) *affection*, 2 Sam. xxiii., 5.

(245) Christ the first Fruits of them that slept.
1 *Cor.* xv., 20.

The first fruits of the harvest were the pledge of the whole, such was Christ's resurrection of ours, or as the *chatak* bird is of the rains, or the budding of flowers of spring; the body which called the worm its sister shall shine as the sun. The first fruits like the first born were esteemed the most valuable, hence the Canaanites caused their first-born to pass through the fire, in order to appease the anger of their deities; one of the *kings of Moab*, when in danger from enemies, offered up his eldest son, 2 Kings ii., 27. *Cain* brought to God the first fruits of the ground, as Abel did the firstlings of the flock, Gen. iv., 4; the Jews always did so, Nem. xviii., 12.

---

(246) Believers are Epistles of Christ not written with Ink.
2 *Cor.* iii., 3.

God's writing things *in a book* denotes his perfect knowledge, exact remembrance, and continued, just regard to them. His writing *bitter things* against one, signifies his gradual afflicting of him with severe and lasting troubles as he did Job. His writing *his law* in men's heart, and sealing them with his Spirit, imports his applying his word by his Spirit to their heart, that they may be conformed to his image and law, and comforted by his influence. His writing men's *names in heaven* in his book of life, with the living, with the righteous, imports his particular and fixed choice of them to obtain everlasting life. His writing his name *in their foreheads* imports his rendering them like him in holiness, and enabling them to make an open profession of his truth. His putting their tears into his bottle, and *marking them* in his book, imports his kind observation, and careful rewarding thereof.

(247) The right Hand of God dashes in Pieces his Enemies.
Ex. xv., 6.

God's *arms*, hands, his fingers denote Almighty power manifested in acts of sovereignty, justice, and grace. God is called the *head* of Christ, to him, as man and mediator, he is the undoubted superior, and it is his to support, rule, and direct him, as such. His *countenance* and face, when represented as set against any, denote the manifestation of his indignation and wrath; in other circumstances, they signify the discovery of his glory and grace. God's *eyes* import his knowledge, his care, and regard; but sometimes the display of his wrath. His *ears* denote his perfect knowledge, his exact observation, and favourable regard. His *nostrils* and nose signify his anger, his approbation, and his exact judgment. His *mouth* and lips denote his will, authority, and wrath. His *back* imports his anger and disregard. His *back parts* denote discoveries of his glory and goodness; but such as are scanty and obscure, in respect of our immediate vision of him face to face in heaven. His *right hand* in the text imports a signal display of his Almighty power, his love, mercy, or wrath. But as relating to the exalted station of Christ, it imports the highest power, authority, glory, and dignity. The *hollow of his hand* denotes his easy comprehension, protection, and support of all things. His *bowels* are his most ardent love, his tender mercy, and unbounded compassion. His *bosom* imports secrecy, safety, eminent nearness, amazing intimacy, and endeared love. His *feet* are the less glorious manifestations of his presence; the exercise of his power and providence, for the relief of his people and overthrow of his enemies.

Elymas the sorcerer was struck blind by God's hand, Acts xiii., 11. Hand denotes strength, thus Ishmael's hand as an Arab robber was against every man, Gen. xvi., 12. Christ sits at the Father's right hand, *i.e.*, the seat of power, Mat. xiv., 63. Pilate, washed his hands in Christ's case to denote his power, was used innocent, Mat. xxvii., 24. Persons were consecrated by the imposition of hands to denote spiritual power imparted, Gen. lxviii., 14—20, Num. xxvii., 8.

---

(248) THE WICKED ARE NAKED AND BLIND.

Rev. iii., 17.

All men return naked to mother earth, but the wicked even in life have a body full of putrefying sores with no covering of holiness.

They have no law-fulfilling righteousness to cover them before God, no inward grace, no holy conversation to adorn them, no spiritual armour to defend themselves from their foes. Hence, how perpetually exposed to the cold, the tempest, the stroke of divine wrath, to the stings of their own conscience, to the injuries of sin, of sinners, of devils, and death ! How shamefully the filthiness of their heart daily discovers itself in their practice ! How unfit for every holy duty for every honourable company ! They do not wish God to array them in fine linen, clean, and white, which is the righteousness of the saints !

The man in the tombs was naked ; the wicked are also blind ; they see not the light of life, discern not the sun of righteousness ; have no true knowledge of spiritual objects ; nothing is nearer them than God, his unspeakable gifts, and their own heart, yet nothing is less known. How oft they stumble and fall into sin without any proper cause! How constantly they wander out of their proper course, and mislead those who follow them! How useless is the clearest light of the Gospel to them!—hence they feed, Is. lxv., 20, on the wind, Hos. xii. 1, and on husks, Luk. lxv., 16. Diseased in every way the wicked have the *blindness* of ignorance, the *deafness* of spiritual unconcern, the *fever* of concupiscence, the *jaundice* of malice, the *swelling tympany* of pride, the *vertigo* of inconstancy, the *quinzy* of cursing and blasphemy, the *dropsy* of covetousness, the *palsy* of stupidity, the *pleurisy* of envy, the *rheumatism* of discontent, the *delirium* of constant levity, the moonstruck *madness* of passion and rage, hardness of heart, and the stings of conscience. By day or night God is infinite in his readiness to visit the distressed!—how He rides on cherubs, on wings of everlasting love to attend them! O! his infinite concern for the welfare of his patients! All of them, though poor and needy, he heals without money and without price.

(249) THE UNLEAVENED BREAD OF SINCERITY AND TRUTH.

1 *Cor.* v., 8.

Hypocrisy and malice are called leaven as being sour, and making other things sour, working secretly, puffing. Leaven also from its diffusive nature symbolised the rapid spread of the Gospel, Mat. xiii., 39.

Nathaniel was an example of sincerity, a man without leaven, Jon. i., 47, so was Paul, 2 Cor. xi., 12.

(250) The Shield of Faith.
Eph. vi., 16.

As the soul is the life of the body, faith is the life of the soul, and Christ the life of faith—faith is the master-wheel that sets the other wheels in motion. Faith is also compared to gold tried in the fire, 1, Pet. i., 7.

A shield was made of hides or even gold, so as to be proof against fiery darts; it was large, so as to defend the vital parts and moveable to protect the head, arms, and chest.

(251) Quench not the Spirit.
1 *Thes.* v., 19.

The Holy Spirit is compared to fire. How absolutely necessary in our cold earth! How powerfully it penetrates into, illuminates, warms, melts, softens, quickens, comforts, and purifies our heart, burns up our inward corruption, and conforms us to its own likeness.

(252) Walking with God.
Gen. v., 22.

Communion with God is represented by going up through the wilderness, leaving on the beloved, Cant. viii., 5. With hope and earnest desire to obtain the better country, Christians therein choose Jesus and his law for their way, and with pleasure proceed from one stage of grace, or act of holiness to another, till at length they appear before God in the heavenly Zion. Thus did Enoch walk with God, and he was not, for God took him.

ORIENTAL PROVERBS & SIMILIES.
ILLUSTRATING
HOLY WRIT.

Illustrations are valuable in every country as the nails to clench an argument, but especially in the East where even the most abstract metaphysical truths are dressed in the garb of metaphor. It has been well said "Arguments are the pillars of the temple of truth: illustrations are the windows to let in light."

The following illustrations are in addition to those used in explaining the emblems: in some cases the emblem has been referred to by a figure in brackets at the end of the proverb or by a quotation from scripture giving another emblem or example.

The Badagas whose Proverbs we give first are an aboriginal tribe in the Nilgheries; their proverbs have been collected by the Missionaries, we have not yet succeeded in getting the proverbs of the Koles, Gonds, Lepchas, Sonthals.

BADAGA PROVERBS.

1. If our silver is bad, why do we quarrel with the gold-smith? Eccl. 7: 29.
2. When he had nothing he was content; now that he is enriched, he is discontented. Eccl. 6: 9.
3. Do every thing at the proper season; some people lose the harvest of a whole year on account of a single meal. Mat. 25: 10. Eccl. 3: 1-8.
4. In trying to save a drop of ghi, he upset the ghi-pot. Mat. 16. 26.
5. If the curry is without savour, you can put salt into it; but if the salt has lost its savour, with what can it be seasoned? Mat. 5: 13.
6. If you yoke a buffalo and an ox together, the one will push for the swamp and the other for the hill top.

7. What knows the monkey of a looking-glass, or the jackal of a temple ? *Mat.* 7. 6. 1 *Cor.* 2 : 14.
8. Of what use is a violin to a deaf man, or a mirror to one who is blind ? *Mat.* 7. 6. 2 *Pet.* 2 : 12.
9. A single coal does not burn well ; a companionless traveller finds the journey tedious. *Eccl.* 4. 9. (100.)
10. If a jackal howls, will my old buffalo die ? if an angry man curses me, what shall I lose ?
11. Will an elephant bring forth a frog or a pig a mouse ? *Mat.* 7. 16. 12: 33.
12. Do you want a mirror for washing your hands ?
13. There is a large number of crows where there is plenty of boiled rice. *Mat.* 24. 28.
14. If he is in the wilderness, he is a robber ; if he comes to a village, he wants to be a Guru. *Mat.* 23. 4-7: 14.
15. Who will give his purse to a monkey ? who will entrust his property to a fool. *Pr.* 28: 26.
16. Three things are equal to each other : a harlot, an adulterer, and a piece of ground which is always in danger of being washed away by a river.
17. Will a child die from the stripes of a mother ? (94.)
18. Even if you give milk to a young snake, will it leave its habit of creeping underneath the hedge ?
19. The whoremonger will vanish away like a handful of mud." (16.) *Isa* 51 : 6.

MALAYALAM PROVERBS.

1. Even milk, when taken by the wicked, is bitter.
2. The inner and outer parts of sugar are alike.
3. Time shows the value of the bridge built with bad wood. *Pr.* 5. 3. 1 *Cor.* 3: 13.
4. What use is it to read the Vedas to a wild buffalo ?
5. Though the ant makes a loud noise, yet it knocks down no tower. *Gen.* 11: 4.
6. Though the dog go into the middle of the sea, yet it will only lap the water. *Heb.* 13 : 6.
7. When we have eaten salt we must drink water.
8. When one has learnt to steal, he must also learn hanging. (74.)

(219)

9. We lie straight only when we are dead. *Rom.* 7: 24.
10. As far as the stream goes it carries sediment.
11. A scalded cat fears even cold water.
12. Among six faces one only is alike. (171.)
13. When we strike mud, we get smeared over. 1 *Cor.* 15: 33.
14. There are many to prepare our medicine ; we are the only ones to drink it.
15. Does the sheep know anything of the bargaining in the market ? *Pr.* 7 : 22.
16. Anger has no eyes. *Pr.* 25: 28.
17. To the hen rice and rice seeds are alike.
18. To give a calf to be brought up by a tiger.
19. It is better to see the king than one thousand of his servants. *Eph.* 2: 18. 5: 12.
20. Are there movements in the sea without waves ?
21. Can we take fish without wetting the hands ?
22. Though you be near the shore, throw not the rudder away. i. e. have two strings to your bow.
23. What profit is it to drive out the rats by burning down the house ? *Mat.* 16 : 26.
24. By running in the boat, do we come sooner to land ? *Jas.* 5. 7-8.
25. Before you leap look at the ground. *Pr.* 22 : 3.
26. Though you dip in the sea, you receive only as much as your vessel will hold. *Phil.* 4: 11.
27. Decorate an ass, it does not make him a horse. *Pr.* 27. 28. 11: 22.
28. Build the house before you make the door.
29. When young you can rub it off with the finger nail.
30. When you seize thorns, grasp them firmly.
31. Before cutting down the forest, is it necessary to consult the axe ?
32. Sport not with a king, nor with water, fire, and elephants. *Pr.* 23 : 2.
33. Make the hedge after you have sown the seed.
34. The elephant's pace is equal to the horse's gallop.
35. We can mount with a leap a fallen tree. (89.)

TAMUL PROVERBS.

 If taken to excess even nectar is poison. *Eccl.* 7: 16.

2. Though the woodlouse be placed on a cushion, it will again seek the dunghill. *Col.* 1: 12.
3. To the timorous the atmosphere is filled with demons.
4. During harvest the rat has four wives. *Mat.* 24. 21.
5. Will the flood that has burst the dam return if one cry after it?
6. The ball rebounds in proportion to the stroke given.
7. Will one enter through a small door-way on the back of an elephant? (28.)
8. The hare in its attempt to lay eggs as the tortoise, strained its eyes out and died. *Dan.* 4: 30.
9. Though it should rain till the end of the world, potsherds will yield no herbs.
10. Though a little bird soar high, will it become a kite?
11. The beaded cat gives religious advice. *Mat.* 7: 15.
12. It is like being offended with the arrow, not with the archer. *Mic.* 6: 9. *Gen.* 45: 5. *Isa.* 10: 5.
13. He publishes the price of the ghi before the buffalo calves. *Luk.* 12: 20.
14. Like burning down one's house for fear of the rats.
15. Rapeseed and sugarcane are profitable when crushed.
16. The flower which is out of reach is dedicated to God.
17. The tears of the oppressed are like sharp swords.
18. Though a man may remove to the distance of fifty miles, his sin is still with him. *Gen.* 42: 21.
19. Will the milk return into the udder? (7.)
20. Plants of learning must be watered with the rain of tears.
21. The crane, hoping to eat dried fish when the sea might be dried up, wasted away in expectancy.
22. Like assafœtida dissolved in the ocean.
23. Is it necessary for one to provide frogs for the well he has dug?
24. Of what use can the news of the country be to a frog in a well? *Mat.* 13: 27. *Eph.* 1: 18.
25. Will the barking dog catch game. *Mat.* 7: 21.
26. What avails height in the dung-hill?—is the town disparaged by being low?
27. A lamp in a pitcher. *Mat.* 5: 15.
28. Desire for moustaches and desire for gruel. *Heb.* 11: 25.

29. If boiled rice be put on the roof, a thousand crows will come. *Mat.* 24: 28. *Job* 39 : 30.
30. Is a looking-glass necessary to look with a sore on the hand ?
31. Will the day break by the crowing of the cock, or the barking of the dog ?
32. If the dog bark at the moon, will the moon be affected by it ? *Ps.* 2, 1-4.
33. The moon shines even in the house of the wicked.
34. If rice be spilt it may be gathered up, but can water ? (7).
35. Will the head-ache be cured by changing the pillow ?
36. To roast a crab and set a fox to guard it.
37. If a dog be washed and placed in the middle of the house it will wag its tail and presently eat filth.
38. The shade is beautiful, but the red ants are troublesome. 2 *Cor.* 12 : 7.
39. Though the thorn in the foot be very small, yet stay and extract it.
40. By pronouncing the word fire, will the mouth be burnt ? (188).
41. Can cotton and fire be stowed together ? *Mat.* 6 : 13.
42. Will the milk be black because the cow is so ?
43. Though a snake be fed with milk, its poison will not leave it.
44. Will that which is born of a tiger be without claws ?
45. Can one make charcoal by burning hair ?
46. What will the mirror effect if the face be ugly ?
47. Though he wash three times a day, will the crow become a white crane ?
48. Water flowing gently will penetrate stones. *Pr.* 25 : 15.

CHINESE PROVERBS.

1. Tanks may be filled up, but man's heart can never be closed. 1 *King* 21 : 1-7.
2. The stag and the tiger do not tread the same path.
3. A hair's breadth out at the bow is a mile beside the butt. *Mat.* 25 : 5, 10.
4. You cannot tell a man by his face, nor measure the sea with a bushel. *John* 7 : 24.

5. Ivory does not come out of the rat's mouth.
6. The egg combats with the stone. *Is.* 45. 9. (9.)
7. The wind and the rain are not to be counted on (a man's fortune is ever changing.) (53.)
8. Disturbing the stream, and complaining that it is not clear. *Gen.* 3 : 12-13.
9. The word once spoken, an army of chariots cannot avert it. *Mat.* 12 : 36.

PUNJABI PROVERBS.

1. As poppy seeds cast before a blind hen. 2 *Cor.* 4: 4.
2. A bitch accustomed to steal will not keep a watch over your *jatabees* (a kind of sweetmeat).
3. The damsel who knows not to dance, makes the pretext that the courtyard of her house is narrow or crooked.
4. A vain man got a cup, and swelled his belly by drinking water again and again.
5. Although a farmer turned a *fakir*, yet he made his rosary of onions. *Col.* 1 : 12.

PERSIAN PROVERBS.

1. The water of life is in darkness, *i. e.* Nothing excellent attainable without labor. *Luk.* 13 : 24.
2. Water below the grass. (18.) *Mat.* 7 : 15.
3. I am flying ducks, *i. e.* Unprofitably employed.
4. It is unprofitable to hammer cold iron. *i. e* Good advice useless to one who will not listen. *Mrk.* 8 : 18.
5. A mirror in an Ethiopian's hand. *Mat.* 7: 6.
6. Two water-melons cannot be taken up in one hand, *i. e.* Attempting too much at once. *Phil.* 3: 13. *Luk.* 10 : 42.
7. Barley at the foot of the steep ascent is useless, *i. e.* You have starved your horse, so that he is become thin and weak, it will be to no purpose to feed him when you come to a steep ascent, *i. e.* Preparation for an enterprise should be made beforehand. *Luk.* 12: 20.
8. An ass cannot be made a horse by beating. (65.)
9. Ten in this world, one hundred in the next, *i. e.* Whatever is given in alms in this world is re-paid tenfold in the next. (49.) *Mat.* 10 : 42.

10. Vegetables do not grow on a stone; what fault is in the rain. 1. *Tim.* 2: 4. *Mat.* 23: 37.
11. She is a tree growing on the wall, *i. e.* An unchaste woman ruins her husband's honor, as the fig tree does the wall on which it grows.
12. A camel and a cat, *i. e.* Ill matched. 2 *Cor.* 6: 14.
13. Without a supple rod the ox and ass would not obey. *Pr.* 26: 5. (94.)
14. It is folly to give comfits to a cow. *Luk.* 7: 32.
15. To pound water in a mortar, *i. e.*, Labor in vain.
16. Should even the water of life fall from the clouds, you would never get fruit from the willow.
17. The river is not polluted by a dog's touching it. *Ti.* 1: 15. 2 *Pet.* 2: 8.
18. He endeavours to extract oil from sand.
19. He flies from his own shadow, *i. e. A great coward.* *Pr.* 28: 1. *Mat.* 26: 74.
20. If you stare at the sun, it will hurt your eyes and not the sun. *Acts* 9: 5.
21. If you put sour milk into a leathern bag for 100 years, it will still be sour milk *John* 3: 5-7.
22. If you be a hen, lay eggs, and if a cock, crow. *Tit.* 3: 3. 1 *Kings* 18: 21.
23. The food of beggars is not lessened by the barking of dogs.
24. He puts the wind in a cage. *Job* 11: 7.
25. The misfortunes of the stable fall on the head of the monkey.
26. The legs of those who require proofs of God's existence are made of wood and wooden legs are exceedingly weak. *Ps.* 14: 1.
27. The breath of a gnat will not put out the sun.
28. A Turkman hearing the name of paradise, asked, is there any plunder or booty to be had there?
29. The arrow once shot, returns not to the bow, *i. e.* The past cannot be recalled. *Eccl.* 11: 3.
30. God's club makes no noise, and when it strikes, there is no cure for the blow. 2 *Pet.* 2: 3.
31. Sweetmeats without smoke, *i. e.* Spoken of any thing without defect.
32. Become dust (*i. e.* be humble) before thou *art reduced* to dust (*i. e.* death.) *Job* 1: 21.

33. My uncle has scraped acquaintance with an ass.
34. An ass that carries burthens, is better than a tiger that tears men to pieces. (89.)
35. Let the ass (even) of Jesus, go to Mecca, when he returns he will be still an ass. (23.)
36. How can a man who is asleep himself, awaken another who is also asleep. *Mat.* 13: 14.
37. The tree that has only just taken root, may be pulled up by the strength of a man.
38. The pains of a lover, cannot be cured by the remedies of a doctor.
39. When one is thirsty, a thousand pearls are not worth one drop of water.
40. Friendship with a fool is like the embrace of a bear.
41. He is tied by the neck, *i. e.* He is married to a bad woman. *Pr.* 21: 9.
42. Give in this world and receive in the next. *Pr.* 19: 17.
43. A black pot makes the clothes black. 1 *Cor.* 15: 33.
44. A pleasant voice brings a snake out of a hole, *i. e.* Gentle means are the most efficacious. *Pr.* 15: 1.
45. A dog without a tail, *i. e.* A foolish, worthless babbler.
46. Love and musk do not remain concealed.
47. Should wood of aloes, and dung, be put in the fire, they will both become ashes, *i. e.* Death levels all.
48. Don't despise pepper because it is small, eat and see how pungent it is, *i. e.* We ought not judge of the powers of people by their size. 2 *Cor.* 10: 10.
49. To entrust the cat with the care of flesh.
50. The humble man is (like) earth, that alike kisses the feet of the king and the beggar.
51. A closed fist is the lock of heaven, and the open hand is the key of mercy. (58) 1 *Pet* 4: 8.
52. Prayer is the pillar of religion. 102. *Acts* 10: 4.
53. The stream which has passed, does not come back to its former channel.
54. Whoever parts scorpions with the hands of compassion, receives punishment. (101.)
55. Every hollow has its hill, *i. e.* Bad may be better.
56. He holds the wind in his hand.
57. He dug up the foundation to finish the roof.
58. He is a cake in the paws of the bear.

59. The lamp gives no light in the presence of the sun.
60. The lamp beneath the clothes, *i. e.* a vain attempt to hide something that cannot be concealed. *Gen.* 4 : 10.
61. Where there is much mire, the elephant's foot slips, *i. e.* The most pious and abstinent are in danger of falling into vice if they go in the way of strong temptation.
62. To hang up grapes in the house of a bear.
63. At forty he began to learn the drum ; he will be skilful by the time he gets into his grave.
64. Much running about wears out the shoes, *i. e.* What is determined must be.
65. Whoever wants a peacock must take the trouble of going to *Hindustan. Mat.* 7 : 7.
66. One pound of learning requires ten of common sense (to apply it.) 2 *Tim.* 3 : 7.
67. Water, which stagnates long in one place, corrupts.
68. Fire seizing a forest makes no distinction between the wet and dry, *i. e.* Any public calamity in which the guilty and innocent are equally involved. *Luk.* 13: 4.
69. To extinguish a flame, but leave the live coals, to or kill a snake and preserve it's young, are not the acts of the wise. *Mat.* 15 : 19.
70. Man comes to man (for assistance,) a mountain comes not to a mountain. (171.)
71. You cannot reach the heavens with your hand from the top of a high house *i. e.* A person who gives himself airs, in consequence of having obtained a high situation. *Gen.* 11 : 4.
72. He should be put in danger of death, that he may be contented with fever. (234.)
73. You may go to the temple of *Mecca* by inquiring the way.
74. What fear need he have of the waves of the sea, who has Noah for his pilot. *Mat.* 8 : 26.
75. God who gives teeth also gives bread. *Is.* 49 : 15.
76. A drop of rain makes no impression on a hard stone. (5.)
77. Your hand in his bowl and your fist on his forehead ?
78. People do not fix their teeth in a rag, *i. e.* One who is eager about trifles.
79. Travel the high way, though it be round about.
80. A bad word is like the sound of a dome. *Pr.* 17 : 14.

81. Patience is the key of difficult affairs. *Heb.* 6 : 12.
82. There is no honey without a sting ; nor rose without a thorn. *Ps.* 119 : 96.
83. Neither is every woman a woman, nor every man a man ; God did not make the five figures alike. 1 *Tim.* 2 : 12.
84. He whose soul is alive his sensual desires are dead.
85. All filth is washed by means of water, but the filth of water cannot be washed by any thing. *Luk.* 4 : 23.
86. One scabby goat infects (spoils), the whole flock.

URDU PROVERBS.

1. Look at your own face in the mirror. (116.)
2. Fire and water are irreconcilable enemies. *Mat.* 6: 24.
3. First there is water afterwards mud, *i. e.* Be in time.
4. The blind heron eats dirt, *i. e.* The ignorant always live in misery and wretchedness. *Luk.* 15: 16.
5. Hunger is the best sauce, and fatigue the best pillow.
6. A stone does not rot in water, *i. e.* A claim, though suspended, is not lost. *Eccl.* 11 : 3. *Pr.* 11 : 21.
7. To make a hole in the vessel out of which one has eaten, *i. e.* To prove ungrateful. (84.)
8. There is moonlight for a few days, and then it is dark as before. (53) *Isaiah* 50: 9. (39.)
9. Can flesh remain in a kite's nest ? *Pr.* 6 : 27.
10. Whether the melon fall upon the knife, or the knife on the melon, the melon is the sufferer. (*Eng.*) The weakest go to the wall.
11. The cat having eaten up seven hundred rats, is going on a pilgrimage to *Mecca*, *i. e.* A very wicked person, pretending to have become penitent and religious.
12. A new thing remains nine days, an old thing lasts 100.
13. The *Nim* tree (which is very bitter) will not become sweet, though watered with syrup and clarified butter. *i. e.* Education is thrown away on one of dull parts.
14. The milk is not yet dry on your lips, *i. e.* A young man who asserts his opinions confidently. 1 *Pet.* 5 : 5.
15. A water pot without a bottom, *i. e.* An unsteady feeble character. *Gen.* 49: 4. *Jus.* 1 : 5.
16. The leaf crackled and your slave fled. *Pr.* 28 : 1.

17. A hair of that man's head will never be crooked, whom God protects. *Luk.* 12: 6-7.
18. The cow will speak in the thief's belly. *Gen.* 4: 10.
19. By throwing dust the moon is not to be concealed.
20. In appearance he is a saint, so that he may catch birds.
21. A jackal's rage, *i. e.* A contemptible thing.
22. There is kindness, but no milk. *Jas.* 2 :15-17.
23. When the Salt dealer's Salt falls he may pick it up again ; but if the Butterman drop his *Ghi* how is that to be recovered. (7.) *Ps.* 103 : 16.
24. A buffalo does not feel the weight of his own horns 1 *Tim.* 5: 8.
25. A lofty shop but tasteless sweetmeats.
26. A wooden pot cannot be often put on the fire, *i. e.* Deceit cannot be oft repeated.
27. Even an earthen pot is rung before being bought. *Tim.* 5: 21.
28. It is a sin whether you steal sesamum or sugar. *Jas.* 2: 10.
29. The friendship of the base is a wall of sand.
30. No twisting a rope of sand. *Pr.* 25: 19.
31. To dig a well after the house is on fire. *Eccl.* 9: 10.
32. Where the flower there the thorn. (52.)
33. Weep before a blind man but you only lose your eyes.
34. Let him touch your fingers he will soon seize your wrist. (129.) *Pr.* 4: 15.
35. To pull down a mosque for a brick. *Heb.* 11: 25.
36. A skin filled with wind, *i. e.* Man's body. *Job* 7 ; 5.
37. The great fish eat up the small. (172.)
38. The cat does not kill mice for God. (98.)
39. The thirsty person goes to the well, not the well, to him, *i. e.* he who want assistance must seek it.
40. Hollow (or rotten) pease sound the loudest. *Luke* 18: 10-14
41. To cut the branch on which one sits.
42. The cloud that thunders much, rains little.
43. He that beats a *Jogi*, dirties his hands with ashes, *i. e.* Unprofitable to oppress the poor.
44. The beauty (which arises from dress) is in the port manteau, and that of the person, is in the platter, *i. e.* Depends on good living. (115.)

45. There is the difference of four fingers between seeing and hearing, *i. e.* There is a great difference.
46. The crows keep cawing, but the corn dries notwithstanding, *i. e.* The business in hand goes on well, notwithstanding the oppositions of cavillers.
47. Do not embark on two boats, for you will be split and thrown on your back. *Luk.* 16: 13.
48. To burn a house in order to kill a wasp.
49. Is it better to go naked, or be hung up by the heels, *i. e.* Of two evils choose the least.
50. He sets up for a druggist with one bit of Assafœtida.
51. Pouring water upon a greasy jar. It slips away like money. *Jer.* 2: 13.
52. A straight finger gets no *Ghi*, *i. e.* the hand must be bent to sip *Ghee* from it, some effect is necessary in every thing.
53. Who washes in the tiger's mouth. *Pr.* 14: 9. 2 *Kings* 2: 23.
54. A wooden owl, (a blockhead.) *Jas.* 4: 13 14.
55. Who has seen to-morrow. Said in reply to a person who procrastinates a day.
56. He who is prepared to die, what will he not attempt.
57. When we die, I shall get a good nap. *Job.* 5: 17.
58. A Service like the root of the castor oil tree. This tree takes little root. *(Eng)* Service is no inheritance. *Mat.* 3: 9.
59. If an elephant were to put forth his strength, a man were but a flea. *Gen.* 9: 2.
60. He rides a steed of air. *Ps.* 73: 20. (153.)

TELUGU PROVERBS.

1. Offering the molasses in the bazar to the idol in the temple, *i. e.* Willing to be liberal at the expense of others.
2. Like ghi poured on fire.
3. If the priest does not come, will the new moon wait for him? *i. e.* Time and tide wait for no man.
4. Lamentations in the the jungle, *i. e.* Of no avail.
5. If you throw a stone into filth, it will fly into your face. *Acts* 9: 5.
6. Not being able to dance, she abused the drum, *i. e.* A bad workman complains of his tools.

7. Making mustard seed into a ball, *i. e.* An impossible combination. 2 *Cor.* 6: 14.
8. Is the bullock's sore tender to the crow? *i. e.* One devoid of sympathy for others. *Rom.* 12: 15.
9. I have cut many boils, but there was never such pain as in my own. Said by a Surgeon.
10. The loss of a wing is the same to a mosquito as the loss of a leg to an elephant, *i. e.* Proportionate losses. *Mark* 12 : 43.
11. The man who has mounted an elephant will not be afraid at the bark of a dog. *Ps.* 112: 7.
12. Clap with one hand will there be any sound?
13. What matters it whether one drinks milk in a dream out of bell metal or gold? *Is.* 14: 9-20.
14. If you put a crow in a cage will it talk like a parrot?
15. He slipped and fell, and then said the ground was unlucky.
16. Will a black dog become a holy cow by merely going to Benares? (118).
17. Could you swim over the Gôdâvari, by catching hold of a dog's tail? *Luk.* 14: 31.
18. Like scratching one's head with a firebrand.
19. Like a snake in a monkey's paw. (101). Jacko is afraid of it but wont let it go.
20. Swallowing crowbars and taking ginger draughts, *i. e.* An insufficient remedy. *Jer.* 2 : 13.
21. The mildness of a young donkey, *i e.* Seemingly good but really useless. *Mark* 7: 19-21.
22. A squint eye is better than a blind eye, *i. e.* Of two evils choose the least. *Mat.* 5 : 29.
23. Will he who planted the tree not water it?
24. A scorpion under a shoe, *i. e.* A ruffian under restraint.
25. A man will not build a hut until he has been drenched nor stoop until he has hit his head. *Pr.* 22 : 3.
26. A man's shadow remains with himself. (74.)
27. Without eating you can't tell the taste ; without going down [into the water] you can't know the depth.
28. Are there sweet diseases, and delicious medicines.
29. Mountains are smooth at a distance, but rugged when near. *Job.* 8: 14. (10)
30. He opens the door for the robber and then awakes his master. *Num.* 23: 10.
31. Among a hundred crows, what could a single cuckoo do.

32. Your mouth is like a sweet plum and your hand is like a thorn-bush. (188.)
33. If the almanacks are lost, do the stars go also?
34. If you talk of work, my body becomes heavy; if you talk of dinner, my body swells [with delight.] 2 *Thess.* 3:10.
35. Friendship with a snake, fencing with a sword.
36. Can rotten food ever be made sweet? *John* 3: 6.
37. Like a cat shutting her eyes, and fancying that no one could see her drinking the milk. *Luk.* 12: 3.
38. Taking hold of a tiger's mustaches and swinging one's self, *i. e.* A rash enterprise. *Job* 15: 26.
39. Like the ant that crawls below a bird flying above.
40. A golden knife, *i. e.* of intrinsic value but of no utility
41. Like sprinkling rose water on ashes. (96.)
42. A cat which kills a rat is a cat, whether it be of wood or mud. *Mat.* 7: 16.
43. The elephant is an elephant whether on high ground or low
44. Putting one's head in the mortar, and then fearing the blow of the pestle. *Heb.* 12: 2.
45. Like putting a bandicoot in a corn bin.
46. A scolopendra with a thousand legs.
47. Cold water to hot water, hot water to cold water, the beneficial union of different dispositions. (171.)
48. Can your house be burnt down with hot water?
49. Sweet words, empty hands. *Mat.* 7 : 21-23.
50. If all get into the palankin, who will be the bearers?
51. If a musquito light on an elephant, what weight?
52. If the thief had said before that he was coming, I would have obtained witnesses. (200.)
53. The cloth which has fallen upon thorns must be taken off slowly. *Pr.* 19: 2.
54. A rat on the Lingam, if you knock the rat off he strikes the Lingam, if he remains the emblem is insulted. *Mat.* 13 : 29.

SAYINGS OF VEMANA* IN TELUGU.

1. Observances void of purity of heart! to what end are they? to what is the preparation of food without cleansing the vessel? *Mat.* 15 : 8.

* Vemana lived in the beginning of the 17th century: he was a ryot of the Kuddapa district, Madras, and is in Telugu literature what Lucian is in Greek.

2. One real and good sapphire is enough, why collect a basket full of glittering sparkling stones ? *Gen.* 18 : 23-32.

3. Even as a lamp shines in a glass vase, thus shineth wisdom dwelling in the bodies of men of understanding.

4· Profitless are some men : what though they be born in the world ? what though they die ? are not the white-ants of the hillock also born ? and do they not die also ?

5. Whatever he devoid of understanding may read, his virtue continues only so long as he is reading ; even as a frog is dignified only so long as it is seated on a lotus leaf. (116.)

6. At the sight of women the lubidinous man is stricken with the pains of desire ; even as the grass-hopper delights in viewing the fire that will destroy it. *Pr.* 7 : 22.

7. No man's disposition will alter, say what we may ; neither can a dog's tail be made straight : the stubborn woman will even put her husband in a basket and sell him (23.)

8. A crocodile while swimming in water will seize and destroy an elephant ; but out of the stream, it is discomfited even by a dog. In the water a ship will float smoothly, out of it cannot crawl even a cubit.

9. A pig will bring forth young, at five or ten at a time ; an elephant produces but one. Is not then one man truly excellent enough ?

10. Any one can instruct a man of understanding, but it is not in the power of others to teach the vile : Is it possible for any one to straighten the bend of a river ? (65.)

11. If you have given your money to an evil man, to follow him about is all folly. If a cat has seized a fowl will it answer your call ? (36.)

12. He that relying on the prince, ruins the land, the sorrows of the people shall reach him, and at last he shall fall. How long, shall the bounding ball, retain its elevation ? (16.)

13. Practising the humility of a fox, and talking obsequiously, he heaps up all his wealth, and does not use it : thus is rice sprinkled at the mouth of a bandycote trap. *Pr.* 13 : 11.

14. Though iron break twice or thrice, the smith knows how to heat and weld it. If the spirit break who shall restore it. *Pr.* 18 : 14.

15. If you behold the fig (ficus glomerata) it is pure gold ; if you open its belly and look in, it is all worms. Such is the ostentation of a reserved man. *Mat.* 13: 25.

16. By the groaning of a buffalo hide bellows (in the world) the five metals are calcined ; when good men grieve, will not a great flame arise to heaven ?

17. As iron by touching the philosopher's stone becomes gold : as camphor unites with the lamp, and both become fire ; or like as the odour in a flower is united therewith, such is the union of our soul with the divinity. *Acts* 17: 28.

18. Like to the flame of a lamp that is placed out of the wind —like to the ocean free from defiling whirlpools,—is the unagitated soul, when free from change. This is named beatitude.

19. By talking and conversing, affection increases : as you continue to eat even the *bitter Nimba leaf*, it becomes sweet, so by practice may we succeed in any art whatever. *Rev.* 10: 9.

20. A single spoonful of milk, from a good cow, is enough : of what use is a pailful of asses milk ? a single handful of food given with faith (zeal or affection) is enough.

21. Without personal experience, the mere savour of the scripture will not remove the fears of the aspirant ; as darkness is never dispelled, by a mere painted flame. 2. *Cor.* 3: 6. *Ps.* 34: 8

22. When the sons of earth see the holy saint they revile him, but cannot understand him. Can the hand discern ambrosia from other tastes ? 1 *Cor.* 2: 14.

23. The six flavours are diverse, but taste is one ; various are the creeds regarding truth, but truth is one : and saints differ among themselves, while he on whom they meditate is one. (171.)

24. If there be one dry tree in a forest, it will produce flame by friction, and sweep away the rest : thus if a base wretch be born in a noble race, he will destroy it all.

25. The teacher who is unable to show the path of holiness to his disciples, and plunges them in an evil creed, his wisdom is like that of a bullock entangled in a field of maize. *Mat.* 15: 14.

26. If you look at a grain of pepper, it is externally black if you bite it you perceive that internally it is pungent. Thus imperceptible is the worth of the excellent.

27. Look closely at musk; its hue indeed is dark, but its fragrance perfumes all things. Thus hidden are the virtues of men of weight. *Is.* 53 : 2. *Heb.* 11 : 4.

28. The man who has crossed a river and reached the shore, cares no longer for the hide-sewn boat; why should the man who has attained *happiness*, trouble himself about the body? 2 *Cor.* v. 1. *Phil.* 3 : 13.

29. It is easy to talk, but hard to stay the mind; we may teach others, but cannot ourselves understand: it is easy to lay hold on the sword, but hard to become valiant. *Mat.* 7 : 26.

30. What mean we by "self," or, "our own people"? knowing, they know not, the mad men! They live like a silk-worm in a cocoon, seemingly secure, but in reality helpless. *Pr.* 7 : 22.

31. We cannot see our own forehead, our ears, or, our backs; neither can we know the hairs of our head; if a man knows not himself how should he know the deity? *Ps.* 9 : 12.

32. Like as what is written in water remains not, so are all the blessings of this life unstable. (53.)

33. Though he roam to Concan, no dog will turn into a lion: going to Benares will make no pig an elephant; and no pilgrimage make a saint of one whose nature is different. *Pr.* 26 : 11. 2 *Pet.* 2 : 22.

34. If authority be given to a low-minded man, he will chase away all the honorable: can a dog that gnaws shoes taste the sweetness of the sugarcane?

35. If you take a bear-skin and wash it ever so long, will it instead of its native blackness ever become white? If you beat a wooden image will it hence acquire any good quality? (23.)

36. A thief if he goes to a holy place will only pick the pockets of the comers; he has no leisure, to draw near and bow to the God. If a dog enters a house will he tend the hearth? 2 *Pet.* 2 : 22.

37. If you know how to swim there is no necessity to sound the stream: if you know how to die there is no grief in the world from which suicide will not release. If you are content with a girdle, no poverty will distress you. 1. *Tim.* 6 : 8 (180.)

38. The dung beetle cares not for the sweetness of sugar.

39. Will a dog recognize the priest; it will only snap at him, seize and tear the calf of his leg. *Mat.* 7 : 6.

40. If an elephant fall into a pit how can a gnat extricate it? *Eph.* 5 : 14.

41. If you catch a monkey and dress it in a new robe the hill apes will worship it. Thus are the luckless subject to the senseless.

42. Though you anoint an ass all over with perfumes, it feels not your fondness, but will turn again and kick you. *Mat.* 7 : 7. *Pr.* 27 : 22.

43. The washerman torments a cloth to take the stains out; and then folds it properly; what then though he who teaches thee chastise thee? (94.)

44. Will plunging them in the *sacred* sea, convert rushes into darbha grass? *Pr.* 27 : 22.

45. What has a cripple to do with bracelets? of what advantage are wooden teeth to the harelipped? will an ass be the better for assuming a beard and whiskers? *i. e.* Mere pretensions are wholly fruitless.

46. Like flies that longing for honey approach it, enter, are intoxicated, and unable to extricate themselves,— so plunged in a multitude of passions, a sinner perishes without escape. (37.)

47. A year to a potter, and a day to a cudgel, *i. e.* The work of a year is destroyed in a day. *Rom.* 5 : 12.

48. Be he stout or tall, or wearing a long beard, devoid of liberality, he is no noble: however large a buffalo is, it cannot compare with an elephant. 1 *Cor.* 13 : 1.

49. The drop that falls into the oyster-shell, becomes a pearl: while the drop that falls into the wave turns to water:—if the situation be suitable, the fruit shall not fail.

50. If he joins himself to the vile, and associates with him, he will be ruined, whoever he be. It is like drinking milk under a palm tree. (Where however innocently, it would be suspected he was drinking wine or toddy.) 1 *Thess.* 5 : 22.

51. If you go with a pail to milk a dry cow, it may kick your teeth out, but you will get no milk.

52. If you suffer a low-minded wretch to creep into your house, you will lament it, whoever you be. If a fly enter the stomach, will it not torment you?

53. Were you to drink milk at a tavern, all would imagine it to be wine; so he who stands where he ought not, will inevitably incur reproach. *Thess.* 5 : 22.

54. Those who mortify their bodies, calling themselves saints, are yet unable to cure the impurity of their hearts. If you merely destroy the outside of a white-ant hill, will the serpent that dwells therein perish?

55. As thorns are produced along with the mimosa tree, springing from the same seed; so does the evil mind of the stubborn fool grow up along with him.

56. If thy heart become calm as the breezeless firmament, and the unruffled waveless deep, changeless and unfluctuating—this is denominated freedom.

57. If an unlucky fool should even find the philosopher's stone, it would never remain in his hands, but vanish, it would melt away like the hailstones that come with the rain. *Pr.* 12 : 27.

58. Even the poison-nut, and the *bitter* margosa, are useful as drugs; but the unfeeling vile wretch is utterly unprofitable. (127.)

59. The good are rarely found, the wicked are as numerous as you will; as gold is more rare than dust.

60. Sweet as the cuckoo warbling in a garden are the charming words of the wise, but the words of sinners are vile as the cawing of a crow. *Pr.* 18 : 8.

61. He who studies the sayings of the ancients, and tries to practice according to them is like a fox that streaks itself in *empty imitation of a tiger*.

62. He who has cut off his lusts and quenched their fire, who has bound his loins, crushed his anger, and given up every desire—this is the only true hermit.

63. If ignorant of his own powers, and those of his opponent, a man blusters and indulges in wrath, he is like a bear performing the torchdance, in which he will of course be burnt. (157.)

64. Imperceptible as the air in the sky, and fire in wood—does the first of beings freely pervade the world, and shine independent of the world. (119.)

65. The tale bearer is the associate of the villain; a stripling is a fit minister for an inflexible king; and the monkey is the only companion for the baboon.

66. Those who roam to other lands in pilgrimage to find the God that dwells within them, are like a shepherd who searches in his flock for the sheep he has under his arm. *John.* 1 : 20 21.

67. Will the application of white ashes do away the smell of a wine pot? will a cord cast over your neck make you twice born? (217)

68. O ye asses! why do you make balls of food and give them to the crows in the name of your ancestors? How can a dung-eating crow be an ancestor of yours?

69. Religion that consists in contriving various postures and twisting the limbs, is just one straw inferior to the exercises of the wrestler. *Is.* 58 : 5.

70. Why bow and fall down *in worship?* Will the hard stone in the temple change its nature? the true temple is the body, the soul is the God therein; empty is the worship ye pay to these worthless stones.

71. Just as a shew man plays his puppets, while he lies hidden; so does the deity, while he conceals himself, admirably govern men.

72. When love is over, the cherry lip of the rosy girl is tasteless as the pulp of the night-shade berry, or the juice of the poison-nut, when you do not care for it, it is as disgusting as the milk of the mango leaf.

73. Though he have read all that can be read, and be an acute disputant, never shall the hypocrite attain to final happiness. His meditations are like those of a dog on the dunghill. 2 *Tim.* 3 : 7.

74. A stone in the shoe, a gadfly in the ear, a mote in the eye, a thorn in the foot, and a quarrel in a family however small in themselves, are unspeakably tormenting. 2 *Cor.* 12 : 7.

75. The root worm destroys the tree; the sap-worm destroy the herb: and the backbiter ruins every good quality.

76. Salt and camphor are one semblance; but if you examine and try the flavours, their tastes are divers: thus do the excellent differ from other men.

77. In an unsuitable place never let us hold ourselves superior. To be low is no humiliation. Small is the image of a hill in a mirror. *Luk.* 14 : 11.

78. It is fit to perform no act tardily; if thou hurry it, it will itself become evil. If thou take and cast down a raw fruit, will it ripen? *Jas.* 5 : 7.

79. The Ganges flows with a tranquil course, but a foul *stream* rushes with a roar. Thus the base can never be mild as the noble. *Luk.* 21 : 19.

80. Like as the fish in the waters, through desire of the delicious bait is fixed on the hook and perishes: so a man if seized with desire is also ruined. *Jas.* 1 : 15.

81. He may ejaculate Nara! (Arjuna) or Namasiva! (a name of the deity) and we may in seeing him say, Good! Admirable! and laud *him*; but he is in no hurry to open his purse and bestow a farthing. *Luk.* 6 : 46.

(237)

82. If the place where you are is troubled, you should pass to a more comfortable land. If the pond dry, will the cranes remain it? (An allusion to a fable in the Hitopadesa). 1 *Chr.* 29 : 15.

83. A good work performed with a pure heart, though small, is not trifling. How large is the seed of the banyan and the mustard tree! *Luk.* 21 : 2.

84. When his passions are redoubled, a man is seized with madness and roams the earth. Cupidity makes a man as restless as a dog. (50) *Mat.* 27 : 5.

85. How should fortune dwell in the houses of those who perpetually tell lies? It is like drawing water in a leaky vessel. *Jer.* 2 : 13.

86. He who knows the truth knows the Divinity, and this will enable him to slay all his lusts. Will he who has swallowed a delicious plantain, swallow bitter venom? (225.)

87. Though a vessel be broken, a new one is easily procured. Is it then marvellous that after a man's death he should acquire a new body? 2 *Cor.* 5 : 2.

88. As metals unite with flame; and a spike with wood; and figures with the walls on which they are painted; so are the body and living soul united.

89. Large is the eye-ball, minute is the pupil; yet in the pupil alone exists the source of vision such are the mediums through which we view the Deity.

90. When one has learnt to speak prudently, why should we think of his youth or age? May not a lamp burn bright though held in the hand of an infant? (166.)

91. Worked chains are various, but all gold is the same; the earthly tenements vary, but the soul is one; viands are many, but hunger is always the same.

92. A feast given without kindness is a mere waste of flour-cakes; worship devoid of piety is a waste of the sprouts used in sacrifice; and gifts devoid of charity are a mere waste of gold. 1 *Cor.* 10 : 31.

93. Why suffer anxiety, O my heart, for the belly? either here or there the belly will be filled. As to having a belly, the frog that lives in a rock is thy equal.

94. The source of final happiness is inherent in the heart, he is a fool who seeks it elsewhere *as at holy places and pilgrimages;* he is like the shepherd who searched for the sheep which was in his bosom. *John* 1 : 21.

95. A stone in the shoe, a gadfly in the ear, a mote in

the eye, a thorn in the foot, and a quarrel in a family,—*however small in themselves* are unspeakably tormenting. (70.)

96. Convert thy *corporeal* dwelling into a candlestick? and the properties *of thy nature* into a wick; let thy acts be instead of oil; and finally, be illuminated with a certain *divine* flame. *Rev.* 2 : 5.

97. How should the holy saint, who is become united with the divine abode, again be mingled with men? When a drop of water in converted into a pearl, will it again unite with its former wave? 2 *Pet.* 2 : 20-22.

98. By devoutly repeating the *sacred* name of Rāma, Vālmīki the savage became a Bramin. Eminence depends not upon birth but virtue. *Jas.* 2 : 5.

99. Riches flourish, like the charms of women, for a season, but rapidly fade away; as moonlight dies when a cloud passes over the sky. (90.) & (53.)

100. A dog instinctively recognizes the kindness shewn to it; how base is the man who feels not the good that is done to him. (84.) *Luk* 17 : 17.

101. It is easy to feel pleasure in the conversation of the learned; but it is more hard to extend the hand and give a farthing: he can easily advise others to be liberal, but cannot become so himself. *Mat* 23 : 4.

102. A fool who knows not right from wrong, if he passes a judgment upon wise men, is like a dog barking against a lion. *Pr.* 14 : 9

103. His forehead is that of a worshipper; his mouth, that of a wolf; and his heart that of a roaming demon: is he so shameless as to say he has learnt of the divinity? (104.)

104. Even a goat can attain to such "corporeal perfection" as consists in living on leaves: how apt men are to fall into foolish whims!

105. Ignorant that the living principle exists in your body, why do you search imagining that it is to be found elsewhere! ye are like one who while the sun shines should search with a lamp.

106. Why should we constantly revile the Pariar? are not his flesh and blood the same as our own? and of what caste is He who pervades the Pariar *as well as all other men? Acts* 17 : 26.

107. Though a Turk go to the sacred hill *of Tripety,* he does not become a palmer; going on *pilgrimage*

to Benares will not make a modest woman of a prostitute; though a dog go to the sacred stream of the Godaveri will it make him a lion? (211.)

RUSSIAN PROVERBS.*

1. The wolf asked the goat to dinner, the goat would not come. *Pr.* 1:10.
2. A fox sleeps, and in its dreams counts hens.
3. The wolf changes his hair every year, yet remains the wolf.
4. However you bend a tree, it will always grow upward.
5. Dog, why do you bark? To frighten the wolves away. Dog, why do you keep your tail between your legs? I am afraid of the wolf. *Mat.* 26:74.
6. A pig came up to a horse and said,—the feet are crooked, the hair worth nothing. (15.)
7. Love, fire, and a cough cannot be hid.
8. A drunkard's money in his hand, goes through his fingers. *Pr.* 23:21.
9. Drink one day; a headache the whole week. *Pr.* 23:31.
10. Make friendship with a bear, but keep hold of the axe.
11. Measure ten times, you can cut only once.
12. Prepare for death, but neglect not to sow.
13. To shoot at a stone is to lose an arrow. *Acts* 9:5.
14. Everything is bitter to him who has gall in his mouth.
15. The hen is not a bird, nor is a woman a man. (19.)
16. Bread and salt humble even a robber. (224.)
17. A stomach filled is deaf to instruction. *Ez.* 16:49.
18. If you hunt two hares, you do not catch even one.
19. His thoughts are beyond the mountains; death is behind his shoulder. *Luke* 12:20.
20. A dream is fearful, but God is merciful. *Pr.* 112:7.
21. The same God who makes you wet, dries you.
22. God is not in haste, but his aim is sure. (71.)
23. Pray to God, but row towards the shore. *Mat.* 26:41.
24. Shut the door on the devil, but he will enter by the window. *Eph.* 6:13.

25. Praise not the crop until it is stacked.
26. The devil when old becomes a monk. *Pr.* 1 : 26.
27. When we are with wolves, we must howl with them.
28. The husband is the father of his wife. *Eph.* 5: 23.
29. The wife must respect the husband as the cross on the steeple. *Eph.* 5 : 33.
30. The baby does not know God, but God loves it. *Luk.* 12 : 24.
31. It is not necessary to plough and sow fools—they grow of themselves. *Mat.* 13: 27.
32. With God go even over the sea; without Him not over the threshold. *Es.* 33 : 15.
33. Truth is not drowned in water, nor burned in fire.
34. One fool may throw a stone into a pond: it may take seven wise men to pull it out.
35. A man thoroughly wet does not fear the rain.
36. Throw bread and salt behind you you get them again.
37. No bones are broken by a mother's fist. (94.)
38. As difficult to look on death as on the sun. *Ph.* 1 : 23.
39. A golden bed cannot cure the sick.
40. Many can give advice; few help. *Jas.* 2 : 16.
41. People may sin like David, but are not sorry like him.
42. A tale is soon told; a deed is not soon done.
43. If you love me do not beat my dog. *John* 12: 26.
44. A man will not be without a dwelling, nor the dead without a tomb (God will provide.)
45. Excepting death you might be tired of everything.
46. Man plans but God fulfils. *Pr.* 16 : 33.
47. God is an old worker of miracles.
48. God lays the burthen according to the strength.
49. God has long patience, but finally He hits hard.
50. To whom God gives employ, he gives understanding.
51. Who goes on the horse must lead him to the water.
52. Eagles catch not flies. *Ph.* 3: 8.
53. Let every one sweep before his own doors. 2 *Thes.* 3 : 11.
54. Grass grows not on the highway.
55. If you wish to eat bread, sit not on the stove. Bitter is labor, but sweet is the bread from it.

56. Whose bread and salt I eat, his praises I sing.
57. Once a thief always a thief. *Jas.* 2:10.
58. All things have two sides. *Ph.* 2:4.
59. A good end crowns all the work.
60. The cat wishes the fish but fears the water.
61. A good fox has three holes. *Mat.* 10:16.
62. Fear has many eyes; who fears the wolf goes not into the forest. *Pr.* 28:1.
63. Great money, great care. 1 *Tim.* 6:9.
64. A good conscience is God's eye. *Rom.* 2:15.
65. The bell calls to Church but goes not in itself.
66. Kill the bear before you deal with his skin.
67. At night all cats are grey. 1 *Cor.* 13:12.
68. As the old live so they learn. *Luk.* 2:25-37.
69. Love teaches even a priest to dance.
70. Boast of the day in the evening. *Pr.* 27:1.
71. Lies march on rotten legs: who lies will steal.
72. When the mouse's stomach is full, the flour is bitter.
73. He who has never been to sea has never prayed fully to God. *Jonah* 1:5.
74. The dog barks, the wind carries it away.
75. Rust eats iron, cares the heart. *Luke* 8:14.

TURKISH PROVERBS.

1. He that falls in the sea takes hold of the serpent to be drowned, *i. e.* from frying pan to fire.
2. Long hair little brain. 1 *Tim.* 2:9.
3. A low ass is easy to ride on. *Pr.* 17:19.
4. He that speaks truth must have one foot in the stirrup.
5. Strong vinegar ruins the vessel in which it is contained. *Mat.* 9:17.
6. The nest of a blind bird is made by god.
7. Poverty is a shirt of fire. *Pr.* 30:8, 9.
8. The dying man regarded not death, but asked if his coffin is made of walnut.
9. Whether sugar be white or black it preservs its proper taste. 2 *Cor.* 10:1.

d

10. To dig a well with a needle. *Gen.* 11 : 4.
11. Though they are brothers, their pockets are not sisters.
12. A cucumber being given to a poor man he did not accept it, because it was crooked.
13. Although the fly be small among insects, yet it has power to turn the stomach of men. *Acts* 12 : 23.
14. The fox goes at last to the shop of the farrier.
15. The camel went in search of horns and lost his ear.
16. If my beard is burnt, others try to light their pipe at it. *Luke* 10 : 34.
17. He is not a man but the roof of a bath, *i. e.* He makes the echo to what you say. 1 *Thess.* 5 : 21.
18. By patience and waiting verjuice becomes wine and the mulberry leaf satin.
19. Few desires happy life. *Is.* 5 : 8.
20. If you go swiftly they think you are running a race.
21. You cannot contract for the fish in the sea.

THE ARABIC PROVERBS AND SAYINGS OF ALI AND ABU TALEB.

1. He is your brother, who helps you in adversity. *Pr.* 17 : 17. (138.)
2. By benefiting the evil-doer you will conquer him. (224.
3. Sell worldly for eternal things, you will gain.
4. The tears of repentance are cool and refresh the eyes.
5. The belly of a man (gluttony) is his enemy. (128.)
6. He gives twice who gives with a cheerful face. 2 *Cor.* 9 : 7.
7. The gaping mouth of covetousness is not filled, except by the earth of the grave. *Ps.* 146 : 4.
8. The garment of salvation never grows old. *Ps.* civ. 2. *Is.* lix : 17. (143.)
9. Food supports life, contentment the soul. *Hos.* 2 : 20.
10. The empire of lies lasts an hour, that of truth to a future life. *Pr.* 12 : 19.
11. That alone is true fame which is not subject to death.
12. Gold is made the ornament to women, learning to men. (115.)
13. Modesty is the covering of a man. 1 *Pet.* 5 : 5.
14. Acid food is better than acid words. *Eph.* 4 : 31.

15. The fear of God makes the heart shine.
16. A heart free from care is better than a full purse.
17. To submit to God's will is the medicine of the heart.
18. Silence is the medicine of the heart. *Ps.* 37 : 7.
19. The money of a miser is a stone that is heavy and useless.
20. The remembrance of youth matter for sighing. The remembrance of death refreshes the heart. (81.)
21. The beauty of the mind is better than that of the body. (9.)
22. He delighting in the world drinks the milk of vain hopes. (10.) (21.) *Pr.* 11 : 7.
23. Covetousness is the punishment of the rich. (27.) A rich miser is poorer than a poor man. (106.)
24. Thy hoary hairs are death's messengers. (199.) *Hos.* 7 : 9
25. Nightly prayers make the day to shine. *Ruth* 2 : 12.
26. The world is too narrow to hold all those quarrelling.
27. The thirst after wealth is more vehement than the thirst after water. *Eccl.* 6 : 9.
28. The shadow of a lame man is crooked. 1 *Tim.* 6 : 17.
29. Live content you will be a king. 1 *Tim.* 6 : 6.
30. The strength of the heart is from the soundness of the faith. *Mat.* 17 : 20. *Heb.* 11 : 33-38.
31. God's word is the soul's medicine. (11.)
32. Riches are the fomenters of desire. (106.)
33. Envy has no rest (4); the wise no poverty.
34. Bad company is venturing to sea. (130.)
35. Forgetfulness of death, the soul's rest
36. It is more useful to flee from yourself than from a lion. *Rom.* 7 : 24.
37. Evil desires are a snake in a man's bosom. *Mat.* 12 : 29.
38. No religion without courage. *Mat.* 11 : 12.
39. Truth is a cutting sword. *Heb.* 4 : 12.
40. Self admiration the mark of folly. *Pr.* 27 : 12, 28, 26.
41. The heart is the treasury of the tongue. *Lk.* 6 : 45-46.
42. Man is the son of an hour. *Job* 14 : 1. (27.)
43. Anger is the fire of the heart. (110.) *Pr.* 25 : 28.
44. The ascent to virtue steep, the descent to vice smooth.

45. A benefactor is alive though removed to the mansions of the dead. *Heb.* 11 : 4.
46. Praying without working is a bow without a string. *Mat.* 26 : 41. *Jas.* 2 : 17.
47. Worldly hope is like the mirage deceiving him that sees it and hopes from it. *Job* 8: 13.
48. A bad companion is like one armed with a drawn sword. (104.)
49. The highest government is governing anger. *Pr.* 18 : 19
50. Your garment in which you clothe another, will last longer than that in which you clothe yourself.
51. The best fighting is against yourself. *Pr.* 16 : 32.
52. The love of the world the fountain of all evil.
53. The sweetness of the future life takes away the bitterness of this. *Heb.* 10 : 34.
54. Spend that which will not remain in you and purchase what will remain. *Mat.* 19 : 21.
55. The poor man's silver shines more with God than the rich man's gold. *Mark* 12 : 41-44.
56. Cure your anger by silence ; it is a plague and emaciating sickness. *Eccl.* 7 : 9.
57. The remembrance of another life is a medicine : the remembrance of this life a grievous disease. *Ph.* 3 : 13.
58. A stumble with the foot and wounds with the tongue destroy. *Pr.* 12 : 13, 18.
59. Meditation in the night watches is the spring to God's friends. *Gen.* 24 : 63.
60. Envy is a man's worst companion and always asking is the worst poverty. (4.) *Pr.* 27 : 4.
61. Doubt destroys faith as salt does honey. *Rom.* 14 : 23.
62. The fasting of desires after worldly pleasures is the best fasting. *Js.* 58 : 4-8.
63. Dim eyes do not injure when the mind's eye is bright.
64. A man's injustice in this life is the forerunner of his misery in the next. (74.)
65. The man is strange—who seeking a lost animal, suffers his soul to be lost—who ignorant of himself seeks to understand God—who doubts the existence of God when he sees his creatures.
66. Knowledge without practice is a bow without a string.

67. The greatness of God meditated on lessons the creatures in your eyes. *Ps.* 8 : 3, 4.
68. Punish your enemies by benefitting them. (224.)
69. The summit of knowledge is self-knowledge.
70. Content enjoys riches, covetousness produces cares, every ambitious man is a captive, and every covetous one a pauper. (106.)
71. Many locks are opened by patience. 2 *Thess.* 3 : 5.
72. Every one living has disease, but to every disease there's a medicine. *Jer.* 8 : 22.
73. Learning without intellect as its companion is profitless, so words without action. 2 *Tim.* 3 : 7.
74. Who questions, learns. *Luk.* 2 : 46. *John* 5 : 39.
75. Only the wise man despises himself, only a fool trusts his own judgment. *Pr.* 28 : 26.
76. He is not dead who leaves monuments of his knowledge behind. *Heb.* 11 : 4.
77. The bitterness of reproof is more useful than the sweetness of flattery. *Pr.* 29 : 15.
78. The prosperity of the wicked is like a garden over a cesspool. *Luk.* 16 : 23 : 17 : 27. *Pr.* 24 : 19, 20.
79. The eyes are little use if the mind be blind. *Mark* 8 : 18.
80. Content lies in three things—satisfied with what is given—no reliance on what is in men's hands—acquiescing in God's decrees. 1 *Tim.* 6 : 8.
81. The gravity of old age is fairer than the flower of youth. (199.)

BENGALI PROVERBS.

1. An excessive noise is of no use. *Eccl.* 7 : 16.
2. Drunk with pride, he wanders through various snares.
3. Having a firm hold on all sides, mount the horse.
4. Look you to your own face—*i. e.*, Mind your own business.
5. The white ant, the cat, and the wicked spoil good things.
6. Unable to fly, the *Shalik bird* is tame—*i. e.*, he makes a virtue of necessity.
7. One man is being impaled, while another counts the joints of the stake—*i. e.*, a man viewing without feeling the calamity of another. *Luk.* 10 : 31.

8. By continual eating he has become an alligator. (28.)
9. When a cow dies she is taken up and carried to the river. When a man dies they cover him up also and do the same—*i. e.*, death levels all distinction. *Eccl.* 3: 19.
10. Not a *sleeping* tiger should awake. *Pr.* 15: 1.
11. A good *horse* is known by his long ears, a benefactor by his gifts. A man by laughing, a jewel by its brilliance.
12. The man who wishes to hear what he can see is a fool not to be equalled. *Job.* 42: 5.
13. A firefly shining by moonlight. 2 *Cor.* 3: 10.
14. On pressure he is only cowdung, yet he swells up as a townbred fellow,—*i. e.*, a fop, a swell. (14.) (9.)
15. The sieve says to the needle, you have a hole in your tail. *Sic.*—"The kettle calling the pot black." "Cast out the mote out of thine own eye." (15.)
16. The rain water never streams up the thatch. 2 *Sam.* 12: 23.
17. Even the sacred cow Kapila, if found in company with a *stolen* one, would be taken up. *Sic.*—One suspected on account of keeping bad company. 1 *Thess.* 5: 22.
18. With a *goat's* foot pounding barley.
19. In a torn coarse bag to put fine rice. (166.)
20. Having drank the *water*, he enquires after the caste of the giver. *Mat.* 25: 10.
21. In the *water* the alligator, on the land the tiger; each aims at breaking my neck. *Sic.*—"between Scylla and Charybdis ;—" "from the frying pan into the fire."
22. Writing on water. *Jer.* 2: 13. 1 *Cor.* 9: 26.
23. Can the dinghy in the water bear a ship's mast—*i. e.*, carrying too much sail. *Pr.* 16: 18.
24. When living he would not give him a snap of the fingers, when dead he bestows fragrant grass.
25. Baldness, natural disposition, and elephantiasis only end with death. (23.)
26. To weed out the thieves would make the village a desert.
27. To employ a bull at the rice pedal—*i. e.*, a man reduced to misfortune. *Judg.* 16: 21.
28. Seeing the wave do not sink the boat—*i. e.*, be not frightened with slight obstacles. *Eccl.* 11: 4.
29. He cuts away the root and waters the branch. *Mat.* 6: 33
30. Begin by making him draw only a load of cotton and you

may make him finally draw a harrow. *Sic*—"the thin edge of the wedge."

31. He eats sweatmeats before curds. *Sic*—"the cart before the horse." *Lam.* 3: 27.
32. A giver is like the cocoanut; a miser like a bambu,—*i. e.*, the former hard without, the latter hollow within.
33. Sand sharpens a knife, a stone an axe. Good words a good man, so giving a thrashing to a rogue. *Pr.* 10: 13.
34. Days go, but words spoken remain. *Sic.—Litera scripta manet. Mat.* 12: 36.
35. Who has *two wives* has much sorrow. 1 *Kings.* 11: 4.
36. An empty stall is better than a bad horse. *Pr.* 21: 9.
37. The grass at a distance looks thick—*Sic.*, cows at a distance have long horns.
38. He who has had *ringworm* knows what it really is. *Heb.* 4: 15.
39. The *carpenter's* daughter wanders through the country and yet she is ashamed to lift the water to bathe herself.
40. He is between two minds whether he should be burnt or buried,—*i. e.*, be a Musulman or Hindu. *Jas.* 1: 6.
41. *Pride* is not in wealth but in the mind.
42. I bind him and he shrieks out; I loose him he wants to fight with me. *Mat.* 11: 16—19. (101.)
43. The cargo of virtue floats. The cargo of vice sinks.
44. The righteous is like a cocoanut, the sinner like Zizyphus Jujuba,—*i. e.* The former inside is soft, the latter hard.
45. The actor's promotion is nothing, lasting only two hours.
46. He who in dreams always sees a tiger eating him has no happy days. *Pr.* 28: 1.
47. The low person's words are like the tortoise's head—*i. e.* which can be put out or drawn in according to circumstances. *Pr.* 18: 4.
48. The lame can leap over mountains by God's aid. 2 *Cor.* 12: 9.
49. The mud sticks not to the body of the *pankal* fish—*i. e.* it is smooth, so calumny to an innocent person. 2 *Cor.* 6: 3.
50. Should the village neighbours be on good terms even a cow without a tail can be sold. (100.)
51. The commission of sin produces the fear of death. (223.)
52. Having crossed the river the ferryman is a rascal.

53. Plastering an old hut. (139.)
54. Affection's boat ascends even mountains. *Gen.* 29: 20.
55. The *heron* a saint, in appearance until the fish come.
56. Straining tight but a loose fastening. *Mat.* 23: 24.
57. He sits down for an hour, during which he could have gone a coss, the road says it is not my fault. *Eccl.* 7: 29.
58. The goat tied up is at the will even of a child —*i. e.*, applied to a man in *debt. Mat.* 18: 28.
59. A bat has sucked the plaintain—*i. e.*, all is gone.
60. With the devotee he is a devotee; with the vegetable seller a vegetable seller. *John.* 2: 14. *2 Cor.* 11. 14.
61. The dwarf hopes to catch the moon. *Js.* 14: 12.
62. Is there a thunderbolt in the cloudless day? *Mark* 13: 4.
63. Young feathers on the neck of an old martin,—*i. e.*, an old man beginning to learn.
64. She went to pray for the gift of a son, she returns having lost her husband.
65. The eggs of the *bol* fish,—*i. e.*, very numerous. (209.)
66. With the mind pure even the Ganges comes into the cobbler's box. *Jas.* 2: 5. *Mat.* 8: 10.
67. A heros words and elephant's teeth remain fixed.
68. A torch-bearer blind,—*i. e.*, one teaching others, untaught himself. *Luke.* 4: 23.
69. A great man's *word* is like an elephant's tusk,—*i. e.*, which once shot out cannot be drawn back.
70. The makhal fruit fair on the outside, but bitter inside.—*Sic.*, apples of Sodom. As Sounding brass or a platter. (18.)
71. He kicked him on the head, but makes a salam at his feet.
72. A child six months after birth is helpless; but a calf when born dances. *Job.* 38: 41.
73. The arrow discharged returns not. (7.)
74. *False* words and sprinkled water how long do they remain? (3.)
75. Sweet mangoes produce worms. *Pr.* 1: 32.
76. For *folly* no medicine. (65.)
77. If a man's *destiny* is crooked, even in a jungle of durba grass the tiger attacks him.
78. He whose religion is not fixed has no fixed conduct.

79. To take a man's grinding stone and pestle and break his teeth with them. *Ps.* 9: 15.
80. Where there is fear of the tiger there it is evening.
81. I feel the *heat* as savage as a tiger. *Jer.* 32: 2.
82. He tears the leaf he eats on—*i. e.*, an ungrateful servant.
83. He sees Jugganath's car, and sells plaintains at the same time.
84. Light sin, heavy punishment. (129.)
85. In fighting cowardly as a lizard, but in talk a tiger.
86. They fetch the salt when the rice is eaten. "The day after the fair." "Locking the stable when the horse is gone." *Mat.* 25: 8.
87. The attachment of the insincere is a razor's edge. (110.)
88. I can believe in your crop of corn when it is gathered into the garner. *Pr.* 4: 18.
89. You may break dry wood, but it will not bend. *Pr.* 1: 20.
90. Faith in God is the root of all devotion, but deliverance from evil is only her servant.
91. On a fire in the city, even the Pir's house is not saved.
92. Reflect five or seven times, then act. *Pr.* 19: 2.
93. Ink on a white surface. *Ph.* 2: 15.
94. By *words* only the moistened rice is not made into a confection. *Mat.* 7: 26.
95. Like Hindu Gods, smooth without, dry grass within. (18.)
96. A Spirit without revenge the highest religion. *Pr.* 16: 32.
97. I will hide my wishes and my age, but when the jaws fall in where shall I hide them. (139.)
98. Put the hand in the fire, whether willingly or no, it will burn. (74.)
99. When they take medicine they think of God, *i. e.*, apply for his aid. *Mat.* 11: 19.
100. He does not know the first letter of the Alphabet, yet disputes about God. *Ps.* 14: 1.
101. Time's march is crooked: time dissolves things. (27.)
102. A blind man losing his stick once will not loose it again.
103. The crow hoping to sing like the cuckow, and the dwarf to catch the moon are both unfortunate.
104. Dancing on an unbaked water vessel. (10) (96.)

c

105. The crow being counsellor all is destroyed. 1 *Kings.* 22.
106. He is the sediment of an earthen vessel, *i. e.*, a quiet person.
107. Fickle as the weaver assenting by nod, but who acts differently. *Mat.* 7 : 21.
108. Blackness leaves the coal when fire enters it, *i. e.* good men, like fire remove sin in their associates.
109. By words he softens the mind, but words will not soften the rice. *Jas.* 2 : 16.
110. The worms got by the young birds to eat, eat the birds themselves. *Jas.* 5: 3.
111. You eat your own head. *Ps.* 7 : 16.
112. By a look from God he can become a king. *Ps.* 75: 6.
113. Many elephants cannot wade the river, the mosquito says it is only knee deep. *Is.* 45: 9.
114. Pull the car the head follows. *Ps.* 24 : 2.
115. Even the very bones of deceivers will prove sorcerers. *Job* 20 : 11.
116. I came alone into the world, I go out alone. (248.)
117. My mind is troubled in collecting to pay the rent, how I can worship Hari. *Luke.* 8 : 14.
118. Where there's a will there's a way. *Pr.* 22: 13.

SANSKRIT SAYINGS.

From *Chanakyea Rajniti.*

1. A learned man and a sovereign are unequal ; the former is respected every where, the latter only in his own dominions. *Dan.* 12 : 3.
2. A learned man is full of virtue ; an ignorant man, of vice ; the former is preferred to a thousand brutes. (15.)
3. A beautiful youth of noble lineage, if illiterate, is not more agreeable than a kinsuk* without fragrance.
4. Parents are the enemies of their children if they refuse them education ; for they appear in society as herons among the flamingos. *Pr.* 22 : 6.
5. To extract nectar from poison,† to pick a gem from a filthy spot ; to draw knowledge even from a vulgar person ; and to choose a female of exquisite qualities even of ignoble birth, are advisable.

---
* A flower which has no fragrance, but is pleasing to the eye.
† Hindu sages maintain that nectar may be found in poison.

6. Shun a wicked person, though endowed with knowledge; just as a serpent, even possessed of a gem‡ inspires terror.
7. It is absolutely necessary to flee 1,000 paces from elephants; 100 from horses; 10 from horned animals, and absolutely to avoid bad company. *Ps.* 1 : 1.
8. A Wise man moves with one foot, stands fast with the other, and does not quit the station he occupies, without well considering that to which he intends to go.
9. Anxiety is the fever of the mind; the burning sun acts like a fever on clothes. *Luk.* 21 : 34.
10. Rubies are not found in every rock, nor pearls in the skull of every elephant,¶ nor an upright person every where, nor sandal-wood in every desert. *Luke.* 12 : 52.
11. Contentment with little, sound sleep, vigilant watching, gratitude and fortitude are virtues inherent in the dog, and are to be learnt from it. (19) *Job.* 12 : 7.
12. A powerful man regards no burden; a tradesman no distance; to a learned man no country is foreign, and a fine speaker finds no enemy. *Eph.* 2 : 19.
13. Strong wind is injurious to shrubs; dew to lilies; thunderbolts to mountains; and the wicked to the virtuous. 1 *Cor.* 15 : 33.
14. The dusk leads one astray; a false woman is like one dead; a small quantity of seeds sown is but a waste, and an undutiful servant occasions disgrace to his master.

From the *Pancha Ratna.*

15. Riches tend to increase pride; worldlings are ever beset with eminent dangers; females alone have the power of attraction; monarchs seldom have friends; no mortal is free from the claws of yama or death.
16. Avarice neutralizes virtue; deceit is the vilest of transgressions; righteousness is the purest devotion; purity of heart needs no *pilgrimage*; generosity is the noblest of actions; wisdom renders other ornaments redundant; education surpasses wealth, and defamation ruins life.
17. The suppression of passions is the noblest heroism; decency adorns a woman; learning is reckoned intrinsic property; patriotism is conducive to real happiness

allegiance secures sovereignty; loss of time is irreparable; following righteousness is the best indication of knowledge; associating with sages is advantageous, and keeping company with unlettered men is disagreeable.

18. Patience is the best defence against evil; wrath is a powerful enemy to mortals; foes are indeed like fuel; invidious fellows are more numerous than serpents; the acquirement of knowledge is the noblest wealth, and the being versed in poetry surpasses sovereignty.

From the *Naba Ratna*.

19. Morality is the chief embellishment of monarchs; humility, of the learned; modesty, of women; constancy, of a married couple; children, of a family; poetry, of ingenious people; and clearness, of speech; beauty is the embellishment of the body; memory, of the mind; tranquillity, of the twice-born; patience, of those who are vigorous; wealth, of the worldly; and health, of the laborious man.

20. An illiterate hermit seeking quietness; a monarch inclined to indolence; an envious man respecting virtue; an indigent family-man desiring respect; a master practising parsimony; a religionist living impiously; a sovereign without the power of governing; a pious man partaking food with others; and a distressed aged valetudinarian becoming the husband of a young girl;—such characters are indeed shameless.

From the *Bánarástaka*.

21. Swiftness is an essential recommendation to horses: modesty, to women; corporal debility, to hermits; knowledge, to brahmuns; temperance, to sages; and vigour, to an armed man.

From the *Maha Mudgara*.

22. Our transient life is like the drops of water, which float for a moment on water-lilies, and soon are seen no more.

23. Day and night, evening and morning, autumn and spring come and go, and time sports with our passing days; yet, the idle winds of hope never forsake mankind.

24. Though the limbs become (feeble,) melted, the hair hoary, the teeth fall, the freshness of countenance decay, the hands tremble that hold the staff, yet, vain hopes are not forsaken.

From the *Shanti Shatak*.

25. How vainly have I passed the whole of my life! Alas; how inestimable a jewel have I bartered for mere glass.

26. Deer are the happiest creatures of the forest, for they are quite unconcerned about their food, live upon bare vegetables, and seem neither to be distressed, nor to lament as we do. Let us then seriously contrast their state with ours, and see the wide difference which exists.

27. The stomach, is satisfied with little food, even with vegetables? but the heart, although gratified with the fulfilment of more than an hundred *desires*, is incessant in pursuing after more. *Eccl.* 6 : 9.

28. Dogs delight to devour human bones, which are so disgusting, filled as they are with worms and moisture, and they eagerly lick the putrid juice as if it was palatable: Thus do mean people appear shameless when perpetrating vile actions. 2 *Pet.* 2 : 22.

29. Why does a hermit retire from the busy world, and feel averse to live in stately fabrics, to hear melodious songs, and to gratify his sensual appetites? Is it not because he knows every thing to be in the same fluctuating condition as the beam of light, which even the wings of a fluttering moth may dissipate? *Jas.* 4 : 14.

30. Censured by an opponent, be not offended at it, but rather strive to adorn the mind and judgment with the invaluable jewel of patience. *Pr.* 12 : 1.

31. All secular affairs are as it were confined in an oven, and all human afflictions are reckoned to be the embers in it. Do not therefore, O ye innocent mortals! wander about in this bewildering maze, like carnivorous casts in quest of eatables, since every thing below is faithless and unstable. *Heb.* 13 : 14.

32. The cupidity of mankind is like an appalling ocean, containing poisonous water, the swelling surges of which no one can cross over; which is surrounded by fanciful and frightful illusions, and in which swim the crocodiles of passion, while hovering birds seem to suspend themselves mournfully over it in the air. This dangerous gulph is however passed over by intelligent sages, with the strong aid of their devotional powers. (50)

From the *Prabodhchandroday Natak*.

1. These tainted natures; these crooked dispositions become the causes of destruction to those who gave them birth, and these perish themselves. Thus whilst, smoke rises

to the clouds, the fire is extinguished and afterwards the smoke itself disappears. *Eccl.* 5 : 11.

2. We might as well expect to find excellent fruit drop from trees growing in the air. (10.)

3. If funeral oblations nourish the deceased, why is not the flame of an extinguished taper renovated by pouring on oil ? *Kings.* 18 : 26.

4. They conceive that you ought to throw away the pleasures of life, because they are mixed with pain ; but what prudent man witll throw away unpeeled rice which encloses excellent grain, because it is covered with the husk.

5. The *equanimity* of rational men is steady as the clear unruffled ocean, so that they bear with reproach from persons whose eyebrows gathered up in black anger, present a fearful appearance and whose eyes are red as the setting sun.

6. Consider the society of friends as a momentary flash of lightning, and revolving this often in your mind, enjoy felicity.

7. *Oblivion* is the only medicine for those severe strokes of grief, which wound, unseen, the mortal parts.

8. How can an answer be given to him who does not *comprehend his own spirit*, any more than it is possible to inform a blind man respecting the figure of his body ?

From the *Atmabodh.*

9. *Knowledge* dispels ignorance, as the light dispels darkness, when the ignorance which arises from earthly affections is removed, spirit, by its own splendor, shines forth in an undivided state, as the sun spreads its effulgence when the cloud is dispersed. *Mat.* 4 : 2.

10. Spirit causes the understanding, organs of sense, &c. to appear, as a lamp renders objects visible.

11. As fire is caused by the friction of two pieces of wood, so by the continual contemplation of spirit a flame of knowledge is kindled which burns up the stubble of ignorance.

12. The emancipated soul is that illuminated person who throws off his former accidents and qualities, and becomes one with the one, living, happy Being ; in like manner as the chorysalis becomes a bee.

13. He himself pervades his own internal essence, and contemplates the whole world appearing. Burnt as fire pervades an ignited ball of iron, and also diplays itself externally.

14. The soul being enlightened by meditation, &c., and burning with the fire of knowledges is delivered from all its impurities, and shines in its own splendour.

From the *Mrichhakati Natak*.

15. He has become impoverished by his liberality; like the lake in the summer which is exhausted by relieving the thirst of the travellers.

16. A preserved pumpkin, a dried *potherb*, fried flesh and boiled rice that has stood for a night in the cold weather, stink when kept too long.

17. You in this world *live*, other men only *breathe*.

18.   Oh then let virtuous youth,
Beware the wanton's charms, that baleful blow,
Like flowers on charnel ground, the ocean waves
Are less unsteady, and the dying glow
Of Eve less fleeting them a woman's fondness.
Wealth is her aims, as soon as man is drained
Of all his goods like a squeezed colour bag,
She casts him off. Brief as the lightning's flash,
Is woman's* love. *Pr. 2.*

19. Nature is woman's teacher, and she learns more sense than man the pedant, gleans from books.

20. The stars are all extinct, as fades the memory
Of kindness in a bad man's heart. The heavens
Are shorn of all these radiance, as the wife,
The glory loses in her husband's absence.

21. Why shave the heart and mow the chin
Whilst bristling follies choke the breast:
Apply the knife to parts within,
And heed not how deformed the rest:
The heart of pride and passion weed
And then the man is pure indeed. *Mat. 23 : 25.*

22. The points of law are sufficiently clear here, but the understanding still labours like a cow in a quagmire.

23.   Love equal smiles
On poor and rich; the bosom's precious balm
Is not the fragrant herb, nor costly ungunt
But nature's breath, affection's holy perfume.

* Refers to women not virtuous.

24.   Fate sports with life
And like a wheel, the whirling world revolves;
Where some are raised to affluence some depressed
In want; where some are borne awhile aloft
And some hurled down to wretchedness and woe.

        From the *Vikram Urvasi Natak*.

25.   Why cherish this alarm
Where its just cause is o'er; unclose those lids—
The lotus opens where the night retires.

26. There he sits *immoveable* like *a monkey in* a *picture*.

27.   The God cements our souls
With mutual fervours—as in one mass combines
Iron with iron where each fiery bar
With equal radiance glows.

28.   The joy that follows grief.
Gains richer zest from agony foregone—
The traveller who faint pursues his track
In the fierce day, alone can tell how sweet,
The grateful shelter of the friendly tree. *Is.* 32 : 2.

        From the *Niti Shatak*.

29. Easier would it be for one by strong pressure to extract *oil from the sand*, or for another tormented by thirst to quench it by drinking the *image of water*, or by wandering round him to catch the *horn of a hare* than to govern the prejudiced mind of fools. *Pr.* 27 : 22.

30. The wealth assigned for each person by God in the book of fate, he shall receive whether he dwells in a desert or in Meru. Be not anxious therefore, whether your water vessel be dipped in the ocean or in the well, it will contain the same quality.

31. Seven things are darts to my soul. The pale moon at day time, a woman whose youth has melted away, a lake without lilies, a beautiful face without meaning, a noble devoted to money, a good man difficult of access, a wicked man admitted to the hall of a prince.

32. In prosperity the mind of the generous is soft as the lotus,
In adversity hard as the mass of rock.

33. The lord of day expands the lotus leaves, the moon the cup of the lily, the cloud unasked gives water : so the good of themselves make exertions for the good of others.

34. The perseverance of a man of constant mind can never be overwhelmed by misfortune, as the flame of the torch turned upward never goes down. *2 Cor.* 6 : 10.

From the *Bhagavatgita*

35. The heart, which follows the dictates of the moving passions, carries away his reason, as the storm the bark in the raging ocean. *Pr.* 25 : 28.

36. As troops of insects with increasing speed, seek their own destruction in the flaming fire; even so these people, with swelling fury, seek their own destruction.

37. The incorruptible Being is likened unto the tree Aswath (Banyan) whose root is above and whose branches are below, and whose leaves are the Veds. *Acts* 17: 28.

Every undertaking is involved in its faults, as the fire in its smoke.

As their old garments men cast off, anon new raiment to assume.
So casts the soul its worn-out frame, and takes at once another form.
The weapon cannot pierce it through, nor wastes it the consuming fire;
The liquid waters melt it not, nor dries it up the parching wind;
Impenetrable and unburn'd; impermeable and undried:
Perpetual ever-wandering, firm, indissoluble, permanent, invisible, unspeakable.

40. The soul floats like the lotus on the lake, unmov'd unruffled by the tide. *Acts* 20 : 24. 16 : 25.

41. He who as the tortoise does with its limbs
Withdraws the senses from the sensual objects everywhere.
His wisdom is confirmed. *Rom.* 6 : 11. *Col.* 2 : 20.

42. As a lamp, standing in a windless place, moves not—that is the likeness.
Of the devotee, whose mind is subdued, who is collected in self-devotion.

From the *Malati Madhava*.

43. All nature's sympathies.
Spring not from outward form, but inward virtue,
The lotus buds not till the sun has risen. *1 Sam.* 16 : 7.

44. Women like flowers are of tender fabric
And should be softly handled. *Eph.* 5 : 25.

From the *Utar Ramcharita.*

45.   A deep and ceaseless sorrow,
Preys on his heart, like a destroying fire,
That lighted in the trunk of some tall tree,
Consumes unseen its sap. 2 Cor. 7 : 10.

From the *Raghuvansa.*

46. She went first followed by the King as *faith is followed by works.*
47. The *storm may uproot the trees* but cannot the mountains.
48. The father can no more destroy his son. than the *cloud* can extinguish by its water. the lightning which proceeds from itself. *Is.* 49 : 15. (82.)
49. The good, like *clouds*, receive only to give away. *Luke.* 16.
50. The iron itself by rust becomes soft. why not the soul with grief. *Ps.* 119 : 67. 2 *Cor.* 7 : 10.
51. They concealed their anger under signs of joy as a lake with its water tranquil on the surface hides the alligator.
52. His countenance freed from the fear of the enemy, shone as a *mirror* which recovers its brightness, when the vapor of the breath is exhaled. *Ps.* 30 : 5.
53. He performed the obsequies for his deceased wife of whom nothing except her virtues was left. *Pr.* 10 : 7. *Eccl.* 12 : 7.
54. The man of feeble mind thinks the death of a friend. a *thorn* fixed within the heart, whereas the wise man looks on it as extracted—for death is the *gate* to happiness.
55. The spear of death however cleft his heart as a shoot of the fig tree does the pavement of houses. 1 *Cor.* 15 : 55. 2 *Cor.* 7 : 10.
56. The king (Dasarath) having enjoyed bodily pleasures, entered on his last stage of life and came near to extinction as the *light of a lamp* in mornings dawn. *Pr.* 4 : 18.

ARABIC PROVERBS.

1. The cloud of summer goes quickly. *Ps.* 90 : 6.
2. The arrow of *truth* is winged and pierces the scope of the argument. *John.* 8 : 32. 1 *Ps.* 91 : 4.
3. A beautiful girl outside, a leopard inside. *Mat.* 7 : 15.
4. The torrent when mixed with mud flows gently on in darkness, *i. e.,* a man who outwardly shows love but hides enemity in his heart. *Ps.* 5 : 9.

5. The noisy cat catches nothing. *Ex.* 14 : 13. *Is.* 30 : 15.
6. The worst day for a cock is when his feet are washed, *i. e.*, previous to being killed. *Jas.* 5 : 3.
7. To show the *mirage* to a thirsty man. *Is.* 44 : 20.
8. More thirsty than the sand. *Heb.* 6 : 7.
9. Satan does not devastate his own vineyard. *Mat.* 12 : 25.
10. One spits out the putrid water in a cistern. *Eph.* 5 : 11.
11. More useless than two nuts in a bag, *i. e.*, only emit sound.
12. Patience is the key of joy. *Ps.* 40 : 1. *Heb.* 6 : 12.
13. The generous can be known by his eyes, as the horses age can by its teeth. *Dt.* 13 : 8.
14. Caution secures not cowards from death—it can come from the sky. *Ps.* 91 : 6. 1 *Kings.* 22 : 34.
15. Iron is to be cut by iron, *i. e.*, no extinguishing a fire with rose water. *Mat.* 5 : 30.
16. Even a noble horse sometimes stumbles. *Pr.* 24 : 16.
17. His nose looks to heaven his legs are in the water, *i. e.*, proud but feeble. *Gen.* 11 : 4.
18. A true brother or friend is a looking glass, who points out all your vices. *Pr.* 27 : 6.
19. Women are parts cut out of men. *Gen.* 2 : 23.
20. The man not performing his *promises*, is like lightning without rain. 1 *John.* 2 : 17.
21. Fatigued with lying on one side lye on the other. *Mat.* 10 : 23.
22. When you roast meat cook it well; when you eat it chew it well. *Eccl.* 9 : 10.
23. Where the mind inclines, the feet lead. Love climbs mountains. *Cant.* 8 : 7. *Gen.* 29 : 20.
24. Though the bow be crooked, the arrow hits the mark. (157)
25. Provoke not a dog. *Pr.* 15 : 1. *Gen.* 19 : 6.
26. Love is the companion of blindness. *Pr.* 10 : 12.
27. More secure than the doves of Mecca. *Is.* 60 : 8.
28. Walls have ears. *Luke.* 12 : 3. *Eccl.* 10 : 20.
29. When the mice and cat are reconciled the shop of the grocer is destroyed. *Luke.* 23 : 12.
30. As long as you are an anvil bear the strokes when you an hammer give it. 2 *Thes.* 3 : 5.

31. The liar's mother is a virgin *i. e.*, he tells impossible things.
32. The servant deceived by the cold of the morning, provided no water for the heat of the day. *Pr.* 27 : 1.
33. Careless as the ostrich depositing its eggs in the sand.
34. Lightning without rain, *i. e.*, a beauty without merit.
35. A fine man of promises only like the camel who at times fondles her young, but will not allow them to suck.
36. A cat's love to her young, *i. e.*, she devours them. *Pr.* 12 : 10.
37. Delays longer than Noahs crow. *Gen.* 8 : 9.
38. Rising before the crow. *Eccl.* 12 : 4.
39. Thorny tress produce gum. *Is.* 53 : 2.
40. To hammer cold iron. *Rom* 12 : 20.
41. His aquria are large, but they contain only croaking frogs
42. A bad friend is like a smith, who, if he does not burn you with iron, will suffocate you with smoke. *Jas.* 4 : 4.
43. With the horse give a rein with a camel a rope, *i. e.* complete a thing. *Eccl.* 9 : 10.
44. He attacks a lion but fears the voice of a crow, *i.e.*, fearing little things : a superstitious man. *Pr.* 28 : 1.
45. The fear of God is a bridle. *Pr.* 14 : 27.
46. The idle man was only moving his head to throw off flies.
47. I escaped hanging by a hair. (203.)
48. Follow the barking of a dog not that of a jackal ; *i. e.* one leads to the village, the other to the desert. Acts 8 :10
49. The trunk of a tree for the camels to rub themselves against. *Job* 29 : 15. *a hack.*
50. Slow drinking quenches thirst, *i. e.*, make a moderate use.
51. Ignorance is the death of the living. 1 *Tim.* 5 : 6.
52. Purchase not an earthen jar before you sound it. 1 *John* 4 : 1
53. A bug touched stinks, *i. e.* contact with the wicked.
54. Like a moth falling on a lighted candle or glue. (39)
55. Creeping as a cat on a mouse. *Acts* 20 : 19.
56. The ass went seeking for horns but lost his ears. *Esth.* 6: 13
57. Good honey in a dirty vessel. 2 *Cor.* 4 : 7.
58. He dived but only brought up mud. 1 *Cor.* 15 : 48.
59. Occasions like clouds pass away. *Jer.* 8 : 20. Sic Agastyca Muni passed south but returned not. 1 *Kings.* 18 : 21.

60. Riding two horses at the same time. 1 *Kings*. 18 : 21.
61. A mule yoked with horses. 2 *Cor* 6 : 14.
62. Little one sitting on a hot stone.
63. The thief for a year did not shear the sheep, *i. e.* making a virtue of necessity.
64. Working like an insect in wood. *Jonah* 4 : 7.
65. The needle clothes others but is naked itself. *Mat*. 23 : 2.
66. Do not spit in the well from which you drink. *Is.* 1 : 2.
67. Who strikes the tree will get leaves. *Mat*. 7 : 7.
68. It follows him as a shadow. *Num*. 32 : 23.
69. If you do not want a fool's medicine keep away from him.
70. The barking dog injures not the cloud neither does broken glass a rock. *Acts* 20 : 24.
71. A summer cloud without rain, *i. e.* a rich miser.
72. Seeking fat in a dog's tail, *i. e.* good things from the vile.
73. Taking a hyena under his protection. *Pr.* 6 : 27.
74. Many who draw the milk but do not look after the flock.
75. Like a whetstone which sharpens but does not cut.
76. The contemplation of vice is a vice. *Pr.* 23 : 31. *Sam.* 11 : 2.
77. Envy is a raging fever. *Acts.* 7 : 9. *Pr.* 14 : 30.
78. More cautious than a chameleon *i. e.* he does not leave one tree until he has secured the other.
79. One rushing between two camels *i. e.* is kicked by both (109.) *Pr* 26 : 17.
80. Every stranger becomes a relative to another stranger (99.)
81. Like an Ethiopian who when hungry steals, when full he is licentious *Pr* 30 : 9.
82. Night is blind (60.) 1 *Thess* 5 : 7.
83. You are not safe from a fool as long as he has a sword in his hand. *Pr.* 17 : 12.
84. A sick person does not relish food, neither one bound by love of the world spiritual admonition. *Mat.* 9 : 12.
85. The eye of man will only be satisfied with so much earth as he can grasp in his hand (the grave.) *Ps.* 146 : 4
86. There are three things which no one knows whence they come—the wind, atoms flying in a house, and a cloud covering the earth. *Pr.* 30 : 19.
87. Those three things are only known in the following way—an hero in war, a wise man in anger and a friend in the time of necessity. *Pr.* 17 : 17.

88. Three things are never hidden, love, a mountain and one riding on a camel. *Mat.* 7 : 16.
89. Covetousness has for its mother unlawful desire, for its daughter injustice, for its companion vileness.
90. Patience is the key to joy, penitence the key to pardon modesty the key to tranquillity. *Luke* 11 : 52.
91. When the crow is your guide he will lead you to the corpses of dogs. *Mat.* 23 : 16.
92. Proverbs are the lamps to words. *Eccl* 12 : 11.
93. An immodest woman is food without salt *Luke* 14 : 34.
94. Silence is the remedy for anger. 1 *Pet* 3 : 9.
95. Four things cannot be brought back—a word spoken, an arrow discharged, the Divine Decree, and past time.
96. He eats an Elephant, but is annoyed by a fly sticking in his jaw.
97. The well lasts longer than the rope. *Ps.* 102 : 26.
98. If your companion be honey, do not lick it all up.
99. In shunning the bear he fell into the pit.
100. Disgrace easier to bear in this world than in the next.

CANARESE PROVERBS.

1. Does a light in the house of a low cast man not burn.
2. An Elephant fears not fishes neither the good the bad.
3. The pearl though originating in the water does not become water again— so the wise. *Pr.* 4 : 18.
4. Knowledge consisting only in words is an earthen vessel with holes. 1 *Cor.* 13 : 1 : 2.
5. Unlawful pleasure first sweet as sugar then tastes as the juice of the Nim tree. *Rom.* 6 : 21.
6. Is a serpent killed by a man beating on his hole—is salvation oftained by castigating the body. *Is.* 58 : 6.
7. Man's stay in the world short as that of a bird on a tree.
8. The riches of the good are like water turned off into a rice field. *Pr* 19 : 17. 11 : 25.
9. The sheep eats on the ground leaves with which it is decorated previous to being slaughtered. *Jas.* 5 : 5.
10. The fly the (poor man) is eaten by the frog (the rich) and both are eaten up by the serpent death. *Pr.* 30 : 23.
11. With legs strong you might go even to Bengal.

12. He has to live on gruel (poor) yet has some one to wipe his moustaches (proud.)
13. He loves his relations, but loves his rice, *i.e.*, he does not wish to spend money on them. *Jas.* 2 : 16.
14. What is extended will tear; what is long will break (ambitious.) *Pr.* 16 : 18.
15. When the washermans corpse is brought out his secrets may be discovered, *i. e.* the clothes he has stolen ; death reveals the true state of things. *Is.* 14 : 4.
16. Will a man pet and bring up a parrot and then throw it into the fire. *Mat.* 23 : 37.
17. Though you go to the wilderness you cannot escape fleas.
18. Though the fruit of the wild fig is beautifully red, inside there is only pulp. *Acts* 23 : 3.
19. Does the owl fly about in the light of the sun. *John* 3 : 19.
20. An ignorant person like the dancer directed by her master.
21. Life like a lamp exposed to the wind. *Jas.* 4 : 14.
22. Alms, are food prepared for a journey. *Rev.* 14 : 13.
23. The body of all men is alike composed of the five elements.
24. Heating a wick by an idiot is wasting cotton and oil.
25. Sandal wood burning gives perfume, so the afflictions of the good. *Heb.* 12 : 11.
26. Is sin an unburnt brick that it shall dissolve by bathing.
27. A word in season good, out of it like a silk cloth torn.
28. A cat is no tiger, and a farmer no scholar.
29. Teaching a fool is pouring water on a stone. *Pr.* 27 : 22.
30. A million of glow worms not equal to one sun.

SCRIPTURE SIMILES ILLUSTRATIVE OF TEXTS.

Adoption Believers have received the spirit of... *Rom.* 8 : 15.
Arm of flesh he trusting in cursed ... *Jer.* 16 : 5.
Bride of Christ the Church ...
Blood woe unto him that builds a town with ... *Hab.* 2 : 12.
Bees Jews chased by Canaanites as ... *Dt.* 1 : 44.
Billows of sorrow went over David ... *Ps.* 42 : 7.
Bullock unaccustomed to the yoke so obstinate... *Jer.* 31 : 18.
Bulls the wicked compass the righteous as ... *Ps.* 22 : 15.
Bulwarks salvation of God as walls and ... *Is.* 26 : 1.

Briar a bribe-taking judge as a	... *Mic.* 7 : 4.
Burthen cast yours on the Lord	... *Ps.* 55 : 22.
Cake not turned Ephraim as a	... *Hos.* 5 : 27.
Cage full of unclean birds. Babylon was *Rev.* 18 : 2. and Sinners are ...	... *Jer.* 5 : 27.
Carts rope sin drawn in as with	... *Is.* 5 : 18.
Candlestick of the unfaithful removed	... *Rev.* 2 : 5.
Cedar righteous flourish as ...	... *Ps.* 92 : 21.
Crooked nation the Jews. *Dt.* 32 : 5. so sinners	*Ph.* 2 : 15.
Crows fed by God, though not sowing	... *Luke* 12 : 24.
Dead the wicked twice dead ...	... *Jude* 12 : 13.
Dish Jerusalem wiped out as a	... 2 *Kings* 21 : 13.
Dream the wicked fly away as a	... *Job.* 20 : 8.
Drop of a bucket the nations before God as	... *Is.* 40 : 15.
Drink Christs to do his father's will	... *John* 4 : 34.
Drowned in perdition by foolish lusts	... 1 *Tim.* 6 : 9.
Dust small of the balance the nations like	... *Is.* 40 : 15.
Drink in iniquity wicked do like water	... *Job* 15 : 16.
Dwelling of Christ in the heart by faith	... *Eph.* 2 : 18.
Enemy death the last to be conquered	... 1 *Cor.* 15 : 26
Father God as a pities his children	... *Ps.* 103 : 13.
Fight the good fight of faith	.. 1 *Tim.* 6 : 12.
Filthy conversation of wicked Lot vexed with ...	2 *Pet.* 2 : 7
Fingers God's seen in Moses miracles	... *Ex.* 8 : 19.
Garment Earth waxes old as a	... *Heb.* 1 : 11
Gaining the world loosing the soul	... *Luke* 9 : 35
Groans of creation for sin	... *Rom* 8 : 22
Handbreadth our days as a before God.	... *Ps.* 39 : 5.
Heath in the desert so he trusting in man only	*Jer* 17 : 6.
Heel lifted up by Judas against Christ	... *Ps.* 49 : 9.
Hiding place from the wind Christ a	.. *Is.* 32 : 2.
Husbandman Christian patient for the harvest as.	*Jas.* 5 : 7.
Hedge of thorns way of slothful as	... *Pr.* 15 : 19.
Horn of the righteous shall be exalted.	... *Ps.* 112 : 9.
Hosts of angels praise God	... *Ps.* 148 : 2.

How y'omb a bad woman's lips like bit her end wormwood	Pr. 5 : 3.
Halting between two opinions	1 Kings 18 : 28.
Helmet the Christians the hope of salvation.	1 Thess. 5 : 8.
Hireling man looks for the reward in heaven as	Job 7 : 2
Hissing Babylon shall be as a	Jer. 51 : 37.
Harvest the of repentance passed	Jer. 8 : 20.
Idolatry; mortify covetousness which is	Col. 3 : 5.
Itching ears to those heaping up teachers	2 Tim. 4 : 3.
Lead Egyptians sunk like in the Red Sea	Ex. 15 : 10.
Lends to God the merciful man does	Pr. 19 : 17.
Madness in the heart of the wicked	Eccl. 9 : 3.
Mother of all to Christians Jerusalem above	Gal. 4 : 26.
Noonday innocence of righteous manifested as	Ps. 37 : 51G.
Nose of Sennacherib God put his hook in	2 Kings 19 : 28.
Nursing fathers kings will be to the Church	Is. 49 : 23.
Ocean depths the Believers sins cast into	Mic. 7 : 19.
Own day of judgment shall burn as	Mal. 4 : 1.
Path of the just a shining light	Pr. 4 : 18.
Pavilion the believer hid in God's	Ps. 27 : 4, 5.
Pierce themselves with many sorrows the rich	1 Tim. 6 : 9.
Plumb line God's judgments as	Is. 28 : 17.
Pillar in God's temple the believer is a	Rev. 3 : 12.
Rags our righteousness as filthy	Is. 64 : 6.
Rain of God's fury on the wicked	Job. 20 : 23.
Rivers broad God a place of	Is. 33 : 21.
Reaping corruption from sowing to the flesh	Gal. 6 : 8.
Schoolmaster the law to bring us to Christ	Gal. 3 : 24.
Scroll heavens will depart as	Rev. 6 : 14.
Sepulchres whitened the hypocrite like	Mat. 23 : 27.
Shadow of evening desired by the servant, so death wished for by Christian	Job. 7 : 2.
Shining of face by wisdom	Eccl. 8 : 1.
Song lovely hearing not doing like listening to	Ez. 33 : 32.
Straight between life and death	Ph. 1 : 23.
Stayed on God mind in perfect peace	Is. 26 : 3.

Sprinkling of the conscience with pure water ...	*Heb.* 10 : 22.
Store for fire earth kept as ...	2 *Pet.* 3 : 7.
Stubble before the wind wicked as ...	*Is.* 40 : 24.
Tooth broken confidence in unfaithful as ...	*Pr.* 25 : 19.
Tower of refuge God to the righteous ...	*Pr.* 13 : 10.
Tree of life a wholesome tongue as a ...	*Pr.* 15 : 4.
Trump of God at last day ...	1 *Thess.* 4 : 16.
Vail on the Jews heart when Moses read ...	2 *Cor.* 3 : 15.
Vessels of wrath fitted for destruction—wicked...	*Rom.* 9 : 22.
Washed their robes in the Lambs blood ...	*Rev.* 7 : 14.
Water as cold to a thirsty soul so good news ...	*Pr.* 25 : 25.
Wave shifting the doubting like ...	*Jas.* 1 : 6.
Wax melteth so the wicked perish ...	*Is.* 68 : 2.
Weaned child David's soul as ...	*Ps.* 131 : 2.
Winepress of God's wrath trodden by the wicked	*Rev.* 19 : 15.
Witness Conscience a ...	*Rom.* 2 : 15.
Wolves the wicked inwardly as ravening ...	*Mat.* 7 : 15.
Wrestling against the, flesh the devil and world...	*Eph.* 6. 12.

ILLUSTRATIONS IN THE BIBLE.
OF
ORIENTAL CUSTOMS.

Abraham entertains angels under a tree, chapatis or flour cakes prepared ...	*Gen.* 18 : 4
A wife selected for Isaac by a *ghatak* intermediate agent ...	*Gen.* 24 : 4.
A stone anointed by Jacob with *oil* ...	*Gen.* 28 : 18.
Laban refused to marry his *younger* daughter to Jacob before the elder was married ...	*Gen.* 29 26.
Esau reconciled to Jacob falls on his knees ...	*Gen.* 33 : 4.
Jacob orders his family to *change* their garments before worship ...	*Gen.* 35 : 2.
Water to wash *the feet* of Joseph's brethren ...	*Gen.* 43 : 24.
The Egyptians would not *Eat* with the Jews. ...	*Gen.* 43 : 32.
Joseph gave his brethren *changes of raiment* after the feast ...	*Gen.* 45 : 22.
Moses ordered to *put off his shoes* on holy ground	*Ex.* 3 : 5.

First born of man and beast sanctified to God ..	*Ex.* 13 : 2.
The Jews *danced* before the golden calf ...	*Ex.* 32 : 19.
The *fire* on the altar perpetually burning ...	*Lev.* 6 : 13.
The *ordeal* by water given to a woman .	*Num. v.* 17-24.
Watering seed with the foot ...	*Dt.* 11 : 10.
Deborah the prophetess lived under a Palm tree.	*Judges* 4 : 5.
David walked on the *house* roof in the evening...	2 *Sam.* 11 : 2.
The servant, Uriah, slept *at the door* of the King's house ...	2 *Sam.* 11 : 9.
David after grieving for his child *anoints* his body, and changes his garments ...	2 *Sam.* 12 : 20.
The *Idol* Baal said to be *sleeping* ...	1 *Kings* 18 : 27.
Naboth refuses to sell his *fathers inheritance* ...	1 *Kings* 21 : 3.
Queen Jezebel eaten by dogs ...	1 *Kings* 21 : 23
A Present from the king to Elisha ...	2 *Kings* 8 : 8.
The Jewish women *tinkled* with their feet ...	*Isaiah* 3 : 16.
God puts a hook in the nose of Assyrian king ...	*Isaiah* 37 : 29.
Women sowing pillows to arm holes ...	*Ezek.* 13 : 18.
Pharisees sounded a trumpet on giving alms ...	*Mat.* 6 : 2.
Two women grinding at a mill on Jerusalem being besieged by Romans'... ...	*Mat.* 24 : 41.
A Woman poured fragrant ointment on Christ	*Mat.* 14 : 3.
The *guest chamber* for Christ's last supper ...	*Mark* 14 : 14.
Christ in a *caravan* when young ...	*Luk.* 2 : 44.
Where the *carcass* is the vultures will be ...	*Luk.* 17 : 37.
Marvel at Christ's talking with a *woman* ...	*John.* 4 : 27.
Blind man's sins of a *former birth* ...	*John.* 9 : 2.
Lazarus' sisters go to his grave to *weep* ...	*John.* 11 : 31.
Christ's Coat *without seam*	*John.* 19 : 23.
Peter went to the *house top* to pray ...	*Acts.* 10 : 9.
For Peter and Paul *garlands* were brought ...	*Acts.* 14 : 13.
Paul brought up *at the feet* of his guru ...	*Acts.* 22 : 2.

See also Gen. 15 : 4. 16 : 3. 24 : 11. 33 : 60. 29 : 18. 13 : 31. Lev. 22 : 13. Num. 6 : 18. 22 : 6. Dt. 23 : 10. 25 : 4. Josh. 15 : 8. 1 Sam. 9 : 7. 17 : 43. 1 Kings 3 : 4. 20. 38. 2 Kings 5 : 12. Job. 21 : 16. Ps. 26 : 6. 41 : 20. 45 : 7. 55 : 4. 5. 78. 63. 80 : 13. 81 : 3. 101 : 2. 133 : 2. Proverbs

11 : 21. 21 : 1. Eccl. 9 : 8. Cantic 5 : 3. Is. 18. 2. 32 : 20. 45 : 3. 46 ; 7. 60 : 4. Jer. 16 : 6. 44 : 17. Lam. 1 : 1. Ez. 9 : 4 23 : 10. 44 ; 25 ; Amos 5 : 19. 6 ; 11. Mat. 1 : 18. 2 : 18, 5 : 8. 6 5, 6 ; 7. 7 : 26. 10 ; 12. 14. 11 21, 18 ; 25. 22 ; 24. 28 : 9. Mk. 7 : 2 10 : 5. 14 : 14. ; 20 ; 52. Luk. 2 ; 7. 3 : 4. 5 : 14. 8 : 27. 14 : 16. 15 : 22. 18 : 15. John 2 : 8. 4 : 20. 5 : 9. 8 : 6. Acts 11 : 11. 1 Cor. 10 ; 25. 11 : 6. Gal. 6 : 17. Rev. 13 : 15.

SPECIMENS OF QUESTIONS ON EMBLEMS *

1	To what	11	objects†	is affliction compared ?
2	„	8	„	the body.
3	„	8	„	the Bible.
4	„	2	„	Christ's coming.
5	„	22	„	Christ himself and his work.
6	„	12	„	Death of righteous or wicked ;
7	„	4	„	Faith
8	„	5	„	God
9	„	3	„	Heaven
10	„	2	„	Hell
11	„	7	„	Holiness
12	„	9	„	The Holy Spirit ?
13	„	4	„	Hopes of wicked, or righteous ?
14	„	4	„	The Idle
15	„	15	„	The Ignorant ?
16	„	10	„	Life
17	„	3	„	Pardon of sin ?
18	„	7	„	Old age ?
19	„	5	„	Prayer ?
20	„	3	„	Providence ?
21	„	8	„	God's punishments ?
22	„	9	„	Regeneration ?
23	„	4	„	The resurrection !

* Where the system of teaching by emblems is taught in school.
† Object include animals, plants, &c.

24	To what	2 birds	The Righteous.
25	,,	4 trees	The righteous.
26	,,	3 animals	Satan.
27	,,	3 metals	Satan.
28	,,	5 objects	Time
29	,,	8 animals	the wicked
30	,,	3 objects	the World

31 To what weapons is sin compared ?

32 The world is compared to a thing found only with the poor.

33 The righteous compared to a thing seen only in great houses !

---

www.ingramcontent.com/pod-product-compliance
Lightning Source LLC
Chambersburg PA
CBHW032118230426
43672CB00009B/1774